The Arena of
International Finance

The Arena of International Finance

CHARLES A. COOMBS

A WILEY-INTERSCIENCE PUBLICATION

JOHN WILEY & SONS

New York • London • Sydney • Toronto

HG
3881
.C673

Library of Congress Cataloging in Publication Data:

Coombs, Charles A.   1918-
  The arena of international finance.

  "A Wiley-Interscience publication."
  Includes index.
  1. International finance.   I. Title.

HG3881.C673   332.4′5   76-19093
ISBN 0-471-01513-X

Printed in the United States of America

10 9 8 7 6 5 4 3 2 1

To

GUIDO CARLI

Preface

Since early 1961, the pound sterling has fallen from $2.80 to $1.70; the German mark has soared from $0.25 to nearly $0.40; the French franc, then quoted at $0.20 has subsequently swung back and forth between a peak of $0.26, a low of $0.18, and its mid-1976 level of $0.21. Meanwhile, the United States dollar has lost since June 1970 roughly 12% of its value against the major foreign currencies.

These currency rate movements reflect major changes for better or worse in the relative standard of living of the countries concerned; a devalued currency buys less in world markets and vice versa. And as these sea changes in the economic life of nations have gone on, the system of international finance set up at the end of World War II in the form of the Bretton Woods agreements has been shattered by a seemingly unending series of world financial crises.

As it happened, my position at the Federal Reserve Bank of New York thrust me into a good many of those international financial crises. From 1961 until my retirement in 1975 I had direct responsibility for all U.S. Treasury and Federal Reserve operations in the gold and foreign exchange markets. Such operations included credits of $8 billion to the Bank of England; $1.4 billion to the Bank of France; $1.6 billion to the Bank of Italy; and $3.3 billion to eight other central banks abroad. They also involved borrowing from foreign central banks on behalf of the United States $5.4 billion of Swiss francs; $4.5 billion of German marks; $2.1 billion of Dutch guilders; and $5.1 billion of other foreign currencies. Because of my operational responsibilities I participated in some of the major financial policy decisions of the times, and was always close to the market action. For 15 years, I met each month with the governors of the major central banks of Europe, Canada, and Japan at the Bank for International Settlements in Basel, Switzerland. Those central bank meetings in Basel became the focal point during the decade of the sixties of a major cooperative effort to keep the world financial system functioning effectively in the face of threatening disintegration. Students of the period may accordingly find in these recollections additional source material for appraising what happened and why.

These memoirs make no pretense of providing a comprehensive historical record of international financial developments during the period. But my account may possibly shed new light on some of the episodes selected. Anyone interested in further data on market developments and operations over the entire period will find them provided in excruciating detail in my semiannual reports in the *Monthly Review* of the Federal Reserve Bank of New York, 1962– 1975.

I have also tried to avoid burdening the narrative with digressions commenting on some of the major policy issues of the period, such as the best way of ensuring an adequate growth of international liquidity or the role of exchange rates in the adjustment process. The main focus of the book is rather the evolution over the period of the machinery of central bank cooperation, with particular attention paid to the development of the Federal Reserve inter-central bank credit network and other types of official credit facilities.

This is hardly intended to suggest that I did not have some fairly strong personal views on the international policy issues emerging during 1961–1975, and on the most appropriate methods of resolving them. I did indeed, and at this point perhaps I would do well to summarize them briefly.

First of all, as early as 1960, it was abundantly clear to me and to my associates at the New York Federal that the Bretton Woods system was heading into serious trouble. At the time, the main problem was the legal commitment assumed by the United States Government in 1945 to maintain convertibility of the dollar into gold on the demand of any foreign central bank acquiring dollars. For various technical reasons noted in the text, this open-ended commitment to defend the dollar with gold could not be indefinitely sustained and meanwhile left unresolved the further problem of providing in some reasonably rational way for an adequate secular growth in international liquidity.

Many theoretical possibilities existed of drastically amending the Articles of Agreement of the International Monetary Fund so as to deal with the problem. But, rightly or wrongly, my judgment, and that of others, was that such sweeping reforms of Bretton Woods, probably requiring many months if not years, could not be negotiated without precipitating a major crisis in the exchange markets. In fact, the very negotiation of the Bretton Woods agreement itself would probably never have proved possible except under such strictly regulated exchange market conditions as those prevailing during World War II.

Consequently, the U.S. Treasury and the New York Federal developed during the early sixties the strategy of gradually reforming Bretton Woods by phasing out gold settlements and substituting a comprehensive range of credit facilities for settling payments imbalances among the major trading nations. The Federal Reserve swap network, the Roosa bonds, and periodic increases in the IMF quotas marked major steps along this route. Subsequently, the open-ended credit facilities provided by members of the European Monetary Union to one another represented further progress in the same direction. And over recent years, the Eurodollar market has provided an abundant, additional source of official financing.

Meanwhile, gold has sunk to the bottom tier of central bank reserves. While the treasuries and central banks of the world will probably cling to their gold reserves as an understandable precaution against unforeseeable emergencies, I doubt that gold will ever again function as the primary medium of official international payments. The initial bright hope of "paper gold" in the form of the SDR has also faded, and as someone who was skeptical of its technical feasibility from the outset I am neither surprised nor saddened. But in any case, the SDR was never really needed. The spectrum of international credit facilities developed since 1961 have provided an infinitely flexible solution to the problem of world liquidity. Moreover, it is essentially a technical solution that can be readily managed by the IMF, the central banks, and the commercial banking community with a minimum of political haggling.

But the second major problem emerging in the late sixties, that of the role of exchange rates in the adjustment process, was not only a technical but also a political problem of appalling complexity.

Devaluations and revaluations of currencies are comparable to major surgery on a human patient. Most central bankers and governments think of parity changes as inherently dangerous policy moves, sometimes essential but always dangerous. I felt the same. In a devaluation, choice of the appropriate cut—5, 10, or 15%—is inevitably rough guesswork with some bias toward drastic action in the interests of credibility. Yet the deeper the cut, the greater the risk that devaluation will boomerang into a new round of domestic inflation and so re-create the original disequilibrium.

To be successful, a devaluation must bring about basic changes in production and income distribution. Real wages must be cut, production must be shifted from domestic consumption to the export markets, and a lot of other politically painful adjustments must be made. And there are troublesome time lags, as illustrated by the familiar J-curve analysis. Accordingly, devaluation should be accompanied, and preferably preceded, by drastic monetary and fiscal restraint, creation of excess capacity, and a firm lid on money wage rates. Yet, all too often, governmental failure to take such domestic policy action is precisely what has eventually confronted them with devaluation by *force majeure*. In the absence of thoroughgoing supportive action on the domestic front, devaluation or exchange depreciation is all too likely to produce an inflationary washout of the corrective adjustment being sought.

Conversely, countries in strong trade surplus who finally decide to revalue despite the bitter opposition of their export trades, generally fail to go far enough to correct the underlying problem. In an expansionary and inflationary environment, moreover, revaluations may actually tend to further enlarge the trade balance of the revaluing country while gilding its currency with the speculative aura of a growth stock. Such was the experience of the German mark during the inflationary years of 1971–1975.

Finally, there is sometimes very real uncertainty as to the relative responsibility of surplus and deficit countries for taking corrective action through exchange rate adjustments. The policy impasse confronting France and Germany in 1968 over the issue of a franc devaluation versus a mark revaluation, or some combination of the two, is a famous case in point and there have been many similar conflicts since then. Quite naturally the deficit country in such bargaining encounters generally finds itself at a disadvantage.

It is understandable, therefore, that governments have frequently delayed so long before nerving themselves up to the harsh political decisions involved in devaluing or revaluing their currencies. And sometimes the struggle to defend an untenable parity has been time well spent when used to introduce, however piecemeal, the domestic restraint measures that were in any case needed to make the eventual devaluation a success. Reserves lost to speculation during such holding actions were generally recovered as the payments leads and lags reversed themselves after the parity change.

Within the councils of government, the central banks were generally the first to sound the alarm when currency troubles developed on the foreign front. Equally generally, with the exception of the Bank of Italy under Governor Carli, they lacked the authority to force decisive action in good time, and were therefore limited to their powers of persuasion. In this advisory role, the central banks invariably urged their governments to deal first with the domestic economic troubles that were in turn breeding embarrassing weakness on the foreign front. I shared their views.

But none of the central bankers I knew ever had any fanatical illusions of defending imperiled currency parities at the cost of massive unemployment. They were sophisticated men of their times, fully cognizant of the social pressures straining the delicate fabric of democratic government. Their advice was mainly focused on the basic need to restrain inflation and so to stabilize the domestic value of their currencies. If that did not suffice to restore a balanced position internationally, no central bank would have countenanced a wasting away of their countries' reserves in futile defense of the prestige value of an overvalued currency. But it was worth finding out whether the root cause of foreign trade losses was eradicable by restoring the health of the domestic economy or instead called for drastic surgery in the form of a currency devaluation.

On a number of occasions, central banks concluded well in advance of their governments that currency parity changes had become inevitable. The German Bundesbank was consistently farsighted in this regard, and so were other central banks from time to time. In November 1968, for example, both the Bank of France and the German Bundesbank were agreed on the need for a simultaneous revaluation of the mark and devaluation of the franc, and were supported in this judgment by all of the major central banks of the world. But this central bank effort to quietly negotiate an appropriate technical solution was angrily rejected by the German government at the Bonn Conference of November 1968, presumably for compelling domestic political reasons.

Thereafter, as we moved into the early seventies, the issue of currency rate adjustments became almost exclusively a political matter reserved to the Treasury officials of the major countries concerned. The role of the Federal Reserve in foreign financial policy was severely curtailed after the accession of the Nixon administration in January 1969. And so, in the absence of new Federal Reserve initiatives, the action center provided over the previous decade by the central bank meetings at Basel fell into disuse.

Such virtual disbarment of the central banks from negotiation at the BIS of exchange rate problems might not have been so damaging if new negotiating machinery at the international political level had been substituted in its place. But the finance ministers and their political lieutenants were not prepared for this new role, and their sporadic negotiations with one another came to resemble a dialogue of the deaf. In effect, it seemed to me, there was a breakdown of communications, more particularly between the United States and Japan, as pressures exerted on the Bretton Woods network of fixed exchange rates by balance of payment disequilibria became more and more explosive.

Faced with a policy impasse that was partly of its own making, the Nixon administration on August 15, 1971, violently broke away from the Bretton Woods system by disavowing convertibility of the dollar in any form and inviting the exchange markets to take over from governments full responsibility for deciding the relative values of the major currencies of the world. While the American government twice accepted, first at the Smithsonian meeting in December 1971 and again in February 1973, new devalued parities for the dollar, it refused on both occasions to make any commitment to defend these parities against market speculation.

The main rationale for this experiment with a free floating dollar, according to Nixon officials, was that the market would provide an accurate and consistently reliable judgment of fundamental economic trends and thereby determine a network of appropriate exchange rates. This was, I thought, an appalling miscalculation of the role and functioning of the foreign exchange markets, which are an indispensible guide but a very poor master of national policy.

By its very nature, the foreign exchange market is a nervous, high risk, ultra-sensitive mechanism, primarily geared to short term developments. Of the tens of billions of dollars in daily transactions cleared through the market, only a fraction derive from such fundamental factors as foreign trade and long term investment. On a day-to-day basis, the market is instead dominated by short term capital movements in search of quick profits or a hedge against exchange rate risks. For months at a time, short term interest rate differentials between New York and Europe can have a far more decisive effect on exchange rates than do current trade figures.

In such an international market, traders are exposed to all the political and economic winds that blow from every quarter of the world. And as exchange rates move in response to the chattering stimulus of news ticker reports, there is an ever present risk that a rate movement in one direction will suddenly become cumulative. The market is characterized by sudden shifts of sentiment that send traders scurrying for cover and violently distort supply and demand relationships. The foreign exchange market has also proved to be highly vulnerable to wholesale gambling as the recent examples of Herstatt, Franklin National, and Lloyds' Lugano have vividly illustrated. In general, I respect the judgment of the foreign exchange markets over the long run but I fear their inherent instability. Many market traders share my view and welcome central bank intervention as needed to protect the market against itself.

Such was the marketplace to which the fate of the dollar was entrusted in August 1971 and again in March 1973. The consequences in the form of a grossly excessive depreciation of the dollar, rampant speculation in the international commodity markets, and 2 worldwide surge of inflation were even worse than I had feared. Only after five years of monetary and inflationary turmoil do we now see signs of returning stability.

I should acknowledge still another value judgment that is probably more crucial than any of the rest. For better or worse, the world constellation of national currencies are simply not coequal in their roles and respective responsibilities. The dollar functions not only as the currency of the largest national trading unit in the world. It also serves by general acquiescence, in the absence of any effective alternative, as the preeminent reserve asset of most foreign central banks as well as the transactions currency of most exchange market contracts. Whether welcome or unwelcome to the United States and its foreign trading partners, there is no practical alternative to this world role of the dollar as a store and standard of value as well as the primary medium of international exchange.

This inescapable conclusion seems to me to involve two major policy corollaries. First, the United States has a duty primarily to itself but also to the entire world to assure the stability of the dollar. This is no less important than our worldwide political and military responsibilities. In an economically integrated world, there is no room for American policies of "benign neglect" of the value of the dollar internationally nor of subsequently seeking an easy way out by a generalized devaluation of the dollar. Second, our foreign trading partners have an equally basic and complementary duty when they move into consistent balance of payments surpluses to upvalue their currencies against the dollar in good time. International agreement on such basic rules of the game is a *sine qua non* of a restructured world financial system.

Finally, I should like to express my gratitude to the Rockefeller Foundation for a fellowship in international relationships that enabled me to work without interruption on these memoirs during the summer months of 1975. I am also deeply indebted to a number of government and central bank officials both here and abroad who reviewed the text and gave me the benefit of many thoughtful suggestions.

CHARLES A. COOMBS

Green Village, New Jersey
June 1976

Contents

Chapter 1 The Gold Trap of Bretton Woods   1

Chapter 2 The Kennedy Gold Pledge   15

Chapter 3 The Basel Meetings   24

Chapter 4 Creation of the Gold Pool   42

Chapter 5 The Federal Reserve Swap Network   69

Chapter 6 Dallas, November 22, 1963   92

Chapter 7 The Sterling Bear Squeeze   107

Chapter 8 The Devaluation of Sterling   131

Chapter 9 The Breakdown of the Gold Pool   152

Chapter 10 Devaluation of the French Franc   174

Chapter 11 Defense of the Dollar, 1965–1968   188

Chapter 12 Collapse of the Dollar   204

            Index   241

The Arena of
International Finance

1

The Gold Trap
of Bretton Woods

John Connally, Secretary of the Treasury during the first Nixon administration, once complained of being caricatured by the press as a "bully boy on the manicured playing fields of international finance." In a way, Connally's complaint is more revealing than any of the accusations. But he was by no means the only politician in recent years to employ strongarm tactics in world financial markets. President de Gaulle during the mid-sixties had ruthlessly exploited the political uses of a strong French franc. And after the Paris riots of May 1968 had brought the franc to the verge of a major devaluation, German political leaders such as Strauss and Schiller flatly refused to assist the French government—and the world financial system generally—by a simultaneous, and urgently needed, revaluation of the mark. Similarly, Nixon officials have blamed the "unfair" exchange rates stubbornly maintained by Japan and other countries for the collapse of the dollar in 1971. Others such as myself would assign major responsibility to the Nixon policy of "benign neglect" of the dollar's value internationally.

By its very nature, international finance is an arena of conflicting national policy interests. In a world of 129 national currencies, each independently managed, the monetary, credit, and exchange rate policies of individual countries inevitably tend to collide rather than to coalesce.

Yet the United States and its major trading partners generally played the international financial game in a fairly civilized and cooperative way from the postwar launching of the Bretton Woods system until the progressive breakdown of the dollar in 1970–1971. The cardinal rule of the game was consultation, and whenever possible, prior consultation, on any national policy move likely to have a financial impact on other countries. National trading and other overseas interests were still hotly pursued but within limits set by a generally accepted if not binding code of ethics.

By the late fifties, moreover, the technological breakthrough in transatlantic jet transport and telephone services had telescoped the ponderously slow official communications of earlier years. From 1961 until the end of the decade, there was an almost instantaneous response of central banks and treasuries to any major financial problem on the world markets. Huge amounts of credit were repeatedly made available by the central banks and the International Monetary Fund (IMF) to currencies falling victim to speculative attack. Even the human factor was altered. Earlier adversary relationships with foreign financial officials yielded to mutual understanding and often personal friendship. The arena was still there, but governments and central banks had now become allies in an interlocking defense against speculation in the foreign exchange markets.

This was something new under the sun. For centuries before, Connally's "manicured playing fields" of international finance had more nearly resembled a merciless battlefield of national rivalries, with no rules of the game save devil take the hindmost. In the twenties, the League of Nations, Norman of the Bank of England, and Strong of the Federal Reserve Bank of New York had initiated new cooperative approaches, but they were swept away by the economic debacle of the thirties. Nor over the years had economic theory devised a plausible blueprint of a world financial system that would combine the discipline of the market place over the longer run with cooperative protection against speculative excesses in the short run.

As a student in the late thirties, most of my instruction in international finance had focused on the causes rather than the consequences of the collapse of the world financial system earlier in the decade. I had become thoroughly versed in the iniquities of the old gold standard, which had allegedly punished inefficient countries with deflation and unemployment while simultaneously inflicting inflation on their more prosperous trading partners. Britain's abandonment of the gold standard in 1931 had seemingly marked the end of an era. Every examination paper quoted Keynes' contemptuous reference to gold as "a barbarous relic." To most students, there now seemed no effective alternative but floating exchange rates.

But in early June 1940, as I took on a summer job at the Federal Reserve Bank of New York, I was startled by the gulf suddenly opened up between my textbook readings and the Bank's perception of the financial policy issues emerging in the late thirties. This was not the fault of the textbooks. Events were moving too fast for scholarly appraisal to keep pace.

At the Bank I soon realized among other facts of life that gold was still very much in the picture. By the late spring of 1940, the bank's storage facilities were being overwhelmed as French and

British warships arrived in New York, laden with their countries' gold reserves for safekeeping. The gold vault, anchored 80 feet underground on the bedrock of Manhattan, normally resembles a quiet mausoleum in which foreign deposits of gold bars are meticulously stored away in individual national compartments, each fronted with iron caging as in a zoo. But in June 1940 the floor of the vault was strewn like a disorderly brickyard with gleaming stacks of gold bars awaiting their turn to be weighed and processed for storage.

It was an awesome spectacle, particularly if one reflected on the appalling history of human avarice, criminality, and suffering that lay behind that mass of metal. As a young student "steeped in Keynes," as Prof. Wassily Leontief once put it, I still thought the whole business pretty barbarous. But I also found, as my summer apprenticeship at the Bank progressed, that the breakdown of the gold standard in 1931 and the subsequent emergence of floating rates had produced a new and even more dangerous form of economic barbarism. Multilateral trade had progressively given way to discriminatory, bilateral trading arrangements, reinforced by exchange controls, amid a welter of charges and countercharges of competitive depreciation through floating currency rates. As early as 1936, American, British, and French policies had consequently turned away from floating rates as a breeding ground of world economic conflict and thereafter moved toward a stabilization of their exchange rates at *de facto* parities.

On returning from military service to the New York Federal in 1946, I found that American and British Treasury officials had negotiated during the war years a sweeping reform of the world financial system at the Bretton Woods Conference of 1944. Gold had again been enshrined as the central value and *numeraire* of a fixed-parity system whose operation would be supervised by the International Monetary Fund with headquarters in Washington.

I also found that during the war years President Allan Sproul and Dr. John H. Williams of the New York Federal had vigorously opposed the creation of the International Monetary Fund, even to the extent of refusing to participate in the Bretton Woods Conference. While solidly supporting the role of gold in international settlements, the New York Bank had urged a less formal stabilization by special measures of the so-called key exchange rates of the dollar, the pound sterling, the French franc, and other major currencies, rather than the global approach embodied and formalized in the Fund.

In the short run, Sproul and Williams were right; the International Monetary Fund could not possibly deal with the postwar financial crisis confronting Europe, and thus it remained inactive as the United States lent billions of dollars to the United Kingdom and subsequently launched the Marshall Plan of 1948–1952. But in a much more fundamental sense, the argument had been over form rather than substance. Nothing in the loosely drawn Bretton Woods agreements precluded an evolution over time toward the "key currency" approach the New York Bank had originally proposed. And subsequently, even as the Bank thoroughly fulfilled its operational responsibilities to defend the Bretton Woods agreements, the key currency approach has reemerged as the only viable route.

But in 1946 we were dealing with the facts of the day. Under the Articles of Agreement of the Monetary Fund, the postwar dollar had been pegged to gold at the 1934 price of $35 to the ounce. The U.S. Treasury had undertaken to maintain this gold par value of the dollar by both selling and buying gold without limit at the request of any and all foreign governments acquiring membership in the International Monetary Fund. In turn, foreign governments had pegged their currencies to the dollar by committing themselves to sell dollars on demand if their currency rates fell 1 percent below par and to buy dollars without limit at currency rates 1 percent above par.

In effect, convertibility of the dollar into gold at $35 per ounce became the lynch-pin of a worldwide fixed exchange rate system. The choice of gold as the *numeraire* and ultimate reserve asset of the system conformed, of course, to historical tradition and the instinctive orthodoxy at the time of every financial community here

and abroad. But the sophisticated architects of Bretton Woods—
not least of all Lord Keynes—thought of gold as no more than a
means to an end, that of locking together through a supranational
standard of value the fixed parities of eventually more than a hundred national currencies. And the fixed parity system was in turn a
means to the end of ensuring that each member country would
forswear competitive depreciations or discriminatory trade arrangements under the watchful eye of the Fund. In this general sense,
Bretton Woods was an idealized, even a noble, concept of a world
financial order under which multilateral trade might flourish to the
benefit of all.

From the very beginning, gold was the vulnerable point of the
Bretton Woods system. Yet the open-ended gold commitment assumed by the United States government under the Bretton Woods
legislation is readily understandable in view of the extraordinary
circumstances of the time. At the end of the war, our gold stock
amounted to $20 billion, roughly 60 percent of the total of official
gold reserves. To government officials, the United States gold reserve
then seemed not only abundant but excessive, allowing ample room
for redistribution of the excess to foreign countries as they recovered from the economic ruins of the war.

Nor did the possible growth of convertible dollar balances in the
hands of foreign central banks suggest any early challenge to the
adequacy of our gold stock to defend the dollar parity. The postwar
exchange market situation was instead one of acute and generalized
dollar shortages abroad which continued for a decade after the
war. As late as 1957, United States gold reserves exceeded by a
ratio of nearly three to one the total dollar reserves of all the foreign
central banks. The dollar bestrode the exchange markets like a
colossus.

An economic and financial imbalance so heavily favoring the
United States could not and did not continue. And as the imbalance
was rectified, largely through processes initiated and encouraged by
the United States itself, the vulnerability of the Bretton Woods
system became increasingly visible. Despite the size of the Amer-

ican hoard, gold was still a scarce commodity internationally and bound to get scarcer. New production would sooner or later be diverted from official central bank buyers at the 1934 price of $35 per ounce to private markets that could and would pay a price more nearly reflecting the rise of commodity prices generally after decades of inflation.

This was a worrisome outlook. As banker for the Bretton Woods system, the United States thus faced at best the longer term prospect of a relatively slow growth of the gold asset side of its international balance sheet, and the interim risk of a continuing erosion of our gold stock if we did not bring the balance of payments deficits emerging in the late fifties under control. By the end of 1960 the American gold stock had in fact fallen from its 1949 peak of nearly $25 billion to somewhat less than $18 billion.

Nor was the liability side, that is, foreign central bank accumulations of dollars convertible into gold, less exposed to future trouble. As long as the dollar and its gold backing was considered invulnerable, foreign central banks clearly had a strong incentive to invest part or all of the dollars thrown off by American payments deficits in interest-earning dollar placements in the New York money market rather than converting them into gold. Such official dollar holdings were convertible into gold and therefore as good as gold, yielded interest income as well, and served to expand international liquidity and thereby encourage the growth of trade.

But the resultant growth in the late fifties of official dollar holdings, and the reemergence of a gold-exchange standard, also gave hostages to fortune. The mounting superstructure of dollar reserves held by foreign central banks rested squarely on foreign confidence in the commitment of the United States to deliver gold on demand at $35 per ounce for the indefinite future. And such foreign confidence in the dollar in turn depended on whether the American government would recognize in time its duty, in its own national interest as well as that of the international system as a whole, to restore a solid balance between its overseas payments and receipts.

But this was a policy problem of infinite complexity. Not least among the difficulties was the political task of persuading the American public, long accustomed to its benefactor role first in the military, then in the economic rescue of Western Europe, that the United States must now accept the same discipline as any other country in the management of its external economic affairs. At all levels of political sophistication, such a reversal of our financial position was littered with potential misunderstandings between the natural desire of the Europeans to regain a selfrespecting and coequal role and the equally natural American feeling that somehow a lot of Europeans still owed us something.

I remember during a walk along the Champs-Élysées in 1957 encountering an elegantly dressed American woman tourist who had apparently just been evicted by an elderly French woman from a collapsible chair for refusal to pay a minor fee. As I passed, my compatriot called on me to witness such ingratitude for the Normandy invasion not to mention the Marshall Plan, while the Frenchwoman, probably a war widow allowed to eke out a meager income by renting her chairs, turned a deaf ear to a familiar complaint.

Nor was the approaching necessity of consigning World War II and the Marshall Plan to the history books, along with Lafayette and Rochambeau, easily accepted by many United States government officials. As United States gold losses mounted in the late fifties, a tendency developed in Washington to classify the foreign central banks buying gold from us as ingrates or worse and those abstaining from gold by accumulating dollars as our true freinds. Washington officials increasingly dropped hints of governmental displeasure over foreign gold purchases without, however, suggesting an alternative policy route.

Ironically enough, the incipient Washington tendencies to classify gold-buying countries as unfriendly and the abstainers as cooperative directly reversed the alignment of World War II. In the case of our former enemies Italy and Germany, twin economic miracles had lifted both economies from the rubble of 1945 into powerful industrial machines, which by the late fifties were generating strong balance of payments surpluses. American economic aid to both countries had provided a powerful stimulus to recovery. Even without American hints, however, it was only natural that the central banks of both countries should shrink from any action that might be interpreted as ingratitude or as endangering in any way still delicate political relations with the United States. Moreover, a sizable portion of Germany's recurrent payments surpluses derived from American military spending in that country. Japanese gold policy was influenced by similar considerations.

On the other hand, several of our former allies in World War II that had been traditionally high gold ratio countries reverted to such conservative policy as soon as their postwar recoveries solidified. The Dutch central bank, for example, had been badly burned by the devaluation of sterling in 1931 and had subsequently limited its uncovered foreign exchange position, including dollars, to no more than working balances. The central banks of Belgium and France were equally well aware of the risks of an open exchange position.

In the case of the United Kingdom, Lord Keynes in the Anglo-American negotiations leading up to Bretton Woods had urged that the discipline of gold and other reserve losses on deficit countries be tempered by provision of automatic credit by the surplus countries. The U.S. Treasury, however, had insisted on the more orthodox and severe arrangements finally embodied in the Bretton Woods agreements. Now in the late fifties, as our balance of payments shifted from surplus into deficit, the Treasury found itself saddled with a formal legal obligation, assumed in 1944 at its own behest, to settle such deficits in gold if the foreign surplus country so requested. And so the Bank of England, which traditionally believes in discipline for everyone, began regularly converting surplus dollars into gold in accordance with the orthodoxy of Bretton Woods. British gold purchases alone came to $1.8 billion during the three years 1958–1960, and Belgium, France, and the Netherlands accounted for another $1.5 billion.

As United States gold losses mounted in the late fifties, Washington had to worry over the further risk that other central banks outside Europe might suddenly shift into the high gold ratio camp. For more than 15 years after World War II, the central banks of Latin America, the Middle East, and the Far East had generally welcomed any influx of dollars. But the frequently changing managements of these banks were particularly vulnerable to scare stories of a weakening dollar, and this too posed a danger of sudden, panicky buying of gold at the first sign of a serious threat to the United States gold parity. As noted by President Marius Holtrop of the Netherlands Bank at the 1961 annual meeting of the International Monetary Fund in Vienna:

> Paradoxically, one might even say that the (Bretton Woods) system's stability is based upon uncertainty. For if it were inconceivable that the dollar price of gold might ever be raised, most of the reserve-holding countries might wish to hold only dollars and the gold exchange standard would tend to be transformed into a dollar standard, the United States having to buy almost all the world's gold. It is very doubtful that this would be a desirable development. If, on the other hand, it were almost sure that the dollar price of gold would be raised, few monetary authorities would wish to continue to hold dollars, and the system would tend to revert to a gold reserve standard, for which no sufficient gold would be available. It is uncertainty, therefore, that presently controls the proper mixture of decisions.

As the balance of uncertainty began to shift against the United States gold parity in the late fifties, the problem of American gold payments became increasingly disquieting. Such gold losses indeed had a useful disciplinary effect on government thinking, as the American architects of Bretton Woods had presumably intended for other countries then ranked as probable debtors. But there was also a growing risk that the disciplinary role of United States gold losses might acquire too sharp a cutting edge and might suddenly inflict a fatal blow to confidence in the dollar before corrective policy measures had time to take effect. Here the age-old mystique of gold began to play a dangerous role, as the gold drain took on a dramatic quality far disproportionate to its real significance. By late 1960 weekly Treasury reports of American gold losses had moved from the financial section to the front page of the *New York Times.* Each weekly report of a new heavy loss threatened to provide fresh precautionary buying by foreign central banks, thereby generating a cumulative drain.

Moreover, the disciplinary effect of United States gold losses operated in a haphazard, almost accidental, way. Small outflows of dollars to Belgium, for example, were immediately punished by Belgian gold purchases, while much larger flows to Germany or Italy might simply disappear into the dollar investment portfolios of the Bundesbank and the Bank of Italy. An even more eccentric feature of the Bretton Woods discipline was that flows of money from a low gold ratio country in deficit to a high ratio country in surplus would result in the latter converting such dollar receipts into gold at the Treasury window, while the deficit country, instead of raising new dollars by compensating sales of gold to the United States, simply paid out old dollar balances

Finally, it was by no means clear in the late fifties just what self-disciplinary action the American government should take in response to gold losses, or the building up of dollar balances by conscientious but nervous foreign holders. The balance of payments problem was a compound not only of incipient economic and financial weaknesses but even more importantly of heavy commitments to spending abroad on various military and foreign aid programs. A realignment of national priorities, involving as they did the military security of the United States, Europe, and Japan, would clearly take some time to work out. Meanwhile, however, the drain of the United States gold stock was telescoping the time available for such a policy review at a truly alarming rate.

Thus by 1960 the Bretton Woods commitment assumed by the United States to settle its balance of payments deficits in gold on demand was fast approaching the moment of truth. Of American payments deficits totaling $11.2 billion over the three years 1958–1960, $6.5 billion had been automatically financed by foreign central bank and private accumulations of dollars. But $4.7 billion of U.S.

Treasury sales of gold to foreign central banks had been required to settle the remainder, with every prospect that more and more central banks would begin to call for gold settlement of dollar inflows generated by the United States deficit.

This was an embarrassing situation all around. Belgium, the Netherlands, and other high gold ratio countries hardly enjoyed the role of administering the Bretton Woods discipline by converting their surplus dollar receipts into gold. And the central banks of Germany, Italy, and other low gold ratio countries were fearful, on the one hand, of provoking by gold purchases drastic cutbacks in American political and military commitments to Western Europe. But on the other hand, they could visualize themselves being charged with failure to protect their countries' reserves if the dollar were to slide into irretrievable difficulty. And in the closing months of the Eisenhower administration, deep policy cleavages began to develop between Treasury Secretary Robert B. Anderson, who saw clearly his financial responsibility for defending the dollar, and equally devoted spokesmen for the Pentagon and the State Department who did not propose to yield vital American interests abroad for lack of dollar financing.

Accordingly, behind a facade of rigid official adherence to the Bretton Woods gold settlements system, financial officials on both sides of the Atlantic quietly began to search for ways and means of stemming the drain on the United States gold stock. These spontaneous reform efforts initially developed in isolation with virtually no consultation across national borders; therefore much time was wasted on proposals having no chance of common acceptance. In France and the Netherlands, for example, proposals that the United States substitute gold guaranteed obligations for gold specie payments gained considerable official support; the United States, however, flatly rejected such approaches as they surfaced.

Moreover, a number of foreign central banks now sought on their own initiative to relieve pressure on the American gold stock by quietly buying gold on the free market in London, where the supply from the South African and Russian mines was still running ahead of private demand. But as such competitive central bank buying on the London gold market gradually pushed the price above the $35 level, speculative interest was kindled and fed by new uncertainties arising out of the American presidential election of 1960.

The London gold market had acquired since its reopening in 1954 a highly respectable, almost quasi-official status, with the Bank of England frequently intervening on a small scale to maintain orderly conditions. By 1960 financial markets all over the world had come to regard the London gold quotation as a true price, hence a barometer of confidence in both the gold-dollar parity and the Bretton Woods system generally. Accordingly, as private gold buying in London mounted, the United States was suddenly confronted with the risk that such speculative demand might drive the London gold price well above the official gold parity of $35 and in so doing pose a major speculative challenge to the dollar.

In September 1960, American financial officials tried to defuse this explosive situation by inviting the Bank of Italy and other central banks identified as buyers on the London market to come to the Treasury gold window instead, thus relieving the pressure on London. But a much more critical issue was whether the U.S. Treasury would directly, or indirectly through the agency of the Bank of England, supply the gold needed to hold the London gold price around the $35 level regardless of the cost to the United States gold stock

This was a dangerous policy dilemma. On the one hand, a sharply rising London gold price might well provoke a crisis of confidence in the United States gold parity, with the probable consequence that central banks all over the world would rush to cash in their surplus dollars for gold. But on the other hand, intervention by the United States on the London gold market to hold the price at $35 would expose our gold stock to the double drain of feeding the gold demand of foreign central banks and the private gold market as well. The latter horn of the dilemma was even sharper then because at the time American residents could buy and hold gold in London while they were prohibited from doing so in the United States.

On this issue of controlling the London gold price, misunderstandings developed between United States financial officials and the Bank of England, and there occurred on October 20, 1960, a spectacular rise of the London price to the $40 level. The breakout of the London gold price in turn ignited an explosion of speculation against the dollar in the exchange markets. Foreign central banks hurriedly cashed in surplus dollars at the United States gold window, and the Treasury found itself forced to put out a press statement formally endorsing Bank of England sales of gold to stabilize the London price at the ultimate expense of the American gold stock.

Thus in late 1960 the dollar had become convertible into gold on demand not only by foreign central banks but also by private speculators all over the world. The United States government had become thoroughly trapped by its gold commitments under Bretton Woods, and a heavy responsibility for devising a safe escape route now fell on the new team of Treasury officials to be appointed by President-elect Kennedy.

2

The Kennedy
Gold Pledge

On December 16, 1960, President-elect Kennedy named C. Douglas
Dillon as his Secretary of the Treasury. Dillon, a former Wall Street
investment banker and a lifetime Republican, had served under
Eisenhower first as ambassador to France and subsequently as Undersecretary of State. Like a number of other liberal Republicans,
however, he had given only token personal support of Richard
Nixon's candidacy in the 1960 election; thus he remained politically
eligible for continuing public service in the new administration.

With the subsequent appointment of Henry Fowler as Under-secretary and Robert V. Roosa as Undersecretary for Monetary Affairs, a remarkably strong and balanced Treasury team took over the direction of American financial policy.

Roosa and I had worked closely together at the Federal Reserve Bank of New York since 1946, he having moved up to Vice-President in charge of the Research Department while several years later I had been appointed head of the Foreign Department. A Rhodes scholar and University of Michigan Ph.D., Roosa had earned a distinguished reputation internationally in both academic and banking circles. His prime interest, however, was policy, and under his driving leadership the Research Department of the New York Federal had pursued its independent view of monetary and economic issues in fearless disregard of the policy bandwagons of Washington. Roosa was a truly gifted advocate of whatever cause he espoused. Even in casual conversation he habitually spoke with flowing eloquence, and at critical moments, as a Bank of England man put it, his appeals for decisive action took on almost a biblical quality. Physically and emotionally he was well equipped to withstand the grueling demands of his new Washington assignment; Gabe Hauge of Manufacturers Hanover Bank once described him as a "tough Scandinavian." Yet he was invariably gentle and considerate in his personal relations and unswerving in his loyalties to a host of friends.

Late in December 1960, Roosa was invited to meet with Dillon at the latter's winter home in Hobe Sound, Florida. Since I had just returned from a swing around the European central banks, I was asked to come along to help in the briefing.

Dillon was an elegantly tailored, handsome man in his early fifties with the quiet assurance of someone having just achieved a pinnacle of personal success. He displayed, as I had noticed in earlier meetings, a capacity for total absorption in whatever he did. As Roosa and I briefed him on current developments, he listened with unwavering attention, only an occasional widening of the eyes revealing any reaction. Subsequently, in his Treasury office, the same habit of concentration was disconcerting to visitors, who after being ceremoniously ushered through a defile of three secretaries, found themselves ignored for minutes at a time before Dillon broke away from the paper he was perusing. His memory for detail was phenomenal, frequently to the embarrassment of his Treasury staff, and he seemed to visualize the machinery of any projected financial operation with only a minimum of technical explanation. His experience in the top echelons of the State Department enabled him to assess realistically in his own mind how far defense of the dollar could be pushed without endangering vital political interests of the United States. But his close personal relationship with President Kennedy also ensured that any strongly held Treasury view went straight to the top. Even in relatively small affairs, the impact of the Dillon personality made itself felt. As Undersecretary of State, he had overcome budgetary resistance to handsome but costly chandeliers for the reception rooms of the new State Department building by donating them himself. Now at the Treasury, he soon swept away the long tradition of frugality as evidenced by worn-out carpeting, unpainted walls, and general dilapidation, and thoroughly refurbished the place.

But what I mainly remember was his professional grasp of his job. In Congressional hearings Dillon seemed always to be the best informed man in the room, making his points quietly but incisively and losing few arguments. And as I later watched him at international gatherings, I could not help feeling a certain national pride in the quality of our representation.

After finishing our briefing session that late December day in Florida, Roosa and I were invited by the Secretary and Mrs. Dillon to stay on for dinner. Later that evening the Secretary opened the *New York Times* and laughed uproariously as he read to us James Reston's Christmas Eve column designating Dillon together with Robert Kennedy as the two prime "hell catchers" of the new administration and counseling both to "let nothing you dismay." But neither Dillon nor his new deputy Roosa was easy prey to dismay;

both seemed to enjoy the thunder and lightning, and their resolute confidence soon jolted the lugubrious, cheeseparing staff of the Treasury out of their bureaucratic routine.

In our briefing session, Dillon had recognized immediately that the prime challenges facing him were the country's payments deficit and the continuing erosion of confidence in the dollar, both symbolized by the drain on the Treasury's gold stock. Meanwhile, however, several policy task forces organized during the Kennedy election campaign had developed proposals for an immediate, sweeping reform of the Bretton Woods system based on some ill-defined master plan. Roosa and I thought such proposals were technically deficient, nonnegotiable, and dangerously likely to distract attention from more urgent issues.

Moreover, President-elect Kennedy, with a lively questioning if not outright suspicion of the same proposals, telephoned Roosa soon after we had returned to the New York Federal to ask his help in forming a nonpartisan committee of financial experts to review the problem of simultaneously reviving a depressed national economy and closing the balance of payments deficit. The president subsequently designated, on the advice of Dillon and Roosa, a three-man committee comprised of Allan Sproul, former president of the New York Federal, as chairman; Prof. Roy Blough of Columbia; and Prof. Paul McCracken of Michigan. Blough had been an economic adviser of Truman, and McCracken had served Eisenhower in this capacity; Sproul was affiliated with neither party and instinctively distrustful of politicians of whatever stripe.

Within three weeks the Sproul committee had produced a terse, realistic policy paper that gave priority to the problem of economic recovery but also sketched out a series of practical measures through which they believed the balance of payments deficit could be eliminated. President Kennedy met with the Sproul committee immediately following his inauguration, and his subsequent balance of payments message on February 6, 1961, incorporated much of the substance and policy thrust of the Sproul report.

The Kennedy message faced the issues realistically. In the short run, no sweeping reform of Bretton Woods could conceivably be negotiated, and even in the long run, no effective restructuring of the world financial system could be achieved without prior action by the United States to balance its external accounts. The President then indicated a scenario of various corrective measures designed to put things right. Inflation control was given top priority. This priority was indeed fundamental, and over the next five years there emerged a remarkable record of price and wage stability. A collection of other specific measures, some important and others of a window-dressing variety, rounded out a balance of payments program that was generally well received by foreign governments and the exchange markets. Having thus chosen to defend the dollar internationally, the President dramatized his commitment by giving his personal pledge to maintain the country's official price of gold. This personal commitment immediately rallied foreign confidence in the dollar, and the free market price of gold in London sank back toward the official $35 level. The jaws of the gold trap began to loosen their grip.

The significance of the Kennedy gold pledge reached far beyond its role in resolving the immediate crisis of confidence, however. Over the next eight years the gold commitment compelled the government to exercise continuing vigilance over trends in the balance of payments and to reinforce its policy defenses of the dollar whenever signs of weakness began to appear. Equally important, and almost paradoxically, the gold pledge also opened the way for a major cooperative effort between the United States and its major trading partners to protect the pledge against any speculative challenge by the gold and foreign exchange markets.

Yet Roosa and I were fully aware that President Kennedy's personal pledge to maintain the gold convertibility of the dollar at $35 per ounce was primarily a holding action that could hardly be sustained indefinitely by his successors. Dependence of the free world's monetary system on a dollar anchored to a fixed gold price would have to give way to broader, more flexible, but equally strong arrangements to assure harmony, and indeed discipline, in the way each country balanced its payments flows to and from the outside world. Our aim was to hold the present official price, through reliance on an evolving series of experimental approaches with new credit arrangements, until gold could begin to sink to the bottom of the reserve barrel. Eventually, we hoped, with a firmly established and tested series of concentric credit rings in full operation, the gold pledge could be withdrawn in an orderly and agreed manner. But that occasion was far down the road. The hard premise for getting any progress on that road had to be continued firm commitment to the gold-dollar price—to make it, in President Kennedy's words, "immutable."

To Treasury and Federal Reserve officials it was all too clear, moreover, that the Kennedy balance of payments program would only gradually squeeze out the deficit. Meanwhile, the recovery of confidence in the dollar achieved by Kennedy remained fragile and vulnerable to new flights of hot money out of the dollar as well as from one weakening European currency, such as sterling, into another. Insofar as such hot money flows found refuge in a high gold ratio country, the central bank involved would reluctantly but automatically cash in such dollar inflows at the U.S. Treasury gold window. Even more troublesome, the Federal Reserve with a recession on its hands was locked into an easy money stance and would have found it almost impossible to defend the dollar against new speculative outflows by a major increase in the discount rate.

In effect, the United States remained imprisoned by the entirely passive role of banker for the world financial system it had chosen for itself under the Bretton Woods agreements. To Roosa as well as to me, it seemed clear that the country must abandon this passive stance and immediately take the initiative in devising new technical defenses for the dollar that would cushion if not completely neutralize the impact of speculation on our gold stock. Any such endeavor clearly depended, however, on the cooperation of foreign governments, whose legal right to convert dollars into gold on demand had just been reaffirmed by President Kennedy. Accordingly, the question now arose of how best to open discreet communications with them.

Although the Washington headquarters of the International Monetary Fund had been intended to provide a center for such intergovernmental financial consultations, various institutional rigidities had frustrated the role originally envisaged for the Fund. The Fund's executive directors, representing its member governments, were generally subordinate officials of their central banks or treasuries, entrusted with little if any discretionary authority and lacking in some cases technical expertise in the intricacies of the gold and foreign exchange markets. Nor did direct contact by the U.S. Treasury with foreign treasury officials offer a more promising route. The European finance ministries had generally delegated to their central banks fairly full authority over their international financial operations. Such delegated authority included the now critical decisions whether to hold incoming dollar reserves or to convert them into gold at the U.S. Treasury window.

With all this in mind, the Sproul committee had recommended that the Federal Reserve should be entrusted with the task of consultation and "quiet negotiation" with its partner central banks abroad, to guard against destabilizing international flows of funds. This task of reopening communications with the foreign central banks quite naturally fell to the Federal Reserve Bank of New York, which had traditionally served as the operating arm abroad of the Treasury and of the entire Federal Reserve System, as well.

In the Wall Street area, the New York Federal is a distinctive landmark and has been graphically described by John Brooks in these words:

> The Federal Reserve Bank of New York stands on the block bounded by Liberty, Nassau, and William Streets and Maiden Lane, on the slope of one of the few noticeable hillocks remaining in the bulldozed, skyscraper-flattened earth of downtown Manhattan. Its entrance faces Liberty, and its mien is dignified and grim. Its arched ground floor windows, designed in imitation of those of the Pitti and Riccardi Palaces in Florence, are protected by iron grilles made of bars as thick as a boy's wrist, and above them are rows of small rectangular windows set in a blufflike fourteen-story wall of sandstone and limestone, the blocks of which once varied in color from brown through gray to blue, but which soot has reduced to a com-

mon gray; the facade's austerity is relieved only at the level of the twelfth floor, by a Florentine loggia. Two giant iron lanterns—near replicas of lanterns that adorn the Strozzi Palace in Florence—flank the main entrance, but they seem to be there less to please or illuminate the entrant than to intimidate him. Nor is the building's interior much more cheery or hospitable; the ground floor features cavernous groin vaulting and high ironwork partitions in intricate geometric, floral, and animal designs, and it is guarded by hordes of bank security men, whose dark blue uniforms make them look much like policemen.

Huge and dour as it is, the Federal Reserve Bank, as a building, arouses varied feelings in its beholders. To admirers of the debonair new Chase Manhattan Bank across Liberty Street, which is notable for huge windows, bright colored tiled walls, and stylish Abstract Expressionist paintings, it is an epitome of nineteenth-century heavy-footedness in bank architecture, even though it was actually completed in 1924. To an awestruck writer for the magazine *Architecture* in 1927, it seemed "as inviolable as the Rock of Gibraltar." . . . To the mothers of young girls who work in it as secretaries or pages, it looks like a particularly sinister sort of prison. Bank robbers are apparently equally respectful of its inviolability; there has never been the slightest hint of an attempt on it.*

The New York Bank had played a major international role in the twenties under Governor Benjamin Strong, who had linked the Federal Reserve with the Bank of England and other European central banks in a series of cooperative efforts to stabilize currency relationships. Since the early thirties, however, such transatlantic central bank cooperation had withered away. As Wall Street became the whipping boy of New Deal legislation, the New York Federal was also subjected to the restrictive if not jealous supervision of governors of the Federal Reserve Board in Washington, who did nothing to fill the void thus created.

The Bank had nevertheless continued to provide to the European and other central banks a broad array of banking and market ser-

---

* John Brooks, *Business Adventures*, New York: Weybright and Talley, 1968. P. 315. Used by permission.

vices, ranging from custody of their gold holdings to investment of their dollar reserves to exchange market operations in support of their currencies. Moreover, the Bank had rigorously maintained a nonpolitical approach. Its policy spokesmen—such as Sproul, Hayes, and Roosa—were regarded abroad as shining examples of professional integrity. The Bank had consequently remained a magnet for foreign central bank visitors seeking advice on operational or policy matters. They had been warmly received, although some may have been disappointed by the absence of wine at the luncheon table. As Per Jacobssen, former Managing Director of the International Monetary Fund, once wryly noted: "The New York Fed gives you good food and all the ice water you can drink."

On being appointed Vice-President in charge of the Bank's Foreign Department in April 1959, I had inherited this fund of foreign good will and respect for the Bank, and I felt considerable frustration that it was not being put to better national use. But in late 1960, a new role suddenly opened up—direct, personal contact on a regular basis with the European central bankers exercising the gold conversion privilege was clearly the starting point. And that starting point was 4000 miles away in the Swiss city of Basel, where the European central bankers regularly met at the Bank for International Settlements (BIS) over one weekend each month to discuss problems of mutual concern. So, with the blessing of William McChesney Martin, Chairman of the Federal Reserve and the Treasury, I made arrangements to fly to Basel to attend the December 1960 meeting of the BIS.

3

The Basel Meetings

Over the next 15 years my monthly trips to the Bank for International Settlements meetings at Basel were both exhilarating and strenuous. Out to Kennedy after the Thursday afternoon directors' meeting of the New York Federal, the overnight flight into the crisp morning air of Zurich's Kloten airport, then to the Schweizerhof Hotel in Basel, a few hours sleep, nonstop business discussions Friday night, all of Saturday and Sunday, and back to Zurich early Monday morning for the return flight to New York. But as the central bankers converged on Basel from all the European capitals, and from Ottawa, New York, and Tokyo, the fatigue of our journeys seemed to vanish as we greeted old friends and listened to the inside story of what was really going on in the financial markets of the world. And if, as so often happened, there were urgent matters to be negotiated, the imminent deadline of Sunday night efficiently concentrated our thinking.

Basel is an ancient city, originally the Roman Basilea, that bridges the Rhine at its uppermost navigable point. There the river turns abruptly north en route to Rotterdam, and as it flows past the terrace of the Three Kings Hotel is compressed into a racing current. On one BIS weekend, the challenge of swimming the Rhine proved irresistible to one of my Bank of England friends, Rupert Raw, an officer of the Scots Guards in the war. As Raw surreptitiously slid into the river in his underwear, a friend carried his London banking attire—dark tie, black-striped shirt, black suit, and black shoes—to a roughly targeted arrival point on the other side. But the velocity of the current had been grossly underestimated. Raw reached the far shore nearly a half-mile downstream, where he was promptly arrested for indecent exposure by a courteous but firm Swiss police-man. Other central bankers from time to time caught in such minor misdemeanors as jaywalking were immediately fined five francs, which was collected on the spot. And on one occasion, Governor O'Brien of the Bank of England was nearly run over by a tram car as he fled a pursuing swarm of journalists across the Basel Bahnhof-platz. Had O'Brien so much as bumped the tram, it would have ranked as a misdemeanor. The Basel tram cars enjoy the supreme right of way, and any injured pedestrian is immediately sued by the tramway authorities as a reaffirmation of the law of Baselstadt.

The passion of the Baslers for law and order is by no means re-served, however, for careless or unruly foreigners. The townspeople meticulously apply the same standards to themselves. Of the forty-odd countries I have visited, Basel is the one place where taxidrivers and waitresses consistently refuse tips when service has been in-visibly included in the charge. The origins of this dour but fierce

sense of civic pride go back a long way. Among other shaping in-
fluences, Basel was a center of the Reformation. To this day, the
Baslers celebrate their pre-Lenten Carnival one week after Mardi
Gras, thus commemorating what was originally a calculated affront
to the resident bishop of the Roman church.

In many respects Basel was an ideal meeting place for central
bankers seeking a refuge for quiet and confidential discussion of
highly charged financial issues. By Friday night, as we arrived,
Basel's excellent hotels and restaurants had been hurriedly vacated
by European business travelers, who thought of Basel as a Swiss
Philadelphia. Tourists and the services catering to them were almost
nonexistent, and no journalist ever came to Basel on a weekend unless forced by direct and intimidating orders to do so. Even among
the Baslers, probably few had ever noticed near the Bahnhofplatz an
office doorway, squeezed between a pastry shop and a jeweler,
identifying in small print the address of the Bank for International
Settlements.

Inside, the BIS offered to its visiting central bankers the spartan
accommodations of a former Victorian-style hotel whose single and
double bedrooms had been transformed into offices simply by removing the beds and installing desks. In between their formal weekend meetings, the central bankers shuttled back and forth in brief
personal visits to one another's private offices, but always stopping
en route to shake hands in the continental fashion with any colleague
going in the opposite direction. These private meetings were in
themselves worth the trip; they provided not only a quiet testing
ground for new ideas and approaches but also an early warning
system when things were beginning to go wrong. More generally,
the BIS weekends were what the French would call *sérieux*. However much money was involved, no agreements were ever signed nor
memoranda of understanding ever initialed. The word of each official was sufficient, and there were never any disappointments. The
day's meetings over, the central bankers returned to their rooms in
the Schweizerhof and the Hotel Euler, less than a minute's walk
away, only to gather later on for working dinners.

Before going to my first BIS monthly meeting in December 1960, I had already become acquainted with most of the European central bank governors through meetings in New York or Washington. But as I joined them in their formal Sunday afternoon meeting at the Bank for International Settlements in Basel, I was even more impressed by the sheer competence and personal distinction of these men who had reached the summit of their profession. Holtrop of the Netherlands Bank, Cobbold of the Bank of England, Baumgartner of the Bank of France, Blessing of the German Bundesbank, Carli of the Bank of Italy, Ansiaux of the Belgian National Bank, Schwegler of the Swiss National Bank, and Asbrink of the Swedish Riksbank were all names to conjure with in their individual countries. And here in this small room in Basel, with Holtrop as President of the BIS in the chair, their joint judgment now focused on the dollar, of which they collectively held more than $6 billion, all convertible into gold at the U.S. Treasury window.

They were very worried men that day, genuinely distressed by the impending clash between their sworn duty to protect the value of their countries' international reserves and their fear of precipitating a dollar crisis by cashing in dollars for gold. They had been particularly alarmed by the October 1960 flareup of the London gold price and welcomed the assurances I brought that the new Kennedy administration would firmly maintain the official United States gold parity and develop an effective program to close our balance of payments deficit. More generally, they felt that Federal Reserve participation in the BIS monthly meetings had now become essential, even though the Federal had never picked up the BIS stock initially allotted to it and our attendance could be in an observer capacity only. Nevertheless, I was extended the great privilege of an invitation to the governors' Sunday evening dinner, the inner sanctum from which all lower ranking officials were normally excluded. Over the next 15 years, monthly invitations to the governor's dinner gave me priceless access to their private thinking. I could generally sense from those dinner discussions which birds would fly and which would not.

Among the European central bank governors, Karl Blessing of the Bundesbank played a towering role during most of the decade of the sixties. As a young man, he had worked on the staff of the BIS and once recounted to me his anguished memories of those days as he watched from Basel the breakdown of international financial cooperation in the early thirties. Now, as President of the Bundesbank with the mark entrusted to his care, he wielded his enormous authority with courage and sensitive discernment of his world financial responsibilities. A cheerfully resolute man, Blessing was an unfailing source of strength and morale in all of our Basel discussions. I thought of him as a truly great man of his times.

My attendance at the BIS meetings also meant stimulating discussions, and sometimes lively arguments, with such international figures as Otmar Emminger, the brilliant Economic Advisor of the Bundesbank, Milton Gilbert of the BIS, Rinaldo Ossola of the Bank of Italy, Kessler of the Nederlandsche Bank, and the successive General Managers of the BIS, Guillaume Guindey, Gabriel Ferras, and René Larre. But the policy influence of these men found their major outlet not so much at Basel as in the intergovernmental meetings of the OECD group in Paris, where such broad policy issues as creation of the S.D.R. were focused. The BIS meetings were instead mainly devoted to operational problems in the gold and foreign exchange markets, and thus had become the primary meeting place of the European central bank officials responsible for such operations.

Accordingly, perhaps the most productive result of those early visits to the European central bankers was the professional understanding and personal friendships that quickly flowered with my opposite numbers, the foreign department men of the European central banks. These officials came to Basel as deputies to their Governors and clearly enjoyed their full trust and confidence. Tüngeler of the Bundesbank, Koszul of the Bank of France, Iklé of the National Bank of Switzerland, Bridge of the Bank of England, Count Vandenbosch of the Netherlands Bank, Ranalli of the Bank of Italy, André of the Belgian National Bank, and Akermalm of the

Swedish Riksbank—all warmly accepted my suggestion that we meet as a group each month to discuss current developments in the exchange markets and possibilities of joint action to control speculation. Those meetings of the so-called Gold and Foreign Exchange group, with all of the original members now in retirement, continue to this day.

There is something deeply satisfying in dealing with fellow professionals in any technical field. Never any speeches, everyone focusing clearly on the issue at hand, sentences frequently left unfinished because everyone instinctively knew the rest, and in an almost uncanny way, a simultaneous realization of the appropriate technical solution. None of us were romantic internationalists. But where we could see a clear overlapping of national interests, our minds instinctively reached out to one another in a true camaraderie of professional cooperation.

It was all to the good, moreover, in my initial meetings with the governors and foreign department heads of the European central banks that I had no policy instructions of the "Yankee trader" variety, which would undoubtedly have produced counterproposals equally inflammatory and time-consuming. At that time, all I needed to do was to predict the Kennedy pledge on gold and to invite their technical suggestions for protecting such a pledge by cooperative action whenever necessary to control speculation in the gold and foreign exchange markets. After years of thorough-going manipulation by the United States of international financial matters, this shift to a low-key, cooperative search for the right answers was probably a refreshing change. In any event, my professional associates in the European central banks rose to the technical challenge and in March 1961 decisively shaped the course of international financial cooperation for the next decade to come.

During the early months of 1961, even after the Kennedy gold pledge, the U.S. Treasury had continued to suffer each week small gold losses as a scattering of central banks cashed in new dollar receipts. Such chipping away of the United States gold stock, together with a continuing small premium on the London gold price above the Treasury's $35 parity, left the well-publicized impression that the dollar was still running a low-grade fever that might suddenly flare into a new speculative crisis. So it was with some apprehension that I received early in March 1961 a telex from the Bank of Italy, indicating that Governor Guido Carli was flying to New York to pay us a visit.

At the International Monetary Fund meeting during the fall of 1960, Alfred Hayes, President of the New York Federal, and I had asked Carli to stop buying gold on the free market in London, where speculation against the dollar-gold parity was beginning to boil up. As a *quid pro quo*, we had invited him to satisfy any essential gold needs of his institution by coming directly to the Treasury gold window. Now in early March 1961, the Bank of Italy had a swollen dollar portfolio of many hundreds of millions of dollars, all legally convertible into gold at the Treasury window. And if Carli now chose to make any sizable conversions into gold, the recovery of confidence we expected from the Kennedy balance of payments program could suffer a major setback.

Carli was a distinguished figure as he arrived on Friday, March 3, in Hayes' office on the tenth floor of 33 Liberty Street. A magnetic personality, with the strong, classical features of a senator or general of ancient Rome, Carli came directly to the point. He had been watching our weekly gold losses and felt that they were frustrating a natural recovery of confidence in the dollar by seeming to challenge President Kennedy's pledge on gold. Believing it essential that we shut off further reported gold losses for at least a few weeks time and thereby allow the recovery of confidence in the dollar to gain momentum during this breathing space, he had come to offer to sell us $100 million of gold, which might suffice to maintain our gold stock unchanged for several weeks to come. And if we agreed to buy it, how soon did we want it?

I replied: "Just telex us next Monday and we'll take delivery from your gold account here the same day." After a few pleasantries, on which Carli generally wasted little time, he left for Idlewild to fly back to Rome.

Robert Roosa was also visiting the bank that day, had joined us in Hayes' office shortly before Carli departed, and had greeted the news of Carli's offer in a gracious although somewhat deadpan manner as befitted an Undersecretary of the Treasury. But in subsequent conversation he was as elated as I. The Carli visit had confirmed our instinctive faith that the Kennedy gold pledge and a meaningful American effort to close the foreign payments deficit would elicit full cooperation from the foreign central banks in dealing with the speculative hurricanes of the future. And as we moved out onto those uncharted and stormy seas, Carli increasingly took over the role of our "Italian Navigator."

As it turned out, Carli's initiative was singularly well timed. That very evening I had invited Wilfrid Guth, then the German Executive Director of the International Monetary Fund, for dinner and the theater in New York. As we met, he told me that for reasons I could probably guess, he would have to pass up the theater and go back to Washington that evening. Otmar Emminger, the Economic Adviser of the Bundesbank, had flown from Frankfurt to Washington that day, to attend a special Fund meeting on the following Saturday morning.

I could indeed guess what was about to happen. During the early months of 1961, the German mark had been pressing hard against its official ceiling in the exchange markets. At the IMF annual meetings the previous September, Emminger had almost passionately urged on Roosa, myself, and others his conviction that the German mark must be revalued if the credit restraint policies of the Bundesbank were not to be washed away by a flood of foreign money attracted by high German interest rates. Since then, Roosa and I had discussed this policy issue on several occasions and we both strongly favored a German revaluation if the revision of the German parity were large enough to persuade the markets that a lasting correction had been applied. We were fearful, however, that the German government would be naturally cautious over inflicting too heavy a penalty on its exporters and would instead revalue by so small a percentage that the markets would consider it as only the first in a series of similar steps, consequently intensifying still further market speculation on a rising rate for the mark.

This is precisely what happened. After IMF approval, the revaluation announced by the German government on Saturday, March 4, was only 5 percent, far below press and market judgments that nothing short of 10 percent would be decisive. The following Monday, March 6, the Netherlands followed with a similar revaluation of the guilder. The exchange markets then erupted in a burst of speculation against sterling and in favor of the German mark, the Swiss franc, and other continental European currencies. The dollar as usual was caught in the speculative backwash. Over the next few days I had many worried calls from the foreign departments of the major Wall Street banks, who could see from the exchange market transactions passing over their books that dollars were piling up in Zurich and other European centers and might well be immediately converted into United States gold by the central banks concerned. All I could do was to take a deep breath and cheerfully tell them not to worry.

But as banker for all the major foreign central banks, the New York Federal in fact knew precisely and somewhat sadly where the hot money was going. Both the dollars being lost by the Bank of England and those taken in by the Swiss National Bank and other continental central banks were immediately reflected in the accounts of these institutions at the New York Federal. By the end of the week following the German revaluation, I could estimate that the potential drain on our gold stock within the next week or so was fast approaching the $500 million mark. Carli's generous gold sale offer on the previous Friday seemed likely to be swamped by the new crisis.

But here again, at this difficult moment, other European central bankers took equally decisive action to bring the situation under control. On Friday morning, March 10, I had a telephone call from Johannes Tüngeler, head of the Foreign Department of the Bundesbank, which had been flooded with speculative dollar inflows since the mark revaluation on the previous weekend. Tüngeler was a courteous, easy-going German from Berlin who managed the huge foreign operations of the Bundesbank with highly professional skill and a remarkable sense of responsibility not only to his own country but to the outside world. Over the years, I have known no other central banker whom I have trusted more. But in early 1961 our professional and personal friendship was just beginning. In February, I had stopped off in Frankfurt and spent an evening at Tüngeler's home, drinking beer before his fireplace, and exploring with him ways and means by which the U.S. Treasury or Federal Reserve could operate in both the spot and forward exchange markets to check speculation against the dollar and thereby insulate the United States gold stock against unnecessary losses. Tüngeler asked a good many technical questions, puffed away on his pipe, and promised to think it over.

When Tüngeler called me that Friday morning in March 1961, the exchange markets were still persuaded that the mark should be revalued by 10 rather than by 5 percent and had pushed the spot rate hard up against its new official ceiling. Even more troublesome, the three-month forward premium on the mark over the dollar had moved up to 4 percent, and at that exaggerated level tended to reinforce speculative anticipations of a further revaluation of the mark. To deal with this disorderly market situation, Tüngeler now suggested to me that the Federal Reserve Bank of New York immediately begin forceful sales of forward marks in the New York market with the objective of driving the forward premium down from 4 percent to no more than 1 percent. Such offers of forward marks would provide the market with readily available insurance at reasonable cost against the risk of a further mark revaluation, thus relieving the pressure of hedging demand for marks on the spot market. Such forward sales of marks—perhaps running to a billion or so—would have to be delivered 90 days hence, of course, and the New York Federal at that moment did not own a single pfennig.

But Tüngeler and his Bundesbank associates had a generous solution for this problem, too. If, when the forward mark contracts matured, the New York Federal could not cover them by mark purchases on the spot market without incurring a loss, the Bundesbank would sell to us against dollars all the marks we needed at the same rates specified in our forward contracts. In effect, our forward mark sales would be fully protected against any risk of loss. Conversely, if the spot mark should weaken and we thereby managed to cover our maturing forward contracts at a profit, the Bundesbank would be content with a 50–50 profit-sharing arrangement. Finally, he suggested, the very appearance of the Federal Reserve in defense of the dollar in the exchange market should have an encouraging effect on market confidence.

My spirits rose as Tüngeler outlined his proposal, and I promised to press hard for the necessary policy clearances on the American side. The New York Federal had no independent authority to undertake such an operation. But I was hopeful that Dillon and Roosa could be persuaded to authorize the Bank, as agent for the Treasury, to conduct this pioneering experiment. With their usual perception and decisiveness, they responded favorably in less than an hour. I called Tüngeler back and by the end of the day all arrangements had been made to launch the operation the following Monday morning, as soon as the New York market opened.

With a feeling of some exhilaration, I left my Green Village, New Jersey home by Bank car around 6 a.m. on Monday, March 13, to leave ample time for a final telephone review with Tüngeler of European market conditions before making our move at the 9 a.m. opening of the New York market. My anticipation turned to angry frustration, however, as a monumental traffic jam on the highway approaches to Manhattan finally forced me to set up shop in a telephone booth at the Newark Airport. This episode was a good lesson; thereafter, whenever a major market operation was planned, one of the senior officers of the Foreign Department stayed overnight at the Bank.

The Federal's offerings of forward marks turned out to be a major success. From March 13 to the end of the month we forcefully resisted the speculative inflow to Germany by selling more than $118 million equivalent of marks for delivery in three months. Market demand for forward marks then tapered off, reflecting the revival of confidence evoked by American official operations on so sizable a scale. But by mid-June our outstanding forward mark commitments had nevertheless risen to $340 million.

As the first of the forward mark contracts began to mature, however, those who had bought our forward marks now had to come up with the dollars to pay for them, and the spot dollar rate gradually rose off the floor to which it had been pinned for many months. Coordinated intervention by the Bundesbank and the U.S. Treasury in the spot mark market also helped to strengthen the dollar rate.

As the tide turned in our favor, it seemed desirable to allow the forward premium on the mark to rise somewhat, thereby increasing the cost of forward cover and further dampening commercial hedging demand. As a consequence, our outstanding balance of forward mark commitments declined rapidly after mid-June as the daily rate of new sales fell far below maturing contracts. In September, in a market also strongly influenced by the Berlin crisis, forward mark sales were discontinued entirely as a normal flow of forward marks from private sources reappeared. And by early December 1961 the Treasury's forward mark commitments had been fully liquidated at a sizable profit to both the Bundesbank and the U.S. Treasury. In general, the forward mark operation had not only helped to hold down short-term capital outflows from New York and the United States payments deficit, it had also calmed a badly shaken exchange market, which needed time and the assurance of intergovernmental cooperation to recover confidence.

While the initiatives of Carli and Tüngeler had provided unexpected new defenses of the dollar against speculation generated by the German revaluation, we were still exposed to gold losses resulting from the flow of hot money into Switzerland and other high gold ratio countries. But here again we had a remarkable demonstration of cooperation by the Swiss National Bank under President Walter Schwegler and his two top directors, Motta and Iklé. Max Iklé in Zurich was in charge of the Bank's gold and foreign exchange operations. Since the end of the war, Iklé and his associates had been guided by one very simple operating rule: the uncovered dollar holdings of the Swiss National Bank were not to exceed 100 million dollars. Any dollar receipts in excess of that figure were automatically converted into gold, either through the London gold market or at the U.S. Treasury window.

But in early March 1961, the Swiss National Bank suddenly found itself flooded in four days' time by dollar inflows exceeding $300 million, most of it the counterpart of reserve losses by the Bank of England, as market traders began to gamble on simultaneous devaluation of sterling and revaluation of the Swiss franc. And this in turn exposed the U.S. Treasury to a $300 million gold loss if the Swiss adhered to their traditional gold conversion policy.

On three trips to Europe during the winter months of 1960–1961, I had had lengthy conversations with Iklé and had enjoyed the hospitality of his home. His personal horizons extended far beyond the cluster of Swiss commercial banks on Zurich's Bahnhofstrasse. He had readily agreed that the rigid gold reserve policy of the Swiss National Bank had become something of an anachronism in the world financial system. The very success of Switzerland in establishing itself as a haven for hot money from all over the world now imposed on the Swiss financial authorities new burdens of international responsibility. The Swiss National Bank could no longer shrug its shoulders at the misfortunes of other major currencies, least of all punish the United States dollar by buying gold with the proceeds of flight capital gathered in from every trouble spot on the globe.

Now, as money poured into Switzerland after the revaluation of the mark, Iklé's good will was put to the test. And as I spoke with him each day by telephone, I was increasingly irritated by the total lack on the American side of any technical facilities to help deal with the problem. I could only counsel Iklé that he could rely on the Kennedy pledge on gold as a binding moral commitment.

By the next weekend, however, when the European central bank governors arrived in Basel for the monthly BIS meeting, Iklé and his associates had found a solution. Early that Saturday morning, Iklé drove from Zurich to the Schweizerhof in Basel, where Roy

Bridge, head of the Bank of England's exchange operations, was staying. Over breakfast, Iklé offered Bridge a three-month credit of $310 million. This Swiss credit provided the all-important nucleus of a billion-dollar package of similar credits from the Continental central banks rounded up by Cobbold and other Bank of England officials over the rest of the weekend.

In retrospect, these so-called Basel credits of 1961 to the Bank of England were a major breakthrough in postwar international finance. At one stroke, European central bank cooperation had not only saved sterling but also had protected the dollar against heavy gold drains. Furthermore, both Dillon of the Treasury and Martin of the Federal Reserve had become fully persuaded that the United States must quickly develop an active role in the international financial markets. Roosa had already initiated new cooperative approaches to the finance ministry officials meetings in Paris, and I was encouraged in my monthly trips to Europe to explore new possibilities of transatlantic central bank cooperation.

By midsummer of 1961 the British had managed to stanch the sterling hemorrhage and were about to repay the Swiss credit out of the proceeds of a medium-term borrowing from the IMF. Accordingly, the surplus dollar position of the Swiss National Bank would be recreated. But here again Iklé was already at work on a new solution. In the late spring of 1961 Iklé had suggested to me both in lengthy letters and in personal meetings that the New York Federal sell forward Swiss francs in volume, thereby reducing the premium on the forward Swiss franc. This would create a small but hopefully adequate incentive for Swiss investors to move short-term funds from Zurich into the dollar financial market on a hedged, or covered, basis. Such investment outflows would in turn reduce the surplus dollar holdings of the Swiss National Bank. Unfortunately the Swiss National Bank lacked the authority to guaranty us, as the Bundesbank had done, that the Swiss francs required to satisfy such forward contracts on maturity would be supplied to us by the Swiss National Bank if market conditions should prove unfavorable.

Treasury Undersecretary Roosa was understandably reluctant to engage in such forward sales of Swiss francs without an adequate cash reserve or other resource for covering them on the maturity date. But a solution unexpectedly turned up in a casual telephone conversation with Bill Heffelfinger, a wise old Assistant Secretary of the Treasury who had served his agency for nearly 45 years and had total recall of all Treasury financing operations since the days of Alexander Hamilton. I was complaining to Bill about the seeming impossibility of building up an adequate balance of Swiss francs to backstop the forward operation when he interjected: "Why don't we borrow them through an issue of Treasury certificates denominated in Swiss francs? Back in World War I, we put out a similar small issue denominated in Spanish pesetas to finance some wartime procurement problem. We still have the authority to borrow foreign currencies."

Dillon and Roosa quickly agreed, and in early August I negotiated with Iklé in Zurich a sizable Swiss franc line of credit against which three-month Treasury certificates could be issued at the Swiss call money rate of $1\frac{1}{4}$ percent. With the backstop of this credit line, the New York Federal now proceeded as agent for the Treasury to undertake forward sales of Swiss francs. By the end of November 1961, such forward sales had reached a total of $153 million, which meant a roughly corresponding reduction in the dollar reserves of the Swiss National Bank and in Swiss gold purchases from the U.S. Treasury. Moreover, the operation proved to be self-liquidating. In February 1962 the Swiss franc began to weaken, and by May the Treasury had bought nearly $140 million of Swiss francs and gold in direct transactions with the Swiss National Bank.

The success of these two Treasury operations in forward German marks and Swiss francs stimulated other European central banks to suggest similar cooperative experiments. At the April 1961 meeting of the BIS, President Holtrop of the Netherlands Bank said to me: "Why don't you get together with my Foreign Department people and see if you can't invent a way for me to avoid buying gold." And so in the fall of 1961 the New York Bank acquired for Treasury account a moderate cash balance of Dutch guilders, which provided reserves for a forward guilder operation launched in January 1962. The results were again favorable, more so in fact than we had anticipated, as a sudden outflow of short-term money from the Netherlands drove the spot guilder rate down to parity and put a severe squeeze on the Amsterdam money market.

Meanwhile, Governor Carli, Emilio Ranalli and other officials of the Bank of Italy had been following closely all these forward market operations by the New York Federal for Treasury account. In fact, when in August 1961 the New York Federal had telexed to all the European central banks information on the issue to the Swiss National Bank of Treasury three-month certificates denominated in Swiss francs, Ranalli of the Bank of Italy had immediately telexed back: "We would be prepared to do the same, and for a considerably longer term."

Now we were getting into much deeper water. The risk to the Treasury of assuming 90-day commitments in foreign currencies, either in the form of forward contracts in the exchange markets or three-month certificates of indebtedness, issued to foreign central banks, was generally not excessive. In so short a period, any prospective revaluation upward of a foreign currency would be fairly visible, if not to us at least to our foreign creditors. But for the United States to assume a two, three, or four-year debt through a Treasury bond denominated in a foreign currency was quite a different proposition. Over such a time span, revaluations such as those by Germany and the Netherlands in March 1961 could be neither foreseen nor ruled out. Accordingly, before assuming such medium-term commitments in foreign currencies, the United States needed formal protection against a revaluation of the currency concerned.

Officials of the Bank of Italy, the Netherlands Bank, and others with whom I discussed this problem fully agreed that the United States should not be penalized by revaluations of foreign currencies in which it was indebted. On the other hand, since few of the European central banks had the legal authority to provide exchange-rate guarantees to the U.S. Treasury, we seemed to have reached an impasse. But on a visit to Amsterdam in late 1961, I was sitting stiffly upright on an uncomfortable settee in Count Vandenbosch's office in the Nederlandsche Bank when the answer suddenly came to me.

I suggested to Vandenbosch that the central bank lending its currency should accept from the U.S. Treasury a standing order to liquidate immediately the outstanding debt, by a direct sale of the creditor's currency against Treasury dollar payment, if and when a revaluation of the creditor bank's currency became imminent. Vandenbosch, a former chess champion of the Netherlands, got up and shook my hand as we both visualized a new, open road of central bank cooperation through this formula.

Back in New York, I immediately drafted my "standing order" proposal and requested an opinion from Bank counsel. After the usual due course, assistant counsel Bill Braun came into my office with my memorandum in his hand and a grave if not doleful expression on his face.

I said: "Well, what do you think of it?"

He said: "It isn't worth the paper it's written on."

I said: "I don't give a damn whether it will stand up in court. In this business, no central bank is going to sue another one. What I want to know is whether acceptance of such a standing order is a binding moral commitment."

He said: "Assuming your foreign central bank friends have a sense of morality, they might find it hard to get off the hook."

I said: "That's all we need."

Roosa fully agreed that the moral commitment assumed by a foreign central bank in accepting such a standing order would indeed be enough, and the route was cleared for subsequent issue by the U.S. Treasury of medium-term bonds denominated in foreign currencies. In the Undersecretary's well-deserved honor, these instruments were promptly dubbed the "Roosa bonds."

By the end of 1961 both the U.S. Treasury and the New York Federal could feel that considerable progress had been made toward tempering the exposure of the dollar to the speculative winds of chance in the foreign exchange markets. During the year, the gold loss had been reduced by 50 percent, with much of the continuing drain accounted for by only four countries: Belgium, Britain, Spain, and Argentina. Most of the operational initiatives in defense of the dollar had come from the European central banks, but none of them would have volunteered such cooperation in the absence of the Kennedy gold pledge and the commitment to close our foreign payments deficit. Meanwhile, however, the U.S. Treasury, with Roosa playing a leading role, had launched negotiations that culminated in a $6 billion enlargement of the lending capacity of the International Monetary Fund. And the New York Federal had also undertaken a major initiative in planning a new defensive bulwark for the dollar against speculation in the London gold market.

4

Creation of
The Gold Pool

The edifice of Bretton Woods rested on the cornerstone of the United States official gold price of $35 per ounce. No direct reference was made in the Articles of Agreement of the International Monetary Fund to the fact that private markets in gold even existed. At the time private ownership of gold was prohibited by the American and British governments, the two major architects of Bretton Woods. Both countries were thus insulated against gold speculation by their own residents. But sterling and the dollar were also international currencies, widely held by foreign individuals and corporations who could switch from dollars or sterling into gold as they pleased. Elsewhere in the world, private gold trading was tolerated if not authorized by many governments.

From the very beginning, therefore, the official United States price of gold was vulnerable to speculative challenge by the private gold markets functioning abroad. Gold was not the exclusive property of the central banks in the Bretton Woods system, nor did our government enjoy full discretionary authority to fix and maintain a universal gold price of $35 per ounce over the indefinite future. Even in 1945, private hoards of gold outside the United States amounted to several billion dollars equivalent, and there was a fair chance that such gold hoarding would continue if not grow over years to come. Artistic and industrial uses of gold were also extensive and sensitive to price relationships with alternative metals. And the supply of newly mined gold obviously depended on a market price yielding an adequate profit. In effect, the official price of gold faced the eventual competition of the private marketplace in gold, which would eventually disregard official fiat and establish a price of its own.

But this threat to the dollar remained largely submerged during the first 15 years of Bretton Woods. Meanwhile, market trading of gold against dollars was being resumed in Tangier, Macao, Hong Kong, and wherever else permitted, mainly involving sales of existing private hoards to new buyers at only slight premia over the official price. In London, the Bank of England allowed a handful of licensed bullion dealers to act as middlemen in such transactions as long as the premia did not exceed 1 percent. Even such small premia above the official price nevertheless sufficed to attract the interest of South Africa and other gold-producing countries. By 1947 such marketing of newly mined gold came under the scrutiny of the IMF policy councils. In June 1947 the IMF issued a policy statement urging its member countries to "take effective action to prevent external transactions in gold at premium prices because such transactions tend to undermine exchange stability and to impair monetary reserves." In response to this Fund request, the British government withdrew permission for free gold market dealings in London, and a number of countries followed suit.

This policy stance of the International Monetary Fund soon began to crumble, however, as the Fund reluctantly yielded to insistence by the French government on establishing a domestic gold market in Paris. Then in February 1949 the Union of South Africa directly challenged the Fund by announcing that it had arranged to sell 100,000 ounces of gold at the premium price of $38.20 for manufacturing or artistic uses.

Since nothing in the Articles of Agreement could be construed as prohibiting such action by South Africa, the Fund had no alternative but to accept the *fait accompli*. The Fund remained concerned, however, that such sales of newly mined gold for manufacturing and artistic purposes were "increasing at a rate indicating that at least part of it finds its way to private hoards, contrary to the gold policy of the Fund established in June 1947." The staff of the Fund was called on to conduct studies of more effective methods of implementing the 1947 policy statement. But these studies ended with the judgment that closer policing was impractical. Accordingly, on September 28, 1951, the Fund reaffirmed the principles of the 1947 policy decision but concluded that it must leave to member countries the practical operating decisions involved in implementing such policy.

In United States government circles the policy issues posed by the free gold market did not receive high level attention during the early fifties, and quite understandably. At the end of 1951 the country's gold stock stood at $23 billion, roughly 64 percent of total world gold reserves. Such wealth naturally encouraged a complacent view of our ability to deal with any problem that might come along in the gold area. Although the dollar price of gold in Tangier and similar exotic markets held around the $40 level during 1952, such premium quotations got little publicity and were almost totally disregarded by other financial markets. Moreover, in 1953 a powerful new influence on the market appeared, that of Russian sales in considerable volume, which soon drove the gold price down toward the $35 official level.

In this new situation some American officials began to see certain advantages in a free gold market, where South African and Russian supplies might well tend to outrun industrial and hoarding demand. Such demonstrated dependence of the free market on a floor price set by the official $35 parity should take the wind out of the sails of Havenga, the South African Minister of Finance, who was already campaigning for an increase in the official price.

Against this background, a British government proposal in 1953 to reopen the London gold market met with no resistance in Washington official circles. But the Federal Reserve Bank of New York perceived two major risks that, with the passage of time, might have serious policy implications. The first risk was that by gathering a large volume of business hitherto transacted in bits and pieces in Tangier, Macao, and other smaller markets, the reopening of the London gold market along prewar lines might give much more prominence and perhaps even quasi-official status to the London price. In troubled times a rising London gold price might well be construed as a feverish weakening of confidence in the Bretton Woods system.

Second, the New York Federal saw the risk that a rise of the London price significantly above parity levels, whether occasioned by shortfalls of supply or speculative buying, would open up possibilities of foreign central bank arbitrage of gold between the U.S. Treasury gold window and the London market. In effect, some central banks might be tempted to sell gold in London at premium prices and then replenish their gold reserves at a profit by new purchases at par from the U.S. Treasury. In fact, if the Bank of England were to exert a stabilizing influence on the London price, it might be forced into such profitable arbitraging of gold between New York and London. Allan Sproul, President of the New York Federal, conveyed his grave concern on these points to both the U.S. Treasury and the Bank of England.

But in Washington the official mood was not to worry unduly over such distant problems, and on March 22, 1954, the London gold market was reopened. Thereafter, London progressively regained its traditional role as the primary gold market, attracting not only South African and Russian offers but also worldwide demand. Restoration of the London gold market was, in a sense, the crowning glory of London's recapture of its historic role as the primary raw material market of the world.

The structure of the London gold market was described as follows by the Bank of England quarterly *Bulletin* of March 1964:

> The daily fixing of the gold price, which takes place at Rothschilds beginning at 10:30 each morning, is the only daily international gold price fixing of its kind in the world. There is no fixing on Saturday or on New Year's Day; but on all other working days a representative of each of the five members of the gold market attends in person at the "fixing room" at Rothschilds, a member of which takes the chair. The chairman will suggest a price in terms of shillings and pence down to a farthing; this price will be chosen at the level where it is thought that buyers and sellers are likely to be prepared to do business. Anyone has the right to bid a higher price or, if the selling interest is uppermost, to offer at a lower price. Finally a point is reached where buyers and sellers come together at a price, and that is the fixing price of the day.
>
> The Bank of England are not physically represented at the fixing. But they are able, like any other operator, effectively to participate in the fixing by passing orders by telephone through their bullion broker, and at the fixing they use exclusively the services of the chairman of the market, namely, Rothschilds. The Bank operate for a number of different parties; they are first the managers of the Exchange Equalisation Account, which may be a natural buyer or seller of gold; secondly, they are the agent for the largest single regular seller of gold in the world, namely, the South African Reserve Bank, which is responsible for the disposal of new production in South Africa; thirdly, they execute orders for their many other central bank customers; fourthly, the Bank aim, as in the case of the foreign exchange and gilt-edged markets, to exercise so far as they are able, a moderating influence on the market, in order to avoid violent and unnecessary movements in the price and thus to assist the market in the carrying on of its business.

For several years after the reopening of the London gold market, private hoarding demand remained at a low ebb; Mocatta and Goldsmid's annual circular for 1956 regretfully reported a "nadir of public interest in gold" and estimated that central bank transactions accounted for as much as 50 percent of total turnover in the London market. The appearance of central banks as strong and persistent buyers of gold on the London market was a natural development. As an entrepôt between gold buyers and the South African and Russian mines, London was far more favorably located than New York. This location advantage was further magnified by a U.S. Treasury decision back in the thirties to impose a ¼ percent fee on both sales and purchases of gold by the United States. For gold deliveries *loco* New York, this decision established a sale price of $35.0875 and a purchase price of $34.9125. Transatlantic shipment costs, then running about 12 cents per ounce between London and New York, meant that the London price would have to fall below $34.80 before shipments of South African gold to New York would become profitable. Conversely, any European central bank wishing to buy gold for storage in London or in its own vaults could afford to pay up to $35.20 in London before finding New York a cheaper source of supply.

The width of such margins on gold transactions *loco* New York gave ample room for the London market consistently to provide a better deal to buyers and sellers simultaneously, and its business prospered with turnover reaching a fairly high level, probably as much as $1 billion annually by the late fifties. On the other hand, London's capacity to handle large-scale transactions remained severely limited by its hand-to-mouth dependence on deliveries of newly mined South African gold and because of irregular Russian sales with only a minimal availability of stocks on hand to meet sudden heavy demands. In effect, a central bank wishing to strengthen its gold stocks could readily carry out a purchase program of a few million dollars a week on the London gold market, thereby taking advantage of the discount below the U.S. Treasury sale price, but would probably have found it impossible to execute an order for $50 million or even $25 million on any single day. Any central bank wanting to buy gold in volume still had to come to the U.S. Treasury gold window.

On balance, these developments were disadvantageous to the United States. The Treasury found itself virtually cut off from access to South African and Russian newly mined gold, while foreign central banks selling gold to meet foreign exchange market pressures also got a better price in London than at the Treasury window. Meanwhile, many foreign central banks, large and small, regularly exercised their legal rights under the Bretton Woods agreement to ask the Treasury to convert sizable inflows of surplus dollars into gold.

From the mid-fifties onward, however, a new phenomenon appeared in the gold settlement area. Several major European countries—Germany, Italy, and France, together with Switzerland and the Scandinavian countries—began to develop inhibitions over buying gold from the United States. Moreover, the adverse trend of our gold stock–official liabilities ratio began to impress itself on the U.S. Treasury. By the late fifties Washington officials were already dropping hints of government concern over the erosion of our gold stock, which further sensitized the qualms already felt by many European officials. And so, behind a formal facade of rigid official adherence to the Bretton Woods gold settlements system, financial officials on both sides of the Atlantic quietly began to search for ways of dealing with an impending shortage of gold in the international financial system.

During the summer of 1960 public and more particularly academic perception of this hitherto submerged problem was suddenly clarified by publication of a lucid and challenging study by Prof. Robert Triffin, who posed the ultimate dilemma of a Bretton Woods system failing to provide either sufficient gold or sufficient dollars to meet the secular growth of international liquidity needs. But the major educational work in this field was soon to appear in ultradramatic fashion, courtesy of the London gold market.

During the first half of 1960 the London gold price had fluctuated over a narrow range of $35.08 to $35.12 in quiet trading. But from July 1960 onward, in the words of one London gold trading firm, "the market could smell thunder in the air." The presidential nominating conventions that summer stridently heralded the November election, which would mark the close of eight relatively tranquil years of the Eisenhower administration. In world financial markets, the November election became regarded as a major crossroads of political and economic policy choices in the United States, with possibly striking initiatives by the new administration taking office in January 1961.

Meanwhile, United States–Russian political relationships had been severely strained by the U-2 episode and Khrushchev's subsequent walkout from a summit meeting with Eisenhower. At home, the economy was slipping into recession; Federal Reserve policy was encouraging a continuing slide of New York money market rates while both the Bundesbank and the Bank of England had shifted to policies of credit restraint; this in turn opened up sizable interest-rate differentials favoring Frankfurt and London over New York. Outflows of short-term funds from New York now widened still further our payments deficit and accelerated gold reserve losses. Much attention was also being focused on the balance of payments burden assumed by the United States in the form of military spending in Germany and economic aid elsewhere. There was lively discussion of the possibilities of either severely pruning such programs or inducing other countries to take over a larger share of the burden. Both suggested courses meanwhile heightened international tensions.

In effect, the United States in the midst of the 1960 presidential election campaign suddenly found itself confronting a domestic recession and a foreign payments deficit, each urgently requiring corrective action. Orthodox policy correctives obviously threatened to relieve one problem while exacerbating the other, and the new policy mix needed to resolve this dilemma was by no means clear. The increasingly acrid debate between candidates Kennedy and Nixon further confused the issues.

In conservative financial circles all over the world, the Kennedy candidacy bred fanciful suspicions that a victorious Democratic administration might suddenly repeat the 1933 Roosevelt tactics of closing the gold window and devaluing the dollar. Not until October 31, 1960, did Kennedy formally commit himself to maintenance of convertibility at the $35 parity, and during the interim the cloud of market suspicion continued to grow. But it is one thing to worry and another to commit money to a judgment. On balance, the position of the dollar still seemed so impregnable that speculative buying of gold in London remained at relatively low levels. Although the Russians were temporarily out of the market, the supply of gold reaching London from South Africa was running well above normal, as the flow of newly mined gold was augmented by sales from the reserves of the South African Reserve Bank to finance a balance of payment deficit.

But a number of continental central banks, probably reflecting policy decisions to avoid any semblance of putting pressure on the United States, now began to buy increasingly heavily in the London market, where their purchases remained invisible to all but a few insiders. The Bank of Italy was a particular heavy buyer in London during the summer months of 1960. As such central bank buying of gold in London persistently swept the market clean of new South African supplies, the London price was pushed gradually upward to a level of $35.25 by September. Private speculators began to prick up their ears.

At the 1960 IMF annual meeting in Washington that month, I was informed for the first time by Bank of England officials of these developments in the London market. The Bank of England, having assumed some responsibility for selling gold to maintain orderly market conditions, was in the awkward position of being squeezed out of the market by other central bank buyers whenever gold became available. Accordingly, the Bank could not offset by market purchases its sales of gold from time to time as needed to maintain an orderly market. The Bank of England could, of course, cover its net gold sales in London by new purchases at the U.S. Treasury window. But here the problem of possible arbitrage profits on such transactions, as foreseen by the Federal Reserve Bank of New York before the opening of the London market, became something to worry about.

Even more worrisome to U.S. Treasury and Federal Reserve officials was the risk that assumption of responsibility for maintaining a ceiling on the London gold price, either directly through American intervention or indirectly through the Bank of England, would over time expose our gold stock not only to central bank demand but also to private demand from all over the world, including our own residents. Federal gold regulations at that time prohibited private purchase of gold in the United States, but curiously enough, permitted United States residents to acquire and hold gold abroad as they pleased. And by 1960 the advent of transatlantic jet service was making London readily accessible to any American with big money to protect against currency depreciation.

In the autumn of 1960, however, the supply of gold from South Africa and other sources was still running far ahead of industrial and artistic demand as well as normal hoarding demands from the Middle East and Far East. If European central bank buying on the London market could be restrained, therefore, there seemed to be a reasonably good chance that the London gold market might accommodate a considerable growth in private demand without an unduly sharp rise of the price. After consulting with Martin and Treasury Secretary Anderson, Hayes and I accordingly suggested to Carli and other European central bank governors attending the IMF meeting in Washington that it might be better for them to satisfy their gold needs by coming directly to the Treasury window, thereby giving the London gold market a chance to cool off.

British financial emissaries attending the IMF meeting in Washington were meanwhile making the rounds of a number of high-ranking American financial officials in pursuit of a clarification of United States policy regarding the London gold market. Bank of England officials, such as Maurice Parsons, welcomed the advice we had given to the Bank of Italy and other European central banks to buy gold directly from the U.S. Treasury rather than from the

London market. But they remained acutely aware of the potential embarrassment they faced in selling gold on the London market, then covering such sales at the U.S. Treasury gold window, perhaps at a handsome arbitrage profit, however accidental.

The policy clarification the British sought was not forthcoming, however, for the very good reason that the United States government itself was still wrestling with the same dilemma. On the one hand, Bank of England officials were given repeated and categorical assurances that no impediment would be placed in the way of British official gold purchases from the United States; in fact, in the course of such discussions the Bank of England bought a moderate amount of gold from the U.S. Treasury. On the other hand, U.S. Government officials confirmed the risk visualized by Bank of England officials of serious embarrassment, and possibly Congressional protest, if it were to become known that the Bank of England was arbitraging at a profit, or even without a profit, substantial amounts of U.S. Treasury gold into the London market to satisfy speculative demand.

More specifically, Bank of England officials got the impression that our government would favor a Bank of England policy of trying to limit its intervention role in the London market to a balancing out, over time, of temporary shortages and surpluses in the London market. In early October the Bank indicated to the Federal Reserve that it would pursue such an operational policy, while reserving full discretion to sell gold on any given day in such volume as it deemed required to keep the market orderly. At the time, I felt that this was a workable solution and so advised the U.S. Treasury.

In effect, this loose, informal understanding represented no more than an effort to buy time until a more fundamental policy decision could be reached. But in retrospect it seems to me to have thrust a worrisome burden of responsibility and political risk on the Bank of England. This in turn inhibited a sufficient delegation of operational authority to the gold and foreign exchange desk at the Bank of England and to its opposite number at the Federal Reserve Bank of New York. In effect, Bank of England intervention in the London gold market now required the personal approval of Governor Cobbold, while any recommendation on market tactics from the American side had to come from both Secretary Anderson and Martin of the Federal Reserve.

This lofty elevation of operational authority eliminated any risk of rash decisions by lower echelon officers. Simultaneously, it laid open the countervailing risk of a ponderously slow official response to any market emergency. Markets seldom wait on the pleasure of high authority.

Meanwhile, Secretary Anderson's strong reaffirmation of the country's determination to hold the $35 official gold price at the IMF meeting had had a reassuring effect, and during the first two weeks of October the speculative demand for gold eased. But as subsequently reported to us by a prominent figure in the London gold market, sentiment abruptly shifted during the weekend of October 15, 1960.

> During that weekend the Continent and, in particular, Switzerland, as well as Canada, seem to have decided that Senator Kennedy was going to be elected with a good majority. They considered that this would bring about more inflation in your country and, as a result, your balance of payments would suffer further. They considered, therefore, that a devaluation of the dollar in the first half of next year was a real possibility, and if done soon, it could be blamed on to the former Republican administration.

On Monday, October 17, Swiss banks began advising customers and probably themselves as well to take a flyer in gold, and the Bank of England was suddenly confronted with a speculative challenge in the London gold market. As buying pressure mounted, the Bank of England allowed the price to rise to $35.24 on Monday, $35.27 on Tuesday, and $35.38 on Wednesday. So far from dampening demand, the rise of the gold price instead confirmed earlier speculative judgments, and orders from Switzerland to buy at best now began to flash in a market suddenly devoid of normal offers.

On Thursday, October 20, the time bomb went off. At the fixing, the supply of gold bars provided by the Bank of England fell far short of balancing out the market and the fixing price shot up to $36.55. The market was now in full cry. Buy at best orders from Switzerland continued to force the price upward, and the chattering ticker services excitedly spread the alarm to financial markets throughout the world.

Market traders were aware of one sobering possibility, the risk that as the New York market opened, the Federal Reserve might suddenly step in with heavy gold offerings and smash the speculative bubble. But as 9 a.m. in New York came and went with no signs of official intervention, the speculative frenzy gathered new strength, and the London price rocketed above the $40 level.

At 9:15 a.m., as I came into my office at the Federal Reserve Bank of New York, all the alarm bells were clanging away. While not surprised that the Bank of England had allowed the gold price to rise still further, I was both astonished and angry that so sharp an increase, more particularly to the magic $40 level, had been permitted. Meanwhile, prominent personalities in Wall Street were bombarding the three top financial officials, Anderson, Martin, and Hayes with irate phone calls demanding to know why the dollar was not being protected against the speculators in the London gold market. The earlier judgment by the New York Reserve Bank that the London gold price would become a barometer of confidence in the dollar was being vindicated with a vengeance.

As the storm broke around our heads, Hayes and I asked Mr. Roche, our chief foreign exchange trader at the time, to telephone his opposite number at the Bank of England to find out what had happened and why. Roche's Bank of England contact politely declined to give him any estimate of the day's turnover, the amount of intervention by the Bank of England, the current and prospective availability of South African supplies, or any indication of intervention plans for the following day. This did not surprise me at all. Our earlier efforts, as the gold crisis was looming, to elicit similar information from the Bank of England had been consistently turned away with the comment that such figures were very closely guarded and were withheld even from Parliament.

It was no particular consolation to the New York Federal to hear that Parliament was equally barred from knowing what was going on in the London gold market. A partial explanation of such reticence, it seemed to us, was that the Bank of England valued and took most seriously its role as marketing agent of the South African gold mines. The Bank was concerned over the potential competition of the Swiss commercial banks as an alternative marketing agent and was consequently fearful of any leakage of information that might impair its agency relationship with South Africa.

More fundamentally, the Bank of England was instinctively inclined to play its cards close to its chest until the United States government made a clear-cut decision to approve or disapprove British official intervention on the London gold market. In reviewing the breakout of the London price, British press commentary at the time suggested that there seemed to be a lapse of communications between the Bank of England and the Federal Reserve. The fact of the matter was that no communications on the gold market intervention problem had ever existed, and it now became our task to develop them in a hurry.

As the Federal as well as the U.S. Treasury urgently pressed for further information on the London gold market, the Bank of England quickly and courteously began to open new channels of communications with us. Maurice Parsons, Executive Director of the Bank of England, had gone on to Canada after the IMF meetings but now returned to New York where he was joined by his associate George Preston, who had been handling among other duties the Bank's operations in the London gold market. Preston was a slim, clean-looking man with one of the sharpest, toughest minds in his field. His manner was candid and direct. I trusted him instinctively, but only later did I realize how stalwart a friend of the Federal Reserve he would prove to be.

Federal Reserve and Treasury discussions with Parsons and Preston in New York and subsequently in Washington yielded two main conclusions. First, as the press and other market observers had already guessed, the volume of turnover on the London gold market on October 20 had been relatively small, probably no more than $20 million equivalent. Accordingly, Bank of England intervention to hold the price within reasonable limits would not have been unduly costly, and a telephone call to the New York Federal warning of an impending speculative challenge might easily have produced *ad hoc* joint official action the next day.

Suspicions naturally flared in many minds that the October 20 breakout of the London gold price had been a deliberate rather than accidental error, and such suspicions quickly became outraged convictions in Paris, Zurich, and other continental centers. My own guess at the time was that the equivocal position of the United States government regarding the London gold market had been the paralyzing factor, and I still hold to this view.

Second, the Bank of England representatives suggested that so much speculative fervor had been generated by the breakout of the London price that it would now prove fairly costly to force the price back down to the $35 level. As Preston put it, "the market had tasted blood," and a major effort would now be required to satiate its appetite. I strongly supported his appraisal, and agreement was reached to push the price back toward a target of roughly $36, but not to expose ourselves to potentially heavy demand below that level.

Immediately following the Washington discussions with Parsons and Preston, the U.S. Treasury issued a press statement noting that the Bank of England had been intervening over the years in the London gold market and stating categorically that the U.S. Treasury had no criticism of such policy. The Treasury statement also noted that in accordance with long-standing practice, the United States both bought and sold gold at the request of the Bank of England at the official price. This statement not only formally reassured the Bank of England that it could count on replenishing gold sold on the London market by coming to the U.S. Treasury window, it carried the even more important implication that the U.S. Treasury would defend such practice against Congressional or other criticism.

The Bank of England thus retained an almost entirely free hand in managing its risk-free intervention on the London market and, so long as the price stayed significantly above $35, a handsome arbitrage profit as well. In the emergency circumstances then prevailing, this was probably the only deal that Secretary Anderson could have made, but it clearly marked the beginning rather than the end of the story.

A lot of the speculative heat went out of the London gold market as implications of the Washington meetings were digested. By late October the price had drifted down to $36 and was held around that level by forceful Bank of England intervention, as market jitters developed just before and after the American election in early November. Thereafter, the market quieted down and the price fell off to $35.60 by year end.

As the dust settled, both the costs and benefits of the speculative explosion of October 20, 1960 became more clearly visible. On the one hand, worldwide confidence in the heretofore sacrosanct dollar had been badly jolted. Anxiety over our balance of payments and the functioning of the Bretton Woods system was no longer confined to a handful of currency experts. From this point on, the international financial markets would mercilessly scrutinize American economic performance and rate the dollar accordingly. Foreign central banks, enjoying as they did a legal right under the Bretton Woods system to convert dollars into gold, could no longer forego this privilege without exposing themselves to charges of imprudent management of the national reserves entrusted to their safekeeping.

During the fourth quarter of 1960, 26 foreign central banks made precautionary purchases of more than a billion dollars in gold from the U.S. Treasury. By the end of 1960 the United States gold stock had fallen to $17.8 billion. Such gold drains continued into the early months of the Kennedy administration, following the inauguration in January 1961.

Such stripping away of the illusion of American economic invulnerability was sooner or later inevitable, of course, and its actual timing came as a fortuitous and stern warning to the economic policy planners of the new administration, some of whom had been nurturing illusions of American omnipotence. Both the departing Eisenhower administration and the incoming Kennedy officials were stung by the challenge mounted by the London gold market, and solid bipartisan support was immediately forthcoming for strong measures to defend the dollar. Late in 1960 President Eisenhower had announced drastic if somewhat impractical economies in military spending overseas, and on January 14, 1961, the U.S. Treasury had belatedly closed the loophole in the gold regulations that had permitted American residents to buy and hold gold abroad.

There was also implicit agreement by the outgoing and incoming administrations that we had to abandon our passive stance in the international monetary field and assume a positive, if not a leadership, role. In particular, there was an urgent need to open full and timely communications with the European central banks, both bilaterally and jointly through their monthly meetings at the Bank for International Settlements. Thus, as previously related, it was agreed that I should attend the December 1960 monthly meeting of the BIS in Basel, stopping en route at the Bank of England, the Bank of France, the German Bundesbank, and the Swiss National Bank.

In London I met for the first time Roy Bridge, who was responsible for the Bank of England's operations in both the gold and exchange markets. Bridge was a small, dapper man with a thin, grizzled mustache, intelligent gray eyes, and the air of an experienced old cat quietly appraising an unwary mouse. Sterling was riding high at the time and so was Bridge; he reacted to the fortunes of sterling as if they were his own, and his ebullient satisfaction with the state of the world at that moment did nothing to improve my own somewhat sour mood. Yet I think our friendship dates from that first meeting in London, when over a late evening drink I mentioned to him my sense of outrage and anguish over the recent speculative attack on the dollar. Bridge had already suffered the same harsh experience several times over in the case of sterling and spontaneously welcomed me as a comrade in arms, facing the common enemy of misguided government policy and consequent speculation in the exchange markets. This sense of professional understanding and sympathy subsequently opened many avenues of technical cooperation between us as sterling and the dollar alike became subject to recurrent speculation.

That December in London, Bridge was naturally delighted with the new arrangements under which the U.S. Treasury had assumed the full cost of his gold market intervention, and he was clearly determined to resist any suggestion of sharing the operation with other central banks. However he was fully prepared to provide the Federal Reserve through coded telephone messages with full information on daily developments in the gold market (and, as always, kept his word). On this note I left for Paris, where I ran into a hornet's nest of deeply worried and angry officials of the Bank of France.

Gold hoarding is endemic in France, and the French government had been forced to allow the opening of a domestic gold market soon after the war. The explosion in the London gold market had had thunderous reverberations on the Paris market and threatened to evoke a new challenge to a still shaky French franc. In short, the French view, put to me with some asperity, was that the United States should immediately ram the London gold price back down to $35 and thereafter should closely police Bank of England intervention operations to make sure that the price did not again get out of control.

The French recognized the potential drain on United States gold reserves from such an all-out intervention policy, but they pointed to the countervailing risk that an uncontrolled London gold price might put heavy political pressure on other central banks, not excluding the Bank of France, to take fuller advantage of the gold conversion privilege. This was the sort of straight talk that I soon became accustomed to hear from Bank of France officials, and in the context of American policy planning then going forward, I found it most helpful.

Again at the Bundesbank in Frankfurt, the Swiss National Bank in Zurich, and the BIS in Basel, which were next on my itinerary, I encountered the same grave apprehension regarding the speculative consequences of an uncontrolled London gold price and a clear readiness to welcome any new American initiative to deal with the problem. The Bundesbank, whose gold ratio had slipped well below the 50 percent level, felt particularly exposed to public criticism.

Such foreign official concern over the London gold market was decisively relieved, however, as President Kennedy in February 1961 categorically asserted his intention to maintain the $35 official price. Further downward pressure on the London gold price was exerted by the Russians, who returned to the market with sizable sales. Then in the early spring of 1961 the gold speculators were thoroughly routed as sterling fell victim to new balance of payments troubles, and the Bank of England found it useful to finance some of its dollar sales in defense of sterling by sizable gold offerings on the London gold market. By May the London gold price had plummeted to $35.05, and market sentiment toward the dollar had shown a major improvement.

Both the new Treasury team, headed by Secretary Dillon and Undersecretary Roosa, and the New York Federal Reserve nevertheless assumed that the gold speculators would be back at the first sign of new trouble. Accordingly, we pushed ahead on devising a new solution to the London gold market problem that would lessen the potentially enormous drain on our gold stock. As I shuttled between Europe and Washington during the spring and summer of 1961, the idea began to take shape in my mind of a central bank syndicate to which various central banks would commit agreed amounts of gold to finance intervention on the London gold market.

In itself, the idea was not new. Shortly before the October 1960 breakout of the London gold price, the General Manager of the BIS, Guillaume Guindey, had visited the Bank in New York and had suggested to Hayes and me the possibility of European central banks as well as the BIS assisting us in keeping the London price under control. We then floated a similar suggestion with Bank of England officials, who immediately and correctly pointed out that there was nothing in this for the United States if such gold sales in London by the continental central banks were immediately replenished by gold purchases in New York, just as the Bank of England felt it must do. And quite clearly, any intervention operations on the London market should be channeled through a single agent, with the Bank of England the obvious choice.

The key question, therefore, was whether it would be possible to negotiate a syndicate arrangement under which the Bank of England and other European central banks joining with us would be prepared to hold for some unspecified period the dollar proceeds of their gold sales on the London market, to ensure that the full burden of intervention did not immediately fall on the United States gold stock. By the late spring of 1961 I had received sufficient encouragement of this idea from the Bundesbank, the Swiss National Bank, and the Bank of Italy to risk opening negotiations with the entire BIS group of central banks. I immediately encountered stiff resistance, however, from several other European central banks who were reluctant to delegate full authority to the Bank of England for intervention operations on their behalf and also feared that other central banks might snap up the gold they sold in London. The French were particularly concerned over the latter possibility.

Meanwhile, the Russian decision on August 18 to put up the Berlin Wall and to exercise other strong-arm tactics had ignited new speculation in the London gold market, and the price moved steadily up during the late summer months of 1961.

In view of the resistance developing in my negotiations in Basel, the gold price trend became a matter of serious concern to Secretary Dillon and Undersecretary Roosa, who then took direct and vigorous action at the political level. At the IMF meeting in Vienna in September, 1961 Dillon made clear to British Treasury officials that we wanted the Bank of England to resist firmly any movement in the gold price above $35.20. He further stressed the need for close consultation with the New York Federal on market tactics and urged British support of Federal Reserve negotiations under way in Basel for creation of a central bank gold syndicate or pooling arrangement. In Paris Roosa and Chairman Martin subsequently talked in similar vein to officials of the French Treasury.

After further telephone consultations with several European central banks, I drafted a memorandum sketching out the main points of a gold pool proposal and, on receiving Treasury approval, Hayes and I took it with us to the November BIS meeting. The main features of our Gold Pool proposal, as presented to a meeting of the Governors in the office of President Holtrop of the BIS, were as follows:

1. All the major central banks had a mutual interest in avoiding speculation on the London gold market through official intervention and in the related problem of minimizing sudden sharp effects of intervention of the U.S. monetary gold stock, by sharing the burden of such intervention.
2. The central banks of the following countries would be asked to commit $270 million of gold to the Pool:

Germany	$ 30 million
United Kingdom	25 million
Italy	25 million
France	25 million
Switzerland	10 million
Netherlands	10 million
Belgium	10 million
United States	135 million
Total	$270 million

3. The Bank of England would manage intervention on the London market by selling its own gold and at the end of the month would be reimbursed by the various participants in accordance with their relative shares in the Pool.
4. The immediate objective should be to keep the London price from exceeding $35.20, which was roughly equivalent to the cost of delivering *loco* London gold purchased in New York. If possible, the price should be pushed below $35.20 insofar as this could be accomplished without unduly heavy intervention.
5. The dollar proceeds of such Pool sales would remain fully convertible by the recipient central bank into gold in New York at all times. But if a central bank's total dollar holdings remained within normal limits, we hoped that the bank would retain the dollar proceeds of such London gold sales. If, on the other hand, the dollar proceeds clearly ex-

ceeded the need for dollar reserves, they would be converted into gold in New York. Since one purpose of the pool would be to soften the immediate impact of United States intervention on the Treasury's gold stock, however, we hoped that such conversions would not take place immediately after receipt of the dollar proceeds. But it would be entirely within the option of the central bank whether to convert in one week, one month, several months, or not at all.

6. The participating central banks and the United States should agree not to buy any gold in the London market nor from any other source, such as Russia or South Africa. Furthermore, we should undertake to persuade other central banks, when opportunities arose, to adopt similar policies.

As on many subsequent occasions, Hayes did a brilliant negotiating job in advancing these Gold Pool proposals at the BIS meeting of November 1961. His personal integrity and tactful persuasiveness almost magically dissolved the national policy differences emerging during the meeting, and we left for New York the following Monday with a gentlemen's agreement to activate the Gold Pool that very day. In the traditional spirit of the BIS meetings, not a scrap of paper had been initialed or even exchanged; the personal word of each governor was as binding as any written contract. For the time being, it was decided that the Gold Pool agreement should remain secret. Publicity, the governors rightly felt, might quickly expose and perhaps inflame the delicate operational problems that undoubtedly lay ahead.

The supply of newly mined gold from South Africa had been falling off sharply as South Africa moved into surplus in its international payments. But the Gold Pool agreement to halt central bank buying on the London market more than offset the shortfall in South African supply, and the London gold price had fallen from $35.20 to $35.15 by the time of the December BIS meeting. In the meantime, Bridge of the Bank of England had succeeded in limiting Pool sales to no more than $17.4 million. Accordingly, the first month of operations of the Pool seemed fairly successful.

I brought with me to the December 1961 BIS meeting several further suggestions I had previously cleared with the Treasury. First, we recommended that the Pool remain in existence, but in view of the decline in the market price to a roughly appropriate level, selling operations should now be suspended, to save the reserves of the Pool for use in a period of more severe strain. Second, we urged the Bank of England to continue to provide the members of the Pool with a monthly accounting of total demand, new production, Russian sales, and such other data as were needed to appraise market developments. Third, we asked all the BIS central banks to continue to refrain from buying gold on the London market, as well as gold offered by Russia and other suppliers through other channels. Fourth, we urged the Bank of England as manager of the Pool to stop making direct purchases of gold from the Russians, to allow such Soviet offerings to exert their full impact on the market price.

The European governors warmly welcomed the recommendations to suspend Pool operations as evidence of our good faith. The Bank of England also agreed to brief the other European central banks on market developments at each BIS meeting, but continued to question the desirability of barring central bank access to the London market or direct deals with the Russians. Here the Bank of England had a point. The whole rationale of the Pool operation depended on the assumption that new production and Russian sales would as speculation subsided considerably outstrip private demand, thereby enabling the Pool to replenish any sales made to deal with short-term speculative situations.

Sooner or later, therefore, continuation of the prohibition of central bank buying in the London market would lead to a surplus of supplies on the London market, which would press down the price to levels at which the South Africans would undoubtedly begin to complain bitterly over the Bank of England's performance as their agent. Alternatively, the BIS group of banks would be in the untenable position of denying themselves access to the London gold market while other central banks throughout the world took advantage of gold offerings in London at bargain prices. Some way out of this dilemma had to be found, and it occurred to me that the natural counterpart of our Gold Pool sales operations would be a joint gold buying program, to be organized when market conditions permitted, again employing the Bank of England as our agent.

On returning to New York I drafted a further proposal that would convert the Gold Pool into a gold buying as well as selling syndicate. Naturally this was enthusiastically endorsed by the U.S. Treasury and, when presented to the January 1962 BIS meeting, by the European governors as well. I stressed the desirability of avoiding a competitive central bank scramble for surplus gold appearing on the London market. Quite clearly, by allowing the Bank of England to function as our purchasing agent, we would confront the two major sellers, South Africa and Russia, with a single buyer representing the United States and Western Europe and presumably could strike a better bargain on the price than if we had acted independently.

There remained a number of technical details to be settled, such as the maximum London price we should be prepared to pay and the even more troublesome question of how to allot Bank of England gold purchases among the participants in the Pool. The BIS governors wanted no part of a haggling encounter over shares that might disrupt the cordial atmosphere of Basel, however, and delegated this delicate problem to Bridge of the Bank of England, Tüngeler of the Bundesbank, myself, and other foreign department men of the BIS central bank group.

At the February 1962 meeting of our Gold and Foreign Exchange group, we found the practical solutions needed. The maximum price for Pool gold acquisitions was set around $35.08, after U.S. Treasury agreement to waive the ¼ percent charge on direct gold sales by the United States to members of the Pool. This fixed the New York price at $35 flat and implied a shipping parity *loco* London of roughly $35.08. After considering various formulas of sharing gold purchases based on balance of payments trends, gold ratios, and so on, we settled for the simple, objective criterion of the previously agreed shares in the selling pool, with the proviso that any Pool member in need of dollars for balance of payments reasons might cede part or all of his share of the Pool's gold purchases to the other participants.

At the March 1962 BIS meeting the governors approved our recommendations for establishment of a Pool for gold buying, as well as selling, and the new arrangement went immediately into operation. During the spring Russian selling appeared in some volume; the Pool was able to recoup the $17 million of gold sold in November 1961, and by the end of May 1962 had built up a surplus of $80 million. Meanwhile the London price had fallen off to $35.07. Late in May 1962, however, a sharp break in the American stock market (largely in response to the confrontation between President Kennedy and U.S. Steel), together with a severe attack on the Canadian dollar, revived speculative buying in the London gold market. By mid-July 1962 the Gold Pool surplus had been exhausted.

After supplying $50 million of Treasury gold to finance further intervention on the London gold market, the New York Reserve Bank requested reactivation of Pool gold sales, and this was approved by the European governors at the July 1962 BIS meeting. Some respite from speculative pressure on the London gold market was gained on July 23, when President Kennedy, in the first televised program carried across the Atlantic via the Telstar satellite, repeated with some vehemence that he would not alter the official price of gold. As noted by Mocatta and Goldsmid in their annual circular for 1962:

> This led, reasonably enough, to the reflection that there were plenty of other things he could do in case of need to protect the international value and prestige of the U.S. dollar and the immediate pressures were at once relaxed.

Further small drains on the Gold Pool reserves occurred in August and September. But in October 1962 a challenge of the first magnitude appeared. During the Cuban crisis, speculative demand erupted, the Bank of England let the price ride up sharply to $35.20, then forcefully intervened for a total of nearly $60 million over the three-day period, October 22–24. Curiously enough, a sizable share of Pool intervention during these three days of crisis was financed by further sales of gold by the USSR. The drain on the Pool's reserves was also sizable, however, increasing its cumulative deficit by October 24, 1962, to more than $80 million.

As the Cuban crisis subsided and Russian sales continued, the Pool quickly recovered $70 million of its earlier losses, leaving a net deficit of no more than $12 million by the end of November 1962. The Federal Reserve then repeated its recommendation that the selling operations of the Pool be suspended until further notice. Over its first year of operations, therefore, the Pool just about broke even. South African deliveries had been running below normal and would eventually recover. But the withdrawal of European central bank buying in London had been largely offset by a strong rise of private demand, which might well continue to grow. At that point the most we could claim for the Pool was that it had been a successful holding operation, in no small measure thanks to Bridge's skillful management of intervention operations.

As we moved into 1963, we were favored by a relatively quiet London gold market in which the price never rose above $35.12. Private demand for gold fell off appreciably from the very high 1962 levels, while South African deliveries rose, and the Pool steadily acquired gold in moderate volume.

Then in the autumn of 1963 the harvest failure in Russia suddenly transformed the whole gold market picture. Heavy imports of wheat from Canada and other suppliers were quickly arranged by the Soviets. We initially anticipated that a high percentage of such wheat imports would be financed by lengthy credit arrangements, with only a marginal increase of Russian gold sales ensuing. As it turned out, however, the USSR, which traditionally puts great store by its impeccable credit rating internationally, objected strenuously to the credit terms available in the international markets and decided to finance its entire cereals import requirement by sales of gold out of reserves.

Suddenly the Pool was flooded with gold. During the final quarter of 1963, Russian sales of $470 million plus other net receipts swelled Pool acquisitions to $639 million, all of which was distributed to the members of the Pool. Further heavy Russian sales totaling $438 million were made during the first half of 1964. South African deliveries also rose by more than 25 percent, and by the end of September 1964 the Pool had accumulated and distributed a further $656 million. In 21 months the Pool had thus augmented the gold reserves of the BIS group of central banks by $1.3 billion, of which the U.S. Treasury's share was nearly $650 million.

At this point the Pool had succeeded beyond the wildest dreams of any who had participated in its creation. Yet the handful of central bankers who were familiar with the Pool's accounts knew all too well that we could not rely on a continuation of such good fortune. The London gold market still represented a time bomb resting at the very foundation of the Bretton Woods system, and as subsequently related, I began in 1965 a major effort to alert the United States government to the risk involved.

5

The Federal Reserve Swap Network

The burgeoning foreign activities of the Reserve Bank of New York in 1961 as agent of the U.S. Treasury aroused mixed feelings among the governors and staff of the Federal Reserve Board in Washington. The wings of the New York Bank had been severely clipped by New Deal legislation in the early thirties. Since then, several governors of the board as well as their staff men had devoted themselves to the task of keeping the Bank grounded. The Chairman, William McChesney Martin, had taken a keen interest, however, in the

Bank's experimental operations in the foreign exchange markets, had personally checked out our operational capacity, and now concluded that the Bank should undertake operations in the exchange markets on behalf of the Federal Reserve System as a whole.

Martin's influence on Washington policy, when he chose to use it, was generally profound. President of the New York Stock Exchange in 1938 at the age of 31, a colonel in Military Intelligence during World War II, he had been appointed President of the Export-Import Bank on returning from the service. In 1949 he had switched to Treasury as an Assistant Secretary, in which capacity he had helped negotiate the "Accord" of 1951 that freed the Federal Reserve from the wartime policy of pegging interest rates. In 1951 he had been appointed Chairman of the Federal Reserve Board of Governors, remaining in that post under five successive presidents until 1970. Martin ran the Federal Reserve in a cheerful and relaxed way, tolerant of clashing views among his fellow governors and the 12 Reserve Banks, and he strongly supported the regional roles of the Reserve Banks against the centralist forces seeking to concentrate all authority in the Federal Reserve Board in Washington.

As a personality, he was refreshingly modest, buying his gray herringbone suits off the rack and in every other way maintaining a low profile. But he had a fierce personal pride in all he undertook and a quiet readiness to rise to a challenge. A former member of the Yale Club boxing team, he had while a young broker on Wall Street accepted a dare to fill in as a substitute in a preliminary bout at Madison Square Garden and had acquitted himself admirably. In the same vein, when in 1965 a showdown loomed between the Johnson administration and the Federal Reserve over the question of a discount rate increase, Martin had insisted on forthright Federal Reserve action, against the timorous advice of many of his colleagues. He was then peremptorily summoned to the Johnson ranch to explain his defiance of presidential authority. Martin won that battle, too, in the same style he dealt with so many other critical issues. His leadership at such times was diplomatic but unmistakably firm.

As a central banker, Martin acquired during his tenure an unrivaled professional prestige, comparable only to the status of General Marshall as head of the military establishment. He had other talents as well, without which his professional qualifications might have been largely wasted. I recall sitting beside Prof. Milton Friedman, no friend of Martin's monetary policy, when Dr. Arthur Burns was sworn in as Martin's successor by President Nixon at the White House in January 1970. Friedman surveyed the assembled political dignitaries, turned to me, and said: "I still think Bill Martin is the best politician in the room."

In 1961 Martin's judgment that the Federal Reserve should assume a major international role was swiftly translated into action. There were solid technical reasons for such an initiative. Abroad, the permanent staff of the central banks, rather than frequently changing finance ministry administrations, had generally been entrusted with the professional task of conducting exchange market operations within broad policy guidelines. Here in the United States there was also an obvious advantage in assuring continuity in the management of exchange market operations through the agency of the Federal Reserve. Moreover, in common with other central banks, the financial capacity of the Federal Reserve to conduct international financial operations extended far beyond that of the Treasury. As the money-creating authority, the Federal could rise to almost any financial emergency, whereas the Treasury was confined, in the absence of new Congressional appropriations, to the existing $330 million resources of its Stabilization Fund.

At the Treasury, Dillon and Roosa were thinking along similar lines and agreed with Martin that plans for a sharing of foreign financial responsibilities between their two agencies should quickly be developed. In this planning endeavor, a major role was played by Ralph Young, Secretary of the Board and of the Federal Open Market Committee (FOMC), who had recently been placed in charge of the board staff's Division of International Finance as well. Young was a polished old professional, wise in the ways of Washington, who brought to his new responsibilities on the foreign side a refreshing readiness to accept the New York Federal as a partner rather than a rival of the Board in Washington. We trusted each other, and for the first time in many years the Board staff and the New York Federal began to work together rather than at cross-purposes on international matters.

Beginning in the summer of 1961, Young and I collaborated with Roosa and other officials of the U.S. Treasury in drafting a series of policy papers that spelled out a projected sharing of responsibility and authority between the Treasury and Federal Reserve in international financial operations. Although not explicitly defined, the key understanding was one of countervailing veto power by each agency. The Treasury, entrusted as it was with overriding authority on international financial matters, retained the right to veto any projected market operation of the Federal Reserve with which it did not agree. On the other hand, the Federal Reserve retained a similar right to refuse to undertake with its own funds, or at its own risk, any financial operation it disapproved, even if formally requested to do so by the U.S. Treasury.

After lengthy debate, the FOMC, which controls all market operations by the Federal Reserve, somewhat apprehensively approved on February 13, 1962, the undertaking of market operations in foreign currencies. The New York Bank was naturally designated as the agent bank by the Committee, and I was appointed special manager of the committee's foreign operations. Over the next 13 years I was to conduct nearly $60 billion of exchange operations on behalf of the Open Market Committee. At that meeting of the FOMC in early 1962, I suppose that it was just as well that neither the Committee nor I could even remotely imagine all that lay ahead.

The FOMC, comprised of the seven governors of the Board together with five of the dozen presidents of the regional Reserve Banks, met at least once a month around the long oval table at the Washington headquarters of the Federal. The foreign operations of the Federal Reserve System were invariably the first item on the agenda. After the Committee had reviewed and approved my operations during the interval since the last meeting, they expected me to alert them to any impending problems on the exchange markets and to call for whatever new authority I needed to deal with the situation. Although there were occasional triumphs to report, most of the time I appeared as a messenger of ill tidings as new troubles continuously erupted on the international markets.

Only a few of the Committee members—Chairman Martin, President Hayes, and Governors Dewey Daane, George Mitchell, and subsequently Andrew Brimmer—were sufficiently well versed in international finance to focus clearly on the technical issues involved and at most meetings their support of my recommendations was decisive. But the Committee as a whole had a very clear concept of the integrity of the Federal Reserve and the ethical standards to which our operations had to conform. At each meeting I was thoroughly grilled on every conceivable exposure of the Federal to Congressional or public complaint, but I quickly learned to enjoy the give and take with such masters of debate as Mills, Robertson, and Mitchell. I was generally ready for them, not least of all because I fully shared their anxieties. But our best protection, I think, was the full and forthright public disclosure of all our actions in my semiannual reports on exchange operations by the Treasury and Federal Reserve.

The primary objective of Federal Reserve foreign exchange operations, as expressed in the Committee's authorization of February 13, 1962, was "to help safeguard the value of the dollar in the international exchange markets." As an initial base of operations, we immediately bought from the Treasury some $30 million of the stronger foreign currencies and opened accounts with a number of the European central banks. There was some thought in Washington circles then that we might endeavor to build up such foreign exchange balances to levels adequate to finance major operations in the exchange markets and even to contribute to a long-term growth of international liquidity.

To me, however, this route seemed littered with pitfalls. Stockpiling European currencies necessarily involved a gamble that they would not depreciate, and those most likely to remain strong were generally unavailable for purchase in volume by the Federal. Buying Swiss francs for dollars, for example, would have correspondingly enlarged the Swiss National Bank's holdings of dollars convertible into gold. Nor, curiously enough, could Federal Reserve balances of German marks be effectively used to settle payments deficits in, say, French francs. The European central banks held only dollars in their foreign exchange reserves. And in the exchange markets, transfers of funds from marks to French francs were executed by selling marks for dollars and then converting the dollars into francs.

In effect, by virtue of the central role of the dollar as the official reserve currency and consequently the "transactions currency" of the exchange markets, the United States was locked into a bilateral pattern of financial relationships with each of the overseas central banks. Strange as it may seem, the European currencies were from the operating point of view of the Federal Reserve effectively inconvertible, one into the others. To foreign central banks, on the other hand, the dollar could be used to settle bills anywhere on the face of the globe. Quite aside from the risk factor and other technical deterrents, it thus seemed to me that a major stockpiling of European currencies would be a relatively inefficient and inflexible way of protecting the dollar.

Consequently my thoughts had turned to the possibility of bilateral financing arrangements with each of our central bank partners. In January 1962 I had broached this subject on a stopover in Paris with Julien-Pierre Koszul, head of the Foreign Department of the Bank of France. Koszul was a quick-tempered French patriot, who nevertheless acknowledged some satisfaction in distant Polish and American ancestors; a huge portrait of a New England divine gazed sternly down at visitors to Koszul's apartment in the Bank of France. He was also a master of his profession, and with Gallic logic immediately drove my problem into a corner and forced it to surrender the solution.

"Mon cher Charlie," he said, "it is very simple. We just do a swap of our currencies: we credit French francs to your account here in Paris against dollars to mine in New York. If you want to use your francs to defend the dollar in the exchange market, fine; if not, at the end of three months we reverse the transaction at the same rate, the money on both sides disappears, and everything is unchanged."

Such swaps of one currency for another, with a forward contract to reverse the transaction, say 90 days hence, had long been a standard trading instrument in the foreign exchange markets. Moreover, back in 1925, the New York Federal under Governor Strong had arranged with the Bank of England a similar swap arrangement of $200 million of United States gold against sterling. As far as the Federal Reserve was concerned, there was therefore no legal problem. And if the swap technique could now be generally adapted to routine dealings between central banks, I could foresee the opening of a long vista of technical cooperation.

But there were still a few problems left. I asked Koszul what amount he had in mind and he replied: "Oh, say 50 million francs— about 10 million dollars." I said: "Julien-Pierre, they would laugh at us—we should need at least ten times that amount to make any impression on the exchange market."

And so to my regret, and perhaps even more to his own, we now faced the question whether the Inspecteurs of the French Treasury, who suspiciously review any sizable transaction of the Bank of France, would condone such a deviation from the orthodoxy of gold. I had almost given up hope, when in late February Koszul telephoned to say that a swap of $50 million, effective March 1, 1962, would be agreeable to the Bank of France. I hastily sent off to him the following telex, which became the prototype of all subsequent swap arrangements:

February 28, 1962

BANQUE DE FRANCE
PARIS
NO. 151
For Koszul from Coombs

Federal Reserve proposes a 3-month French franc–dollar swap in the amount of $50 million. On March 1 we shall credit your account $50 million. Please credit French franc equivalent to "Federal Reserve Bank of New York Account A" advising by cable amount credited and market rate of exchange. The swap will have an initial maturity of three months. On maturity the swap will be liquidated at the same rate of exchange.

It is understood that you will place the resultant dollar balance on March 1 in a nontransferable U.S. Treasury certificate of indebtedness which the Secretary of the Treasury is prepared to issue to you at par to mature three months after date of issue but redeemable upon two days notice and to bear interest at a rate based upon the average rate of discount on the auction of the last issue of three-month Treasury bills. The certificate will be issued and redeemed at the Federal Reserve Bank of New York as fiscal agent of the United States. It is further understood that our franc balance with you will bear the same rate of interest.

This swap arrangement, including the U.S. certificate of indebtedness, will be renewable on agreement of both parties.

To protect both parties against the remote risk of a revaluation of either currency we suggest the following procedure: We place with you a standing order to be executed when necessary for that purpose to purchase for our account French francs in any amount sufficient to replenish any earlier drafts upon our franc balances created by the swap. We accept from you a similar standing order to be executed when necessary for that purpose to purchase dollars against French francs for purposes of replenishing any earlier drafts upon your dollar balances created by the swap.

FEDERAL RESERVE BANK OF NEW YORK

As central banks endowed with the privilege of creating money, the Federal Reserve and the Bank of France thus produced out of thin air on March 1, 1962, an increase of $100 million of international reserves by the simple process of a Federal Reserve payment of $50 million dollars to the Bank of France account at the New York Federal against an equivalent payment of French francs by the Bank of France to the account of the New York Federal in Paris.

A British journalist cynically described this cross-crediting of reserves as "monetary incest." But the essence of the transaction was a 90-day loan by the Bank of France of $50 million equivalent of

French francs to the New York Federal at our request. The Federal could either spend the French francs in the exchange markets to resist selling pressure on the dollar exchange rate or use them to buy up surplus—and gold convertible—dollars on the books of the Bank of France.

Meanwhile, the Bank of France would hold an I.O.U. from the New York Federal in the form of a $50 million dollar credit, sold forward against French francs, on which it would collect interest at the U.S. Treasury 90-day bill rate. By thus incurring a debt in French francs, the Federal would become exposed to a risk of a revaluation of the French franc. But the Bank of France undertook to safeguard the Federal against this eventuality by accepting a standing order to sell, on the eve of any French revaluation, whatever French francs the Federal needed to cover its debt against payment by the Federal in dollars.

On the other hand, if the Federal did not have occasion to disburse the French franc proceeds of the swap, the Federal would earn a precisely offsetting interest return on its French franc balance. In effect, the swap credit cost the United States interest charges only when and to the extent it was used. All this may seem to be an excessively roundabout way for the Federal to borrow foreign currencies. But apparently when the Federal Reserve Act was drafted, no one had contemplated such a need, and no explicit statutory provision for such borrowing was made. The swap technique, on the other hand, was clearly authorized and yielded precisely the same results as a direct borrowing from a foreign central bank.

As it happened, the New York Federal decided not to spend in market intervention the French francs made available under the swap. Money was still coming into France in some volume. To both Koszul and myself, the limited scope of market operations from a $50 million reserve base could easily appear as no more than a quixotic gesture. Accordingly, after one renewal, the swap was liquidated on August 2, 1962.

More importantly, however, the Bank of France–Federal Reserve swap arrangement was thereafter formally maintained on a standby basis. Thus that initial $50 million swap subsequently set the pattern for a spreading network of similar reciprocal lines of credit between the Federal and other major foreign central banks. When I took early retirement from the New York Federal 13 years later, those reciprocal lines of credit—or swap facilities—had mushroomed into a $20 billion dollar network linking the Federal Reserve with 14 foreign central banks and the BIS.

Encouraged by this evidence of French readiness to cooperate, we next approached the Bank of England with a proposal for a similar swap of dollars against sterling. At the March 1962 meeting of the BIS, I met with Lord Cromer, who had succeeded Lord Cobbold as Governor of the Bank of England in July of the previous year, and outlined our thinking as follows. Sterling and the dollar were subject as reserve currencies to volatile movements of funds. If suddenly reflected in sizable gold or reserve losses, such hot money flows could easily become a speculative onslaught. There was, therefore, a need for a reciprocal credit facility between sterling and the dollar that would temporarily cushion the impact of such money flows, thereby providing breathing space for consideration of whatever correctives might have to be applied. In view of the experience of March 1961, when many hundreds of millions of dollars of hot money had suddenly flooded across the exchanges in a few days time, it might be imprudent to leave the negotiation of such reciprocal credit facilities to last-minute emergency action. What was instead needed was establishment well in advance of credit facilities that might be invoked on very short notice, over the telephone if necessary. We thought that such reciprocal credit facilities might most simply and effectively be provided through a swap arrangement between the Federal Reserve and the Bank of England. Such a swap arrangement might conceivably involve an amount ranging up to $300 million.

In British parlance I got a fairly dusty answer, not so much from Cromer as from some of his senior associates at the Bank of England. To them, the new American initiatives on the foreign exchange markets looked suspiciously like an attempt to devise means of blocking access to the Treasury gold window. This was not too far from the mark, although we rather thought of our approach as one of providing a temporary alternative to international gold settlements in the form of central bank credit facilities.

To complicate matters further, the British Treasury staff had meanwhile swung to much more ambitious schemes of converting the IMF into a largely automatic credit facility. And so to them the central bank swap facilities we proposed seemed both inadequate and yet more likely to command international support. After a certain amount of Anglo-American political squabbling, Bridge of the Bank of England was sent over to the New York Federal to discuss the matter further, and agreement was finally reached on a swap of $50 million, executed on May 31. At the end of August this swap also remained unused by either party and so was liquidated and placed on a standby basis identical with the Federal Reserve arrangement with the Bank of France. But we had not been simply spinning our wheels. The New York Federal had meanwhile thoroughly tested the telex, investment, and other technical procedures involved in both the French and British swap experiments and was now ready to operate in any emergency.

In June 1962 a sharp break of Wall Street stock prices followed the confrontation between President Kennedy and U.S. Steel, and a speculative flight from the Canadian dollar further unsettled the international financial markets. Hot money began to flow from New York to Amsterdam, Brussels, and Zurich, raising the dollar reserves of the central banks concerned and again threatening heavy conversions of such surplus dollars into gold. Meanwhile, however, I had had encouraging discussions with Governor Ansiaux of the Belgian National Bank and President Holtrop of the Netherlands Bank regarding swap credit facilities. Now, with the approval of the FOMC, I negotiated in mid-June new swap arrangements of $50 million each with the Dutch and Belgian central banks.

The swap technique was then given its first test as an actual instrument of international settlements. In late June 1962 the Federal Reserve not only drew but disbursed $60 million of Belgian francs and Dutch guilders under the two credit facilities as needed to mop up surplus dollars on the books of the two central banks and thus enabled them to forego buying gold at the Treasury window. More importantly, the guilder and Belgian franc debt thus incurred by the Federal Reserve was quickly repaid over subsequent weeks as speculation subsided and the two central banks found themselves in renewed need of dollars. The Belgian and Dutch swap facilities then also reverted to a standby basis.

The speculative wave generated by the Canadian crisis and the break in the New York stock market resulted in even heavier flows of dollars into the Swiss commercial banks, which in turn unloaded them on the Swiss National Bank. In July, the FOMC accordingly approved my recommendation to extend the Federal Reserve swap arrangements to Switzerland, where I negotiated with President Schwegler and Max Iklé $200 million dollars in swap facilities, dollars against Swiss francs, with the Swiss National Bank and the Bank for International Settlements.

In July and August $110 million of Swiss francs was drawn by the Federal under these two arrangements and immediately used to buy back an equivalent amount of dollars on the books of the Swiss National Bank. Concurrently the U.S. Treasury defended the dollar by selling Swiss francs in the forward market. Thus we weathered this period of intense speculation with only relatively small losses of American gold to the European central banks.

With these successes behind us, the FOMC readily approved extension of the swap network to the Bundesbank, the Bank of Italy, the National Bank of Austria, and the Swedish Riksbank. On subsequent monthly trips to Europe, I negotiated these facilities, each in the now standard unit of $50 million. By early 1963, a visible rampart of credit defenses for the dollar thus linked up the Federal Reserve with all the major European central banks.

Meanwhile the deepening crisis in the Canadian dollar had opened the question of whether a Federal Reserve swap arrangement with the Bank of Canada would be appropriate. Between January and late June of 1962, about $900 million, or nearly 45 percent, of Canadian gold and foreign exchange reserves of $2 billion had been swept away by payments deficits which now threatened to force the Canadian dollar off its newly established parity of $0.92½. In the judgment of both the Canadian government and the International Monetary Fund, the new exchange parity still seemed to be fully appropriate; the root of the problem was instead a crisis of confidence that was feeding on itself.

In this emergency, the Canadian government introduced on June 25, 1962, an effective program of fiscal and other restraints and simultaneously announced the negotiation of more than $1 billion of stabilization credits from abroad. This financial support operation, which had been put together in four days time, included a $300 million Canadian drawing on the International Monetary Fund, a $400 million standby credit from the Export-Import Bank, a $100 million credit to the Bank of Canada from the Bank of England, and a $250 million swap between the Federal Reserve and the Bank of Canada.

With this announcement, the speculative attack on the Canadian dollar immediately collapsed. Between June 25 and the end of August, 1962 the Bank of Canada recovered more than $500 million of its earlier reserve losses. By December 1962 the Bank of Canada no longer had need of the Federal Reserve swap arrangement which then reverted to a standby basis. Once again, the capacity of central bank and intergovernmental cooperation in defending currency parities against flows of speculative funds had been dramatically demonstrated. The Canadian dollar crisis also provided a good test of the effectiveness of telephone communications in any emergency. My numerous discussions with Governor Louis Rasminsky of the Bank of Canada regarding the $250 million swap arrangement were conducted by telephone. Approval by the FOMC of the Canadian swap was also secured through a telephone conference call of the Committee at which I recommended the action.

Only a few months later, the suddenness of the Cuban crisis further highlighted the necessity of close and continuing communications between the Federal Reserve and its European central bank partners. On Monday, October 22, 1962, I could sense from telephone calls to and from Washington that something highly unusual was under way. But not until I had checked into my Washington hotel room that evening and watched President Kennedy's televised threat to "turn the full nuclear power of the U.S. against the USSR" if Soviet missiles in Cuba should be used against us, did I realize the awesome gravity of the situation.

After a few hours sleep, I awoke at 3 a.m. and from my hotel room checked by telephone the opening of the London, Frankfurt, and Zurich markets. Since the London gold market was particularly vulnerable, my first call was to Bridge of the Bank of England. We quickly agreed to let the London gold price ride up to $35.20, then intervene in unlimited amount to hold the line. Similarly, telephone conversations with Iklé of the Swiss National Bank and Tüngeler of the Bundesbank revealed that our mutual instinct was to dig in at existing exchange rate levels and, through cooperative exchange market operations, demonstrate our intention to maintain orderly conditions.

This we did. Later that morning at 9:30, in a regularly scheduled meeting of the FOMC, Chairman Martin called on me, in my usual lead-off spot on the committee agenda, to report on the reaction of the European financial markets to the President's speech of the previous evening. As messengers continued to hand me telephoned reports of market developments, I assured the Committee that our European central bank partners were joining with us in a solid line of defense against speculative developments. Curiously enough, as the crisis subsided over the next two days, we were assisted by sizable sales of Russian gold on the London gold market, probably reflecting a Kremlin decision to build up liquid dollar balances against the risk that Russian borrowing facilities in the Eurodollar market might suddenly disappear. In a world momentarily shadowed by the risk of nuclear annihilation, Russian financial officials thus continued to carry out their technical responsibilities, along with their counterparts in London, Zurich, Frankfurt, and New York.

The sudden, fast-breaking nature of the financial crises triggered by the German revaluation, the attack on the Canadian dollar, and the Cuban confrontation had convinced me that we must constantly maintain in our swap arrangements a large margin of safety to deal with the unforeseen. Moreover, the volume of hot money capable of being moved from one country to another seemed to be constantly growing. In particular, the steady expansion of the Euro-dollar market had built up a huge reservoir of dollars that could suddenly flood onto the exchange markets.

With the support of Chairman Martin, Undersecretary Roosa, and most of my foreign central bank associates, I therefore sought and secured FOMC approval of major increases in our swap lines with the major foreign central banks. By the end of 1963 the Federal Reserve swap lines with the Bundesbank and the Bank of Italy had risen from $50 to $250 million, with the Swiss authorities from $200 to $300 million, and with the Dutch and French central banks from $50 to $100 million. And in the spring of 1963 a major new commitment of central bank cooperation had been made after Lord Cromer handed me, at the May BIS meeting, a formal suggestion that the Federal Reserve–Bank of England swap line be raised at one stroke from $50 to $500 million. Finally, in October 1963, the Bank of Japan had joined with the Federal in a reciprocal credit line of $150 million. Within 18 months the swap network had thus grown into a defensive ring linking the Federal Reserve with 11 of the largest foreign central banks through reciprocal credit lines totaling somewhat more than $2 billion.

Thus expanded, the Federal Reserve swap network, together with other central bank credit facilities, played a major role in absorbing exchange market pressures generated by a number of dramatic events in 1963–1964. Sterling came under pressure following de Gaulle's rejection of the British bid for membership in the Common Market in early 1963; during the spring of 1963 heavy capital outflows from New York weakened the dollar; the assassination of President Kennedy occurred in November 1963, and a speculative attack on the Italian lira reached crisis proportions during the winter of 1963–1964. The lira crisis was a particularly instructive test of international financial cooperation.

In late 1963 the Italian currency came under increasingly heavy selling pressure as a result of a widening payments deficit on current account, capital outflows, and precautionary repayments of debt in foreign currencies by Italian commercial banks. To deal with the situation, the national authorities took various corrective measures that would need at least a few months to produce results. Meanwhile, heavy drains on the Bank of Italy's reserves continued, and the need for short-term credit and other assistance became clear.

Under the $250 million swap line with the Federal Reserve, the Bank of Italy made three successive drawings of $50 million each in October 1963, January 1964, and March 1964. During this period the U.S. Treasury also made advance repayments of the entire $200 million of lira bonds issued to the Bank of Italy in 1962. Meanwhile, however, efforts by the Italian government to round up additional credits from its Common Market partners had broken down as the political negotiators on both sides became involved in some ill-tempered bargaining. Its pride affronted, the Italian government arranged for Governor Carli of the Bank of Italy to call on the IMF and the World Bank in Washington as alternative sources of financial assistance.

Carli attended the March BIS meeting en route to Washington and somewhat to my surprise showed no interest in arranging new credit facilities with his fellow governors of the BIS. As we traveled together by train from Basel to Zurich, Carli related to me the unsympathetic response of Italy's Common Market partners to the plight of the lira and suggested an increase in the Federal Reserve swap line with the Bank of Italy from $250 to $500 million. I indicated some preference for a package of central bank and other assistance and offered to help enlist the support of the Bank of England, the Swiss National Bank and the Bundesbank.

A few days later, while Carli was in the midst of his Washington discussions, the lira was suddenly struck by a burst of speculation that drove the three-month forward rate to a discount of 7 percent. In this dangerous situation, an immediate and massive reinforcement of the Italian reserve position was clearly called for, and Treasury Undersecretary Roosa took the initiative in putting together a credit package. Within 48 hours the Italian authorities were able to announce that approximately $1 billion of external assistance was at their disposal. This credit package included: (*a*) a $100 million swap arrangement offered by the U.S. Treasury (in addition to the partly drawn $250 million swap facility with the Federal Reserve System), (*b*) a $200 million standby credit from the Export-Import Bank, (*c*) $250 million in credits of up to three years from the U.S. Commodity Credit Corporation, and (*d*) short-term credit facilities of $250 million from the Bank of England and the Bundesbank, which I helped to round up.

Announcement of this credit package immediately broke the speculative wave. Moreover, provision of such sizable credit assistance to Italy more or less coincided with a turning point in the Italian economic scene. During the first quarter of 1964 the Italian balance of payments had registered a deficit of $436 million. This turned into a surplus of $226 million in the second quarter, as the corrective policy measures previously initiated by the Italian authorities began to take effect and as a reversal of the leads and lags brought about a covering of short positions in lire. As the reflux of funds developed, the Bank of Italy proceeded to repay its entire swap debt of $150 million to the Federal Reserve as well as the credit drawn under the facility provided by the Bundesbank. Other credit facilities provided in the March credit package had remained unused.

Over the first two years of the Federal Reserve swap network, major operations were thus conducted in defense not only of the dollar but also of two foreign currencies—the Canadian dollar and the lira—with effective results in each case. The speculative and other market pressures involved consistently proved reversible. Of total credits of $1.8 billion extended under the swap network through the end of June 1964, nearly all were paid in less than six months as the waves of unsuccessful speculation receded. By mid-1964, therefore, the Federal Reserve swap network and other forms of central bank cooperation had already transformed the functioning of the Bretton Woods system. As noted in a report dated August 1964 of the finance ministers of the Group of 10:

> . . . these demonstrations of close central bank cooperation are themselves an effective deterrent to speculative movements. Their informality, speed and flexibility make them especially suitable as a first line—and short-term—defense against sudden balance-of-payments pressures. Over the past several years, they have mobilized massive resources in a short time to combat and limit speculative and crisis situations. Their success has greatly reduced the threat to official reserves from disequilibrating movements of private short-term capital.

Nevertheless, as the scale of Federal Reserve operations mounted in 1963–1964, we became increasingly conscious of the risks involved. In requesting the massive increase to $500 million of the Bank of England swap line in May 1963, Lord Cromer had made two warning comments that coincided with apprehensions already felt by Chairman Martin and other members of the FOMC as well as myself. First, if both sterling and the dollar were under pressure, we should "avoid giving the appearance of two lame ducks helping each other." Second, it would be inappropriate to use the facility to finance a structural balance of payments deficit on the part of either country. In short, both Cromer and Martin were keenly aware of the risks of political abuse of central bank credit facilities on the scale now emerging, and they sought to establish some safeguards.

The most effective safeguard, of course, would have been a solid restoration of reasonable balance in both the British and American balance of payments accounts. But the British Conservative government was soon to embark on the ill-fated policy of administering a strong financial stimulus to the economy in the futile hope that expansion would somehow lead to improved efficiency and so generate a strong growth of exports. And on the United States side, progress in closing the balance of payments gap had been disappointingly slow. Although the deficit had been cut from $3.9 billion in 1960 to $2.4 billion in 1961 and $2.2 billion in 1962, prepayments of debt by foreign countries and other special intergovernment transactions had accounted for much of the improvement. The dollar remained particularly vulnerable to continuing heavy outflows of both short- and long-term capital funds.

For my own part, I was acutely aware of the danger that some of the swap borrowing and lending operations I was conducting might prove irreversible. We had prudently refrained from drawing on the French swap line in view of the emergence of a chronic surplus in France's balance of payments. But other exchange market situations threatening the dollar were frequently a mixture of short-term speculation and much less discernible longer term trends.

In most emergencies, it seemed to me, we would probably have to mount a temporary holding action by drawing on the swap lines with little basis for judging whether the speculative pendulum would quickly swing back or would instead prove to be the signal of a basic disequilibrium. I had accordingly resisted suggestions by various FOMC members that stern criteria be established limiting swap credit to the financing of clearly reversible payments situations. To me, the only meaningful safeguard against abuse of the swap network was to establish firm rules requiring the repayment of such central bank financing within a relatively short maturity span.

In fact, by the spring of 1963 Federal Reserve drawings of Swiss francs made in July 1962 had already become a troublesome case in point. Continuing market speculation in favor of the Swiss franc had frustrated their reversal. Accordingly, I recommended to the FOMC at its meeting of May 28, 1963, that the committee fix a firm working rule of paying off any swap debt outstanding for as long as a full year. As I noted:

In our various published statements as well as in conversations of System officials with foreign central banks, we have repeatedly stressed the short-term nature of the swap facilities. The integrity of the System has thus become involved and we should now make crystal clear this integrity of purpose by taking the initiative and arranging a full repayment of the $50 million drawing upon the

Swiss National Bank on or before the July maturity. In this connection, there may well be future occasions in which foreign central banks may make drawings upon their swap lines with us and encounter difficulties in effecting repayment. If in the meanwhile the System establishes, in the conduct of its own borrowing operations, a tradition of unconditional adherence to the short-term nature of such swap drawings, we can help to clarify the rules of the game applicable to all central banks involved in the swap network.

FOMC approval of this one-year time limit on credits extended under the Federal Reserve swap network quickly produced an unwritten understanding with our foreign partners that the debtor central bank should begin exploring ways and means of liquidating its swap debt well in advance of the one-year time limit. Such Federal Reserve insistence on limiting its swap operations to short-term commitments in turn thrust on the U.S. Treasury the burden of providing a "take-out" for the Federal Reserve debts to foreign central banks that proved irreversible within a year. Dillon and Roosa were not looking for an easy escape from their own responsibilities at the expense of the Federal, however, and the Treasury readily accepted the time limit the FOMC had placed on its international financing role.

Meanwhile, the Treasury had developed medium-term financing facilities in the form of the Roosa certificates and bonds. Such Treasury issues to the European central banks of certificates and bonds denominated in the currency of the foreign central bank had been frequently employed since 1961 to deal with exchange market situations that seemed likely to drag on beyond the short-term focus of Federal Reserve operations. In 1962 the Treasury had made repeated issues to the Bank of Italy of lira certificates that were converted late in the year into $200 million of medium-term Roosa bonds. Similarly, $129 million of such bonds and certificates had been issued to the Swiss authorities and in early 1963 a $200 million issue of Roosa bonds was used to absorb surplus dollars on the books of the Bundesbank.

But neither the New York Federal nor any other institution could predict with consistent accuracy which market situations would prove reversible and which would not. In August 1963 the first miscalculation occurred as the Federal encountered lengthening delays in repaying a $50 million swap drawing on the Bundesbank. With heavy flows of funds to Germany continuing, both the New York Federal and the Bundesbank could see little hope of reversing this particular transaction within the prescribed time limit. Accordingly the U.S. Treasury agreed to take over $50 million of the Federal Reserve obligation by issuing to the Bundesbank a medium-term Roosa bond, denominated in German marks. Until the closure of the gold window in August 1971, other lingering Federal Reserve swap debts were similarly liquidated by similar Treasury issues of Roosa bonds.

Finally, before settling payments deficits in gold, the Treasury could call on its credit facilities with the International Monetary Fund. In his initial balance of payments message in February 1961, President Kennedy had indicated his readiness, if and when appropriate, to draw on the Fund for financing our payments deficits. But in early 1961 this possibility was more theoretical than real. Though the Fund held plenty of dollars, reflecting the disproportionately large United States quota, its available supply of other major currencies was closely limited by the relatively low quotas initially assigned to Germany, Italy, and other countries in the early postwar years.

With the powerful support of Per Jacobsson, Managing Director of the IMF, Dillon, Martin, and Roosa had pushed through in 1961 a major negotiation with the finance ministers of nine foreign countries that gave the Fund new access to the currencies it needed. The countries involved—quickly dubbed the Group of Ten (G-10) —formally agreed to make available up to $6 billion of their currencies to the Fund under the so-called General Agreements to Borrow. Switzerland subsequently volunteered a parallel arrangement in the amount of $200 million. Selective quota increases, together with a 25 percent across-the-board increase of all quotas approved at the 1964 IMF annual meeting in Tokyo, further substantially enlarged the lending capacity of the Fund.

As a result of all these initiatives, there now began to emerge a pattern of concentric defense lines shielding the dollar against speculation and other exchange market pressures. On the perimeter was the Federal Reserve swap network, reinforced as needed by Federal and Treasury operations in the forward exchange markets as well as by spot and forward operations conducted by our foreign central bank partners. When pressures on the dollar at any point could not be contained by such temporary holding actions, we could fall back to a second line of defense in the form of the Roosa bonds. The final defense line protecting our gold stock was the IMF, through which the United States could borrow at medium term foreign currencies up to $5.2 billion equivalent as determined by its quota.

Meanwhile, however, a full-dress debate had developed over how best to ensure an adequate growth of international liquidity to support an expanding volume of world trade. Quite clearly, the stock of gold in central bank hands was unlikely to grow fast enough; we were instead faced with the risk of its being dissipated by official sales on private markets such as London. As new and ever more ingenious schemes for creating world liquidity proliferated, the cooperative efforts of the central banks to deal with the problem through a broad spectrum of credit facilities had little appeal to most university economists. To them, such *ad hoc* devices as central bank swap arrangements seemed to be patching up the world financial system with "chewing gum and baling wire," as they often put it.

Curiously enough, such solidly based arrangements as the swap line between the Bundesbank and the Federal Reserve, the central banks of the two largest trading countries, seemed somehow less promising than the vision of a new global arrangement, imposing a uniform pattern of external financing on more than a hundred national governments with widely differing views of their national interest. In an effort to persuade the skeptics, Tüngeler of the Bundesbank, Iklé of the National Bank of Switzerland, Ranalli of the Bank of Italy, and I collaborated in August 1963 on a joint article, published in the *Monthly Review* of the Federal Reserve Bank of New York, where we said:

> There has been a tendency in certain quarters to regard these central bank and other intergovernmental defensive arrangements as no more than temporary and unreliable expedients. It is quite true, of course, that many of these defenses were quickly improvised, sometimes within a matter of hours, to deal with sudden emergencies. In most cases, they were negotiated on a bilateral basis and may give the impression of being no more than an unrelated patchwork. But these bilateral defenses have the most important advantage of being solidly based on market and institutional realities in each country and are capable of being flexibly adapted to new and unforeseeable needs. One cannot overemphasize the importance of being able to move quickly—on the basis of telephone consultations if necessary—against speculative pressures before they gain momentum. In our view, the central bank and intergovernmental defenses developed during the past two years should be regarded as a permanent reinforcement of the international financial machinery.

We believed what we said, and a little more than three months later, as the first ticker reports that President Kennedy had been assassinated rocked the financial markets, the European central banks joined forces with us in an all-out defense of the dollar against speculation.

6

Dallas,
November 22, 1963

In the New York metropolitan area, late November generally means
cold and rainy weather to bedevil still further the commuters from
New Jersey, Long Island, and Westchester who supply the management cadres of Wall Street. But the morning of Friday, November
22, 1963, was that rare gift of a golden Indian summer day, with
continuing fair weather forecast for the final weekend of the college
football season.

The Harvard–Yale game was set for New Haven that year, and

my college roommate, who had moved from Cambridge via Iwo Jima and Tarawa to a partnership in a preeminent New York law firm, had months ago lined up our respective families for adjoining seats at the game. This cut two ways: our individual seniority, with both of us pushing close toward our twenty-fifth class reunion, would by itself have staked a claim to excellent seats close to midfield, in accordance with the time-honored code of the Harvard Athletic Association. The H.A.A. inflicts severe penalties on marriage and children, however, and our combination of two wives and four children seemed all too likely to drag us back behind the goal posts. On balance, it still seemed worthwhile; with our former classmate Jack Kennedy in the White House, traditionally torpid college loyalties had been awakened, and a resounding defeat of Yale to clinch the Ivy League football title would be something to cheer on the spot. And so that morning, as my wife drove me through the clean little city of Madison, New Jersey, to the Erie-Lackawanna station, we happily agreed to meet in Grand Central around six that evening, in good time to take another train to Connecticut for a pregame dinner party with our host and his family.

The Erie-Lackawanna commuting trains almost invariably run on time; they did in 1963 and more than a decade later they still do. The equipment is antique, sauna-hot in summer and over- or underheated in winter. But the 8:28 that morning was precisely on schedule, and the conductor, pocket watch in hand, nodded pleasantly to familiar passengers as they climbed on board. As I settled down for the jolting trip to Manhattan with other middle-aged commuters, reading with heads uptilted the *New York Times* or the *Wall Street Journal* through the lower window of their bifocals, the overnight news seemed as placid as the morning's weather. President Kennedy had begun his tour of Texas before welcoming crowds but was already engaged in seemingly petty local issues, or as the *Times* put it, "the volatile passions of the faction-torn" Texas Democratic party. His host at a reception the previous evening, Governor John Connally, had not invited his fellow Democrat, Senator Ralph Yarborough, who had in turn denounced Connally as "uneducated governmentally." Abroad, the Congolese government had broken off diplomatic relationships with Moscow, Cambodian President Sihanouk had refused to accept further aid from the United States, and the Ecumenical Council convened in Rome by Pope John XXIII had approved non-Latin forms for the sacraments. Generally speaking, a fairly peaceful world. On the sports pages, the Princeton–Dartmouth and Harvard–Yale games were appraised, with Harvard favored to win the Ivy League title.

The business news was so scanty that it permitted coverage of a speech I had made at St. John's University the day before on central bank cooperation during the Cuban crisis of October 1962. To my relief, the *Times* story was warmly sympathetic to such coordinated action to control speculation on the foreign exchanges. Only one cloud seemed to be looming on the financial horizon. The day before, the *Wall St. Journal* had broken wide open the "Salad Oil Scandal," which had forced the suspension of two leading brokerage houses and pushed down the Dow-Jones index by more than seven points. Now both the *Journal* and the *Times* developed the story further. Various well-known names in the Street had been providing sizable credits against soybean and other vegetable oil allegedly stored, just like gasoline, in a so-called tank farm near Bayonne, New Jersey. But now, as the borrower's insolvency focused closer scrutiny on his collateral, it appeared that some of the tanks were filled with nothing but water. All of which suggested heavy losses to individual firms, but no serious threat, it was hoped, to the financial markets as a whole.

And so, along the aisle, the pages of the *Times* and the *Journal* kept turning slowly, if for no other reason than to avoid even a passing glance at the sprawl of aging industry in the Jersey meadows. With train and reading schedules thus ritually synchronized, most commuters turned to the final page as the train pulled into the gloomy Hoboken terminal, across the Hudson River from Manhattan. A quick look uncovered no additional scraps of news—only a full-page advertisement in the *Times* of a current movie thriller *Seven Days in May,* apparently involving a military conspiracy to take over the presidency.

Arriving in Hoboken, commuters to Wall Street then enjoyed the privilege of choice between crossing to Manhattan under the Hudson River in crowded, antiquated subway cars or of churning in a downstream slant across the river in an equally antiquated, wooden-hulled ferryboat that occasionally lost arguments over the right of way with steel-prowed freighters hurrying upstream. On November 22, 1963, the weather tipped the scales, and that Indian summer morning the ferries were unusually crowded with Wall Street men.

Anyone reflecting on the state of our country and indeed of the rest of the world, as the profile of lower Manhattan loomed above the morning mist of the river, might have found much to be grateful for on Thanksgiving Day, less than a week away. The Bay of Pigs and the Cuban missile crisis seemed to be well behind us. The American economy was healthy and thriving. President Kennedy had awakened America's conscience on racial discrimination. Inflation was running at less than 2 percent. Unemployment was steadily declining. The trade surplus was swelling to record proportions. In its *Annual Report* for 1963, the Federal Reserve Bank of New York, which instinctively avoids complacency like the plague, was forced to admit that ". . . the 1963 performance of the United States economy and, indeed, of the international economic and financial system as a whole, gave grounds for solid satisfaction."

As the ferry lurched into the slip at Fulton Street, we were caught up by the tempo of Manhattan and hurriedly fanned out through the streets west of Broadway, lined with ugly buildings awaiting demolition in favor of the towers of the World Trade Center. And so through the old Dutch streets of Cortlandt and Maiden Lane, to the massive, Florentine presence of the Federal Reserve Bank of New York.

In my office on the tenth floor of the Reserve Bank the telex, telephone, and ticker reports indicated quiet markets in London and on the Continent. No particular selling pressure on the dollar was discernible anywhere. Sterling, which would soon become a major problem, was riding close to parity. The London gold market, which had helped provoke a severe burst of speculation against the dollar shortly before our 1960 election, had subsequently been brought under control by the Gold Pool established in 1961 by the Federal Reserve and other major central banks. Indeed, the Pool was now skimming from the London gold market the bulk of huge gold sales by the Russians to finance grain imports against their 1963 harvest failure. The French franc stood proudly at its ceiling. More than a year before, the Bank of France had initiated a program of monthly gold purchases of $30 million from the U.S. Treasury, but this had been done in a discreetly precautionary way with no hint yet of the aggressive policy on gold subsequently launched by President de Gaulle. The morning passed in a pleasant routine, and our luncheon table in the Bank's dining room when I arrived around one o'clock was busily engaged in analyzing the Salad Oil Scandal.

In distinct contrast to the European central banks, lunch at the New York Federal has never been a quiet interlude of respite from the pressures of the business day. I recall being present in the office of an executive director of a European central bank when he received an urgent telephone message clearly deserving the immediate attention of his governor, who was prolonging his lunch. The decision finally made to interrupt the governor's digestion was a carefully balanced judgment. At the New York Federal, in contrast, lunch is generally no more than a continuation of the business day with a telephone cubicle close at hand. The phone rings several times during lunch, usually for officers of the Foreign and Domestic Trading Desks, but this has become so routine that the conversation on banking problems around the table is hardly ever interrupted.

Around 1:40 p.m. that Friday the phone rang again, and a junior officer of the Foreign Department sitting beside me shrugged and went into the telephone cubicle to answer. He never managed to get the door closed after taking the phone but instead clutched at the jamb with one hand as an expression of horror spread across his face. After several insistent questions, I finally got an answer from him as to what in hell was going on.

"Kennedy has been shot! Several times! He may be dead!"

The young officer then said thank you, hung up the phone, returned without another word to his place at the table, and, as he told me later, automatically finished his lunch in a state of near total numbness.

As for myself, I felt as if I had suddenly plunged into a deep underwater dive. But within seconds or minutes later, a hand came down hard on my shoulder and a rasping voice said: "Charlie— Kennedy has been shot—you've gotta tell Hayes—you've gotta do something—let's go!"

The voice came from one of our operations managers, promoted late in life to a post requiring the buck-sergeant toughness of mind to ensure that certain vital services of the Bank continue, come what may. He had already heard the news and had indignantly reacted to my stunned inertia, as he would have to an elevator stalled between floors. Obediently, I got to my feet and followed him, my head clearing somewhat as I walked along the corridor to President Hayes' private dining room, where a lunch in honor of upstate New York bankers was in progress. Hayes was silently fingering a ticker clipping just handed to him, and immediately I saw that he knew. I just said "I'm going down to the Foreign trading room—we may have work to do." He nodded in his imperturbable way, the lunch broke up, and I hurried down to the Foreign Department, passing by secretaries quietly weeping before their typewriters.

In the Foreign Department, the trading room ticker not only confirmed the telephone report but opened new and even more sinister possibilities of Vice-President Johnson also falling victim to what might be a fantastic conspiracy against the government. Now even more shaken than before, I turned away from the ticker, slumped down on one of the chairs at the trading desk, and struggled to concentrate. After a moment I looked up and found that the traders who had been huddled with me around the ticker had returned to their places before their individual telephone turrets and were sitting stiffly at attention, as if awaiting immediate instructions for market action. One of them, a solid, experienced man, took out a cigarette to relieve his tension, but his hand shook so badly that he managed only after several attempts to set it alight.

In that shaking hand, I caught a glimpse of what must have been the state of mind of the foreign exchange market, where thousands of transactions were in midstream and hundreds of millions of dollars of uncovered positions outstanding, with none of the market participants knowing any more than I what was really going on in Dallas. Meanwhile the stock market was struck by an onslaught of panic selling, with the Dow-Jones index plummeting 21 points within 30 minutes on turnover of more than 2 million shares. Action to close the stock exchange was presumably already under way, and the thought crossed my mind that a similar prohibition of trading in foreign exchange might succeed in forestalling a similar wave of panic selling of dollars across the exchanges.

This route was replete with technical, time-consuming complications, however, requiring coordinated decisions at the highest political levels in both the New York State and federal governments, in a situation that cried out for immediate action. But what action? If the dollar were to ride out the storm undamaged in any way, our main hope lay in providing tangible proof to the market that President Kennedy's personal commitment to defend the country's currency would be honored by his successor, whoever he might be. The problem was essentially one of assuring the market of a continuity of policy. Here again, any effort to close the New York exchange market would probably have boomeranged as being nothing but a prelude to closure of the gold window, with all the speculative consequences flowing from such a market judgment.

There was still another difficulty—the foreign exchange market is an international market, and suspension of trading in New York could hardly prevent continued speculation against the dollar in Europe. Finally, for various technical reasons, including the time differential, the volume of dollars traded across the exchanges in Europe generally far exceeded that in New York. Opening rates on the dollar in Europe the following Monday—or even in unofficial trading on Saturday—would point to either stabilization or a slide in the international value of the dollar.

All at once it seemed quite clear that immediate and massive offerings of foreign currencies to defend the dollar by the Federal

Reserve Bank of New York could do more to maintain international confidence in the continuity of United States financial policy than any other step. Moreover, with the European markets having closed for the day, our exposure would be limited to speculative or hedging demand originating in the United States time zones. But where was the foreign money to come from? At that critical moment, we had on hand hardly more than $16 million of foreign currency scattered over a broad range of countries, with no balances whatsoever in certain important European currencies. Under usual market practices, any foreign currencies we might offer that Friday afternoon would not have to be delivered until the following Tuesday. We could, of course, readily backstop such offerings of foreign currency by subsequent sales of gold to the foreign central banks involved. But we still had no idea of how far-reaching the reports from Dallas would turn out to be. And if we were forced to publish a heavy gold loss the following week, further speculation against the dollar might explode. In all probability, it seemed to me, the Treasury would flatly refuse to accept such a risk.

Our only realistic hope of defending the dollar, therefore, lay in borrowing and selling foreign currencies through the Federal Reserve network of $2 billion of reciprocal currency lines, the swap arrangements, with the Bank of England and other foreign central banks. Any foreign currency debts we might pile up by drawing on these credit lines would not have to be repaid, or even reported, until months afterward.

But under the Federal Reserve swap network, it was prudently and explicitly provided in each reciprocal credit line that neither central bank could draw on the line without the prior approval of its partner central bank. And here the clock had outrun us. Because of the time differential with Europe—it was now nearly 6:30 p.m. in London and 7:30 p.m. on the Continent—the news of the President's assassination broke shortly after the European central banks had closed for the day. All their top officials were now presumably on the way home after stopovers at official receptions and other way stations on a Friday night. Could we afford to wait until we reached them at their homes? This could involve delays of an hour or more, by which time the New York market might have worked itself into a panic. Or could we in such emergency circumstances count on their subsequently underwriting our sales of their currencies, possibly running into hundreds of millions of dollars, without their prior consent? I knew each of these foreign central bankers personally and well, and concluded that we could.

For a moment I considered trying to get Chairman Martin, President Hayes, and Treasury Undersecretary Roosa all on the phone at once, to give my recommendations and to request their joint approval. They were, after all, personally responsible for any action I might take, particularly if it failed. But they were busy men, and probably never more pressed for time than at that moment. Even if I could get them all on a conference call in the next few minutes, which was highly doubtful, what general advice could they give me other than there must be some presumption of a continuity of policy? And as for any specific technical measures we might take, the New York Foreign Trading Desk was already entrusted by the Federal Open Market Committee with broad discretionary authority to intervene with Federal Reserve resources in the exchange market. In this emergency, if we now sought clearance from higher authority on specific measures, we might seem to be trying to escape responsibilities already fixed on us and in the process undermine the very credibility of our own recommendations. Finally, and to me the clincher, we could not risk the paralysis of being shunted off onto subordinate Treasury officials in Washington who might play it safe by advising us to do nothing until their principals had an opportunity to break clear of other demands on their attention to focus on mine.

So I decided to go ahead on my own, and for the rest of the afternoon thought and acted in a coldly technical way, drained of all the emotional reactions of the previous quarter-hour. At 2:00 p.m., 20 minutes after the first ticker report from Dallas, I asked our Foreign Trading Desk to place in the market an offering of 10 million marks at the rate prevailing at 1:40 p.m. and to make clear to the Wall Street bank acting as our market agent that we would be prepared to follow up with additional offerings at the same price.

The Federal offering of marks suddenly flashed in a virtual market vacuum, all other bids and offers by commercial traders having been pulled back to await the next news on the ticker, and so had a dramatic impact on market psychology out of all proportion to its size. Conversely, of course, and this had been my major concern, a comparable bid for marks one minute earlier by some frightened trader could have triggered an avalanche of other demands for foreign currencies. So far so good. As our mark offering remained blessedly untouched over the next five minutes, we followed up with sizable offerings of sterling at 2:08 p.m., and of Dutch guilders at 2:14 p.m. Still no takers in any volume. I then instructed the Trading Desk to inform the market that we would supply Swiss francs at the upper limit for that currency, only slightly above the rate prevailing at 1:40 p.m. Meanwhile we heard from the Bank of Canada, which had instantaneously reacted to the ticker reports from Dallas by stabilizing the United States–Canadian dollar rate, and we reinforced the Canadian action by similar support at the identical rate in New York. The French franc was already at its ceiling, and at this level we had in hand a standing order from the Bank of France to sell francs as needed to hold that ceiling rate. With defensive action thus taken in six important foreign currencies, I felt that the other two, the Belgian franc and the Italian lira, would not move far out of line on their own and, if they did, we could of course pull them back.

As minutes went by, with the market doing no more than nibble at our offerings of foreign currencies, I decided that we could risk going all the way by officially informing the market that we stood prepared to supply foreign exchange in unlimited amounts to defend the dollar, calling on the entire $2 billion of swap facilities, if necessary. This was done, at roughly 2:30 p.m., and for the rest of the trading day we froze the whole pattern of international exchange rates at the levels prevailing just before the assassination.

Having thus committed the Federal to an all-out defense of the dollar, I left the trading room for my office close to that of President Hayes on the tenth floor to report on what had been done. While I was talking with Hayes, who was Vice-Chairman of the Federal

Open Market Committee, a call came in from Ralph Young, then committee secretary. Both men strongly supported my decision to intervene, agreed that we should maintain an unyielding defense of the dollar on the exchange markets for the rest of the afternoon, and undertook to seek the support of Chairman Martin.

I still had not cleared any aspect of our intervention with the U.S. Treasury, however, although staff members of the Treasury had been kept currently informed by our Trading Desk. In normal circumstances, any important market action by the New York Federal without so much as a by-your-leave to top Treasury officials would have been a serious breach of the courtesy and substance of Federal Reserve understandings with the Treasury, which bears full political responsibility for the country's international financial policy. Subordinate commanders in the field rarely find the rule book of much help in emergencies, however, and for better or worse must stake their reputations on their judgment of what has to be done. So, as I placed a call to Treasury Undersecretary Roosa, I could only hope that the operation would succeed, in which case all would presumably be forgiven.

Meanwhile, Roosa had already reached Hayes on another line. As I joined in the conversation, I asked what was the latest on President Kennedy's condition. Roosa replied grimly, "He's dead." Such was our concentration on the operating problems at hand that without another word we plunged into a discussion of the foreign exchange market. Roosa, with Secretary Dillon still over the Pacific en route back to Washington, was carrying an enormous load of responsibility and had vividly in mind the speculative panic in the stock market which, at his request, had been closed only minutes before. He was clearly shocked, and understandably so, that I had not cleared with the Treasury the potentially massive operation I had just launched in the exchange markets. I did not argue the issue. But as I explained the market situation, a temporary vacuum in which the Federal's aggressive offers of foreign currency should forestall speculation against the dollar, he immediately grasped the point and ended by giving his blessing. He understood markets.

Meanwhile, our telephone operators had been hunting down the foreign central bank officials whose money we were using, and one by one I reached them at their homes within the next hour. Roy Bridge, the senior official in charge of gold and exchange operations at the Bank of England, subsequently recalled our initial telephone conversation in a talk before a symposium on central banking sponsored by the Federal Reserve Bank of Boston.

I remember very well that Friday night when your former president was assassinated. When I am in London on a Friday evening I often have a drink with a couple of foreign exchange brokers to discuss dealings for the week. So I left the office at 6 o'clock, and after a drink I took a train from Waterloo down to Richmond, and a taxi from Richmond up to Kew Gardens. I arrived home at 7:30, so I had been out of touch for an hour and a half, during which time these events had broken.

After the taxi door shut my second daughter came rushing from the house. She said, "Daddy, President Kennedy has been shot. The Governor (of the Bank of England) wants you to ring him immediately and Charlie Coombs is trying to get you on the phone from New York." So I said, "I'll take New York first." Charlie Coombs then told me what he was doing. I said I thought his plans extremely sensible, because the essential thing at that time was to maintain confidence. I told him that so far as we were concerned, he could ask for all that he wanted and if I thought of any other currencies that he could use he could have them on Monday. I then immediately reported to the Governor what I'd done and received his full approval.

Mr. Johannes Tüngeler, Director of the Foreign Department of the Bundesbank, who spoke at the same symposium, reported his reactions in these words.

Recalling the situation on my side on the day of President Kennedy's assassination, things developed as Mr. Bridge has explained. When I arrived home at about 7 p.m. I switched on the radio and, while the alarming news from Texas was broadcast, a telephone call from Charlie came through. It goes without saying that I confirmed all necessary drawings on the existing mark-dollar swap facilities to meet any speculative pressure on the New York market. In addition we took care to show ourselves as buyers of dollars in the Frankfurt exchange market early next morning.

All the foreign central bank officials we reached by telephone that Friday afternoon fervently concurred in the stabilizing action we had taken and further agreed that we could draw on the swap lines to whatever extent might prove necessary. In the case of our Swiss franc swap lines, then amounting to $200 million, $150 million had been already used up by previous drawings, and tentative discussions on increasing the lines had already been initiated. Since the Swiss franc has been a traditional refuge for hot money during periods of crisis, the projected enlargement of the credit line with Zurich now became a matter of some urgency. I accordingly requested by telephone the immediate approval of the Open Market Committee of an increase of $100 million, or 50 percent, in our Swiss franc lines, and then secured, again over the telephone, Swiss agreement to the increase.

As I talked that Friday afternoon to my central banking friends abroad, I began to realize for the first time the extent to which President Kennedy had captured the trust and admiration of the outside world. Central bankers tend to be a fairly hard-nosed breed, particularly when appraising the frailties of political leadership, whether at home or abroad. But even in Zurich, which hardly ever drops its deadpan, unemotional mask, the effect of the assassination was shattering. All through the afternoon, the expressions of personal grief that came over the telephone from Zurich, London, and elsewhere were so spontaneous and insistent that on several occasions I had to cut them off with a harsh reminder that we had urgent business to do.

In the New York market, as I came back down to the Trading Desk, our earlier action to underwrite without limit the exchange value of the dollar against the major European currencies had been accepted as a formal, official reassurance that American financial policy would continue unchanged. In those days official assurances enjoyed a full measure of credibility. Those with short positions in foreign currencies felt terrifying personal risks suddenly lifted from their shoulders, and our Trading Desk was deluged with calls expressing relief over the firm stand we had taken. As such business worries subsided, the emotional impact of the Dallas tragedy overwhelmed everything else, and market activity faded away well before the close. Total sales of foreign currencies offered by the Federal in New York amounted to only slightly more than $23 million, and Bank of Canada operations came to less than $27 million, for an overall total of just about $50 million. I too felt as if a considerable personal risk had been lifted from my shoulders.

For most of that Friday afternoon the absorbing technical job I had been trained to do had shielded me from the surrounding emotional turmoil, almost as if I had been enclosed in an isolation booth. But by late afternoon, as the pressure eased off, I suddenly remembered that I was supposed to meet my wife and daughter in Grand Central at 6 o'clock en route to the football weekend. Still ensconced in my technical world, I telephoned home to check whether they were going to make it on time. The answer was no, a vividly indignant no, with the further suggestion that I must be absolutely out of my mind to think of going to a football game with the president lying dead.

And so I came back to reality. The Harvard–Yale game would of course be postponed, the day's work was over and a lot of other things as well, and the full impact of the tragedy hit me for the first time. I felt sufficiently shaken to ask for a ride home in a Bank car and was driven by an old friend on our guard force, a tall, soft-spoken man named Tony Angotta. Like many other people that day, Tony was deeply apprehensive of a Texas conspiracy behind the tragedy and sadly commented: "This time they really put Dallas on the map." I shared that evening his suspicion, but my mind kept returning to my technical worries. Should I not have waited for Treasury clearance before taking all-out defensive action in the exchange markets? And what would we do on Monday if the European exchange markets, perhaps inflamed by further shocking developments over the weekend, should challenge with big money the power play we had just launched?

All these professional anxieties were soon to be relieved, however. Over the weekend the decisive takeover of White House authority by Lyndon Johnson provided worldwide assurance of a vigorous continuity of policy. On Monday the European exchange markets opened for business with a sober appreciation of the united front of the central banks against dollar speculation and a dramatically heightened sense of political solidarity between Europe and the United States. Indeed, the worldwide mood on that day of drums in Washington was symbolized for me by the Swiss reaction. It was early evening there when the last journey of President Kennedy was made to Arlington, and the President of the Swiss National Bank subsequently wrote to us of the empty streets and how the church bells suddenly began to toll in the darkness "from Zurich, from the villages on the lake and from the mountains." By Tuesday the financial crisis was over, the stock market staged a strong recovery, we gradually defrosted the frozen structure of exchange rates and allowed the market its head again. And a few days after that, the New York Reserve Bank received the commendation of both Treasury Secretary Dillon and the new President of the United States on the emergency action we had taken.

Emboldened by the success of the operation, I issued with Treasury approval standing instructions to the Foreign Trading Desk to react instantly to any new emergency of major magnitude by similar defensive tactics in the exchange markets. In the late sixties those instructions were quietly withdrawn. With the progressive erosion of the dollar's strength, the risks of all-out defensive action had simply become excessive. It was a bitter decision.

7

The Sterling Bear Squeeze

The strength of sterling during the United States election campaigns in late 1960 did not delude Governor Cobbold of the Bank of England into thinking that any fundamental improvement was under way. He and his associates knew all too well that inflows of hot money from New York were mainly responsible for the buoyant sterling rate. Such funds could take flight from London as suddenly as they had moved in. Tough measures by the new Kennedy administration to cut our payments deficit might thus inflict on sterling the double jeopardy of competition from a resurgent dollar as well as from a German mark that was already being touted as a candidate for revaluation.

In the background was the familiar story of the price Britain had paid for its gallant role in World War II. Official reserves and foreign investments had been severely depleted, while heavy new liabilities to the sterling area and other countries had been incurred. Cobbold and his associates were rightly apprehensive of any major speculative challenge to sterling. London already faced an acute shortage of international liquidity.

Accordingly, British financial officials had assiduously promoted during 1960 the debate then getting under way on the most appropriate technique of assuring an adequate worldwide growth of international liquidity. In the British Treasury official thinking seemed to be leaning toward the creation of some new international money unit. But in late 1960 I got the distinct impression that the top echelon of the Bank of England had instead concluded that a major increase in the official gold price of the United States was the only realistic way out of the world liquidity dilemma.

When I stopped off at the Bank of England in early February 1961, en route to the monthly BIS meeting, there was considerable interest in any news I might be bringing of the financial plans of the Kennedy administration, inaugurated only days before. I was immediately ushered into a meeting in Governor Cobbold's office with Parsons and other senior officials also present. In response to questions, I outlined in a general way the intention of President Kennedy to make a personal commitment to defend the $35 gold parity of the dollar and to demonstrate the force of this commitment by various new measures designed to bring the country's balance of payments back into equilibrium.

Cobbold and his associates listened in silent, deepening gloom. Quite aside from evident disappointment on the gold price decision, they could now anticipate a strong recovery of the dollar, which would in turn pull hot money out of London. To me, their reaction confirmed the urgent necessity of new cooperative arrangements to defend the world monetary system against speculation. In particular, some way must be found for London and New York to accommodate through technical cooperation the inevitable ebb and flow of money between them.

Sterling did in fact weaken in response to the Kennedy program, but the major damage was done instead by the surprise revaluation of the German mark on Saturday, March 4, 1961. As money flooded out of London into the continental financial centers, the whole international monetary system was suddenly faced with a major challenge. The Bank of England needed financial help to stem the reserve drain, while the Swiss and other continental central banks were swamped with dollar inflows. If the continental banks now exercised their legal right under the Bretton Woods agreement to convert such dollars into gold at the U.S. Treasury window, the crisis might spread from sterling to the dollar, with unpleasant consequences for all concerned.

The inflow of money into the Swiss National Bank had been particularly heavy, $300 million in four days. At this critical juncture, the Swiss National Bank decided, as previously related, to lend back to the Bank of England most of the incoming dollars as well as $110 million of gold. At one brilliant stroke, this decision provided urgently needed financial support to sterling and simultaneously relieved the U.S. Treasury of the risk of Swiss conversion of surplus dollars into gold. Even more significant, the Swiss credit of $310 million provided the all-important nucleus of a billion dollar package of central bank credits from the Continental central banks rounded up by Governor Cobbold and other Bank of England officials during the March BIS weekend. At the close of the BIS meeting, the governors put out a cryptic communique stating that they were "cooperating in the exchange markets," without any reference whatsoever to the major reinforcement of British reserves that had been negotiated.

Though impressed by the speed, flexibility, and effectiveness of these Basel credits, American financial officials found it difficult to understand the secrecy surrounding the truly impressive total of central bank credits provided to the Bank of England. To us, it seemed that an immediate announcement of so massive a reinforcement of the British reserves would have had a highly favorable effect on market psychology. Moreover, at monthly BIS meetings later in 1961, I ran into a good many complaints from other European central banks that the credits to the Bank of England had been secretly negotiated on a strictly bilateral basis. None of the continental banks knew how much the others had provided nor under what terms and conditions. Here again, we were inclined to favor a full exchange of information within the circle of cooperating central banks.

Meanwhile, during the summer and autumn of 1961, the U.S. Treasury had supported Federal Reserve initiatives to resume operations on the foreign exchange markets, and in February 1962 the Federal Open Market Committee formally approved such action. As previously related, a swap contract providing the Federal with $50 million dollars equivalent of French francs was executed on March 1, 1962. A similar swap arrangement with the Bank of England also in the amount of $50 million was put on the books at the end of May 1962.

In early 1963, however, British reserves were swollen by seasonal inflows and the Federal Reserve drew $25 million on the swap line with the Bank of England. Shortly thereafter the situation was abruptly transformed as President de Gaulle rejected the British application for Common Market partnership. Immediate outflows of hot money from London shifted the role of the Bank of England from lender to borrower under the swap line. Meanwhile, the Bank of England, in an effort to demonstrate the continuity of European monetary cooperation, had negotiated new lines of credit from the continental central banks. On April 3 Chancellor Reginald Maudling announced that credits from the continental central banks totaling $250 million had been made available. The Federal welcomed these precautionary arrangements.

Much more, of course, would be needed to withstand a new speculative attack on sterling, and British financial policy officials saw no alternative but to turn to the Federal. Earlier fears by the Bank of England that Federal Reserve swap arrangements were designed to shut off British access to the U.S. Treasury gold window seemed to have subsided considerably since the appointment of Lord Cromer to succeed Lord Cobbold as governor in June 1961. At 42 Cromer had already made a distinguished career in merchant banking with Barings, his family firm, and subsequently as the British economic minister to Washington. In the latter post he had made frequent visits to the New York banking community, where he seemed to feel more at home than in the political and bureaucratic labyrinths of Washington. A congenial man, unfailingly courteous and considerate, and seemingly incapable of dissembling, Cromer always reminded me of Hayes of the New York Federal. The friendship that quickly developed between the two men communicated itself down the line, and technical cooperation between their two banks became the order of the day.

Cromer was also enterprising and decisive. I heartily welcomed his bold suggestion to me at the May 1963 BIS meeting of a tenfold increase of the Federal Reserve swap line with the Bank of England from $50 to $500 million. This massive enlargement of the dollar-sterling credit line, which was approved with hardly a dissenting murmur by the Open Market Committee on May 28, 1963, had an immediate salutary effect on market confidence. Over the rest of 1963 and on into 1964 the sterling market remained relatively calm.

By the summer of 1964, however, as the October date of the British election drew nearer, the storm signals were again flying. Cromer then proceeded to reinforce the credit facilities of the Bank of England with an enlarged support package, this time totaling $500 million dollars, from the European and Canadian central banks. Meanwhile the British government had also negotiated a standby credit of $1 billion dollars from the International Monetary Fund, thereby providing the Bank of England with a backstop for any central bank credits reaching their final maturity dates.

But probably no one was more apprehensive of the speculative consequences of a Labor party victory in the 1964 British elections

than James Callaghan, the Labor shadow chancellor. Some time
before, Callaghan had come to lunch with Hayes and me at the
New York Federal. Callaghan was a thoroughly professional politician with an easy-going, ebullient style. Over the luncheon table he
acknowledged that the main reason for his visit to New York was
his grave concern over a flight from sterling if Labor should come
out on top in the British elections.

Like the incumbent Conservative Chancellor Maudling, Callaghan was considering many relatively long-range possibilities of
increasing international liquidity, and the reserve backing of sterling
in particular. Hayes and I gave him our flat judgment that none of
these long-range proposals could conceivably mature in time to
help deal with a postelection sterling crisis. In the short run, the
only hope of defending sterling lay in central bank credit facilities,
backed up by the medium-term credit resources available from
the International Monetary Fund. We made no effort to counsel
him in financial orthodoxy but did stress the overriding necessity
of maintaining market confidence. To Hayes and me, Callaghan
seemed a decent, honorable man, pragmatic rather than doctrinaire
in his approach, and deserving of sympathetic support. Whether
he or any other Labor politician in the thankless role of chancellor
could bring about a rational wage policy was another question.

In the British election of October 15, 1964, the Labor party
gained a paper-thin majority of 317 out of 630 seats. The new government was immediately confronted with the major policy decision of whether to defend the existing sterling parity of $2.80.
Largely reflecting the overstimulative budget introduced by Chancellor Maudling the previous spring, the British balance of payments
had gone far into the red during the summer months of 1964.
Perhaps the Labor government in its first few days in office did not
fully appreciate how far the payments situation had deteriorated
nor how strenuous an effort would be needed to set matters straight.
In any event, Prime Minister Wilson announced on October 26 the
historic decision to defend the sterling parity of $2.80.

With the advantage of hindsight, many commentators have subsequently castigated the Wilson decision as a major policy blunder. But as I recall the situation, there was little support anywhere at the time for the devaluation option. Lord Cromer, together with top career officials of the ministries primarily concerned, have subsequently confirmed to me that deliberate resort to devaluation as a policy tool was discussed in British official circles in no more than a perfunctory way. The Wilson decision to defend sterling was generally welcomed by worldwide opinion at the time. The main problem seemed to be that of arresting the inflationary surge originating in the Maudling budget.

Having made such a policy commitment, the Labor government's first order of business should have been to restore some measure of confidence in the badly shaken exchange markets. But over subsequent weeks much of what Labor spokesmen had to say served only to frighten the exchange markets still further. The truly alarming deterioration of the British payments position under the Conservative government was set forth in detail, but the corrective policy program enunciated in bits and pieces by Labor fell far short of persuading the market that an effective solution would be found.

In fact, the major defensive move was to impose a temporary import surcharge of 15 percent. This was construed on the Continent as an effort to shift the burden of adjustment to Britain's trading partners, and the supplementary budget produced by Chancellor Callaghan on November 11 did little to slow down the fiscal engine of inflation. On the monetary side, despite strong appeals by the Bank of England, no action in the form of a bank rate increase or related credit control measures was permitted by the Labor government.

At the November BIS meeting, Lord Cromer made a skillful defense of the Labor government program but was unable to persuade his European central bank colleagues that any revival of confidence could be achieved in the absence of an increase in the Bank of England discount rate. Toward the close of the governors' Sunday evening dinner, one of the continental governors leaned across the table and whispered "Lord Cromer, on behalf of all of us, please be careful!" In private conversations all the foreign department men from the European central banks I met that weekend felt that we faced an explosive situation in both the gold and foreign exchange markets. They were particularly fearful that a massive speculative attack on sterling would react back on the dollar as well.

Meanwhile the Bank of England had been forced to draw heavily on its $1 billion of short-term credit facilities with the Federal Reserve and the European central banks. In September and October, $415 million had been drawn to finance intervention in support of the sterling rate, and in November the drain accelerated still further. Back at my office in New York, I was now on the telephone several times a day to Bridge of the Bank of England, as we coordinated intervention operations in New York with those in London. I watched with mounting apprehension as each Thursday—the traditional bank rate fixing day—went by without an increase in the Bank of England's discount rate, and was immediately followed by a new speculative onslaught on sterling. Friday, November 20, was a particularly bad day, and reserve losses of $180 million were posted. By evening the Bank of England had exhausted its short-term credit facilities of $500 million with the Bank of Canada and the continental central banks and had drawn $355 million of the $500 million available under the swap line with the Federal Reserve. In our telephone conversations, Bridge was seething with anger over the sheer futility of pouring reserves into the exchange market without decisive discount rate or other policy moves, and eloquently cursed the Labor left-wingers responsible for the inaction.

That Friday night I left the Bank with the feeling that the Labor government was about to throw in the sponge. But over the weekend, I had a call from Hayes reporting that the Labor government had agreed to a dramatic increase in the Bank of England discount rate from 5 to 7 percent, to be announced the following Monday. So I stayed overnight at the Bank on Sunday and was on the phone to Bridge early Monday morning to assess the London market response to the discount rate increase.

The discount rate announcement caught the market by surprise and had the immediate effect of inducing a scramble to cover short positions in sterling. The sterling rate rose sharply, giving Bridge an opportunity to take in about $70 million. By midday Monday, however, the return flow of funds subsided. An ominous lull persisted through Tuesday morning. Then, around Tuesday noontime on the Continent, big selling orders of sterling suddenly began to flash in the French and German markets. By the time of my first phone call to Bridge around 8:00 a.m., New York time, sterling was already in full retreat. Shortly after 9 o'clock, Bridge called to report that he was now losing dollar reserves at a rate of more than $1 million a minute.

The dramatic increase of the Bank of England rate to crisis levels had clearly failed to produce the traditional market response. Some have attributed the psychological failure of the bank rate increase to its surprise announcement on Monday rather than the traditional Thursday date. This might have suggested to the market that the British government had spent the preceding weekend debating the alternative of devaluation but had finally decided on a last despairing effort to hold the line by resort to the discount rate. The market was probably also guessing that all the central bank credits available to the Bank of England in September had now been exhausted and that the British drawing scheduled for late November of $1 billion on the International Monetary Fund had already been committed to refund the central bank credits. And if the full cost of defending sterling were now to fall on the Bank of England's scanty remaining reserves, the battle would be over and lost within a matter of days.

As I sat in our New York trading room watching the flight from sterling, it seemed to me that the market was challenging not only the British government's defense of the sterling parity but also the whole structure of international financial cooperation built up since Bretton Woods. Prime Minister Wilson's decision on October 26 to hold the $2.80 parity had been strongly supported with money as well as words by all the major governments represented in the

International Monetary Fund. However misguided the parity decision might turn out to be, and I was already beginning to feel some
doubts on this score, the few short weeks that had elapsed since
the Labor government had taken office hardly constituted an adequate test of its exchange rate and other policies.

Nor did the market onslaught on sterling seem primarily moti-
vated by longer range judgments of the fundamental economic
problems confornting Britain. From bitter experience, exchange
market traders have learned that they can lose their shirts by betting
on the longer term fundamentals. The sterling crisis was essentially
a crisis of market confidence in the Labor government. On that
morning of November 24, 1964, market traders were gripped by the
immediate and exciting chance that sterling—and perhaps the Labor
government as well—might from one day to the next be toppled
by lack of money, lack of financial expertise, or lack of nerve. All the
ingenuity of the market now concentrated on how to get rid of
positions in sterling or, better still, to sell it short.

In the eleventh-hour emergency facing us, no real possibility
existed of the British government putting together some crash program of new austerity measures and least of all, any possibility of
intergovernmental discussions conditioning further foreign aid on
certain measures of British self-help. In fact, the only chance of resolving the policy options of the British government in an orderly
way lay in an immediate and major reinforcement of sterling by
new and unconditional foreign credit. Such a demonstration of foreign official support of the decision of the British government to
maintain the official parity might temporarily stabilize the exchange
market and give the Labor government a breathing space in which
basic corrective measures could be taken.

But if a new credit package of central bank and other assistance
were to be put together, a nucleus of at least one major credit commitment was immediately needed. That initiating role seemed to
fall naturally to the Federal Reserve and its swap network of reciprocal credit facilities with other central banks. Moreover, because

of the time differential in which New York lagged six hours behind continental Europe, a new Federal Reserve credit to the Bank of England would have to be approved by the Federal Open Market Committee at least a full day before any approach for similar credit facilities to the continental central banks.

With all this in mind, I advised President Hayes shortly before 10 a.m. of the hurricane of speculation on the sterling market and the clear danger that the British government would be forced either to devalue or to impose a sweeping system of exchange controls before the week was over. As a nucleus for a new credit package, I suggested an emergency telephone meeting of the FOMC to recommend an increase in our swap line with the Bank of England from $500 to $750 million; I also suggested that the Export-Import Bank be asked to provide a standby credit on the order of $250 million.

Hayes agreed and immediately telephoned Chairman Martin, Dillon, and Roosa of the Treasury to apprise them of the gravity of the situation and of our recommendations for action. Both Dillon and Martin accepted our recommendations. Martin called a telephone meeting of the FOMC for 3 p.m., that afternoon, while Roosa undertook to enlist the support of the Export-Import Bank. Later in the morning I telephoned Bob Beattie, the Deputy Governor of the Bank of Canada, regarding our plans, and asked whether the Bank of Canada might be able to join in a rescue package for sterling to the extent of roughly $200 million. Beattie was personally sympathetic and indicated that he would immediately take up the question with Governor Rasminsky and the Canadian Ministry of Finance.

That afternoon a telephone conference of the Open Market Committee linked up the Board of Governors in Washington with the New York Bank, as well as the Reserve Banks of Cleveland, St. Louis, Richmond, and San Francisco. Chairman Martin called on me to give my analysis of the situation and recommendations for action. I began by noting that the Bank of England had already lost that day more than $210 million in reserves and that the Federal Reserve swap line and other central bank credit resources of the

Bank of England were now exhausted. The FOMC minutes read as follows:

> The British Government, Mr. Coombs continued, thus faced the prospect of a severe depletion of their already limited reserve availabilities unless the present crisis of confidence could somehow be countered. As he saw it, there were now two main alternatives. First, the British might decide to devalue sterling. This would probably precipitate an international financial crisis of the first magnitude. He would expect to see a major speculative drive on the London gold market and sooner or later an even more dangerous attack on the U.S. dollar. If the British devaluation were to trigger devaluations of other currencies, such an attack on the U.S. dollar might develop swiftly and in huge volume.
>
> Mr. Coombs thought, therefore, that it was essential to avoid at all costs recourse to the devaluation alternative and to try to deal directly with the confidence factor by putting on a display of international financial cooperation through a new and very large package of short-term credit to the U.K. He thought that the situation was extremely dangerous and that a "now or never" effort should be made. In round figures, Mr. Coombs said, the Committee might think in terms of a total international credit package of $2 billion over and above the present swap line of $500 million and the short-term European and Canadian bank credit of $500 million, both of which would be presumably repaid out of the British drawing on the IMF.
>
> In building up such a $2 billion package, Mr. Coombs thought, the U.S. share would probably have to be about $500 million. He was hopeful that the Treasury or the Export-Import Bank might be able to provide $250 million, one-half of the U.S. share. The remaining $250 million from the U.S. side should, he believed, be provided by an increase in the Federal Reserve swap line with the Bank of England from $500 million to $750 million.
>
> Chairman Martin said that, in his judgment, the issue before the Committee now was whether the Federal Reserve was prepared to increase the reciprocal currency agreement with the United Kingdom by $250 million if a package of credits such as that outlined by Mr. Coombs was put together. The British might decide not to

request such credits, but that matter, he thought, was outside the purview of the Committee at present. He would hope that the System would adopt a posture of being as helpful as it could.

The committee unanimously approved my recommendations, and the Bank of England was immediately informed of the conditional action taken.

I stayed on at the bank again that night. Around 8 p.m. Parsons of the Bank of England telephoned to say that after consultations with the British government, they were now prepared to go for a new credit package and would welcome our assistance. In the course of the evening, Secretary Dillon advised me by telephone that the Export-Import Bank credit of $250 million was assured.

So then, with a billion dollars of credits firmly in hand, I slept for a few hours and at 4 a.m. began a series of telephone calls to our central bank friends in London, Paris, Rome, Frankfurt, Zurich, Amsterdam, Brussels, and Stockholm. In London the speculative drive on sterling was continuing unabated, and by 2 p.m., New York time, another $260 million of British reserves had gone. My immediate objective was to convince the continental banks that we faced an emergency of the first magnitude. A new package of credits for sterling of unprecedented size had to be assembled within the next few hours if a sterling devaluation were to be averted. In this first round of calls I could not get into specific figures, since the Bank of England had meanwhile run into further delays occasioned by last-minute discussions with the British government.

By 6:00 a.m., New York time, however, the Bank of England was ready to talk specifics with its prospective creditors. President Hayes had meanwhile arrived and joined me on the telephone in my office. We quickly worked out with Lord Cromer a schedule of possible contributions from the central banks of Canada, the European Continent, and Japan, adding up to a target figure of $2 billion which, with the $1 billion already committed by the United States, would create a total package of $3 billion.

Cromer from London and Hayes and I from New York then began

to bombard the governors of the European central banks with telephone calls stressing the urgency of immediate decisions, and the package gradually began to take shape. A difficult problem of timing now arose, however. Several central bank governors, most notably those of the Netherlands, France, and Switzerland, were unwilling to make definite commitments before consulting with their ministries of finance. As these clearances were pursued, the hours slipped away, and by the 9:00 a.m. opening of the New York market, the package was still incomplete. And as we had feared, sterling was then inundated by sell orders from the New York market.

Moreover, we ran into a major and unyielding roadblock when Walter Schwegler, President of the Swiss National Bank, advised us that he would have to delay a decision until the following day. We informed Washington of this impasse, and Undersecretary Roosa telephoned Schwegler with a brilliant improvisation: the U.S. Treasury Stabilization Fund would initially take up the Swiss share, leaving Schwegler with the option to take over the commitment subsequently if he saw his way clear to do so. Schwegler agreed to this arrangement and subsequently exercised the option.

Although the financial resources of the Bank of Japan at that time were not particularly strong, we felt that a small contribution from them would also be useful in the interests of solidarity. But to my dismay, I realized that, with a 13-hour time differential, it was now past midnight in Tokyo. The head of the Foreign Department of the Bank of Japan, Haruo Mayekawa, was an old friend, however, so I thought I could presume on this personal relationship. As he answered the telephone and listened to my apologies, he commented that the moment the phone had rung, he had guessed it was me; no Japanese would ever dream of calling at that hour. Within 15 minutes, however, he was back to us with confirmation of a $50 million Bank of Japan contribution to the package.

The last remaining commitment being sought was that from the Bank of France, and here we had to contend with the political background of recent criticism by President de Gaulle of the role of sterling as a reserve currency. As we were considering going forward with an announcement of a slightly smaller package leaving the French out, a call from Cromer shortly before 2:00 o'clock reported that the Bank of France had finally joined in, and we had our $3 billion package complete. Over a stretch of 10 hours, we had made 55 overseas telephone calls, receiving almost as many others.

NOVEMBER 1964 CREDIT PACKAGE

Bank	Millions of Dollars
German Bundesbank	500
Bank for International Settlements	250
Bank of Canada	200
Bank of France	200
Bank of Italy	200
Swiss National Bank	160
Swedish Riksbank	100
National Bank of Belgium	75
Netherlands Bank	75
Bank of Japan	50
Austrian National Bank	50
Federal Reserve Bank of New York	750
Export-Import Bank	250
Other	140
Total	3000

Joint announcements of the credit package by the Bank of England and the Federal Reserve Bank of New York were immediately issued to the press, which in New York had been fully alerted by market contacts to the gravity of the emergency and the probability of major policy decisions being made that very day. The Bank of England, at 7:00 p.m., London time, put out a brief communiqué saying simply: "The Bank of England have made arrangements under which $3 billion are made available for the support of sterling" and pretty much let it go at that. In New York, however, the head of the Reserve Bank's Public Information Department, Tom Waage, could not escape holding a major press conference.

Waage took most seriously indeed the dictum of President Hayes' predecessor, Allan Sproul, that "if you are operating in the public domain you have to explain what you are doing." As noted by John Brooks, "Waage's communiqué, although falling somewhat short of the mood of, say, the last scene of *Die Meistersinger,* was nevertheless exceptionally stirring as bank utterances go, speaking with a certain subdued flamboyance of the unprecedented nature of the sum involved and of how the central banks had moved quickly to mobilize a massive counterattack on speculative selling of the pound."* At the press conference Waage apparently also gave a fairly full and dramatic account of the events of the day in New York; he had in fact been present in my office during most of the telephoning. He had little information to convey about the Bank of England's role; he simply did not know any of the details of what had gone on in Cromer's office and, in any case, assumed that his opposite number at the Bank of England would be covering the British side of the operation.

The next day, which was Thanksgiving Day, Hayes called me early in the morning at my home, and told me with grave concern in his voice that we were "plastered all over the *New York Times* and the *Herald Tribune.*" As I got the papers, I could readily see why Hayes was upset. The press reports from New York on the sterling rescue operation were accurate as far as they went, but the imbalance between full reporting by the New York Federal and almost total reticence by the Bank of England had inevitably left the impression that the entire operation had been engineered by the New York Bank. Cromer's major role was almost invisible. An angry attack on the *New York Times'* coverage by the Bank of England press officer did nothing to help matters, but in succeeding days Waage managed to secure a more balanced press appraisal of the cooperative effort of the Bank of England and the New York Federal.

Meanwhile, to the deep regret of Hayes and myself, Cromer had been seriously and unjustifiably embarrassed. Moreover, his enemies in the Labor government construed the incident as further proof

---

* John Brooks, *op. cit.,* pp. 366–367.

that Cromer was trying to deny them credit facilities that the Americans and others were fully prepared to provide. Nothing could have been further from the truth. The Federal Reserve credits and those of the other central banks were based squarely on our confidence in the Bank of England and its governor. If Cromer had so much as hinted at any reluctance to continue borrowing in defense of sterling, the whole operation would have been instantly called off.

In any event, the provision of $3 billion of new credits to the Bank of England signally failed to generate a real recovery of confidence in sterling. After jumping sharply in New York on the afternoon of November 25, following announcement of the credit package, the sterling rate sagged once more as the market remained unconvinced that the Labor government possessed the resolve to defend sterling effectively.

Returning from the December 1964 BIS meeting, Hayes and I stopped off in London and saw Chancellor Callaghan. He was clearly shaken by the November onslaught on sterling and asked us point blank what could be done if another major wave of speculation suddenly materialized. I told him quite candidly that I thought there would be little or no hope of raising additional central bank credit. Meanwhile, however, the financial resources available from the November 1964 credit package could and should be protected by heavier operations by the Bank of England in the forward market. Such forward operations would not only have a salutary effect on market confidence but would also relieve pressure on the spot market and British dollar reserves by providing at reasonable cost the alternative of hedging in the forward market.

After the turn of the year sterling began to show faint signs of recovery. But new complications arose in January 1965 as Federal Reserve action to restrain commercial bank lending abroad led to some withdrawal of funds from London. And in April Chancellor Callaghan's budget message fell far short of the fiscal austerity required to curb domestic demand and restrain the inflationary trend of wage settlements. Speculation erupted once more, and heavy support had to be given by the Bank of England in both the spot and forward markets.

On May 25, 1965, the British Government drew the remaining $1.4 billion available from the IMF and proceeded to repay all the $1.1 billion of central bank credits drawn since November 1964. The $2 billion of six-month credit lines provided in November 1964 by the European central banks, the Bank of Canada, and the Bank of Japan then lapsed, leaving available only the $750 million swap line with the Federal Reserve.

As the market appraised this partial closing down of the Bank of England's credit facilities, the speculative drive on sterling now gathered fresh momentum. In June 1965, massive outflows from London forced the Bank of England to make heavy new drafts on the Federal Reserve swap line; $360 million was drawn during June, several hundred million more in July, and by late August the $750 million line had been exhausted. At the end of August 1965, the Federal Reserve and the U.S. Treasury provided additional special credits totaling $140 million. Over the previous year, the Bank of England had thus spent on market intervention nearly $3 billion of central bank credits, plus more than $1 billion from its own reserves, while also assuming heavy commitments in the forward market.

Bridge of the Bank of England was in charge of this costly rearguard action, which had been primarily fought in the London market. As we discussed market tactics each day, I increasingly appreciated both his professional expertise and his personal style. In adversity, Bridge never bluffed or complained but acknowledged with devastating candor just why the markets were losing confidence in sterling. Aside from our daily telephone conversations, my frequent visits to London also enabled me to see Bridge in action at moments of crisis in the foreign exchange markets. There, in his office, I could watch the true professional, alert to all the technical and psychological forces of the market, as he took decisions whether to hold a certain rate level at possibly heavy cost or to retreat and risk even heavier losses. Those were not easy judgments, but they were made decisively and courageously as Bridge paced the floor between crackling telephone calls and snarling commentaries on whatever had brought matters to such a pretty pass.

Meanwhile, however, the enormous losses suffered by the Bank of England in defending sterling over the previous year had been accompanied by a buildup of very large short positions in the sterling market in anticipation of an inevitable devaluation. Costly to maintain, these short positions were consequently vulnerable to even a temporary recovery of confidence in sterling. But the market had shrugged off a substantial improvement in the British trade figures during 1965 and remained convinced that wage inflation would inevitably bring sterling down.

During the summer months of 1965, however, our hopes were kept alive by Bank of England reports that the British government seemed to be finally moving toward effective action to check the inflationary trend of wage rates. If such action was taken, we should be able to count on some tentative recovery of market confidence. And if we could exploit this recovery of confidence by driving the sterling bears to cover, a major reversal in the fortunes of sterling might be achieved.

I broached this idea of a bear squeeze to Bridge, who was weary of his dismal task of feeding out the dollars demanded by the market and avidly looked forward to an opportunity to take the offensive. But the Bank of England, after suffering a $3 billion drain on its credit lines, plus heavy reserve losses, during the preceding year was hardly in a position to gamble on an aggressive bidding up of the sterling rate.

As I studied the problem, it occurred to me that the Federal Reserve with the help of other central banks might themselves execute a bear squeeze in the market by aggressively buying sterling. But this would depend on reaching an understanding with the Bank of England that the sterling we thus acquired would be not only convertible on demand at the Bank of England but also fully guaranteed in terms of the dollar. As a *quid pro quo*, we would naturally show due restraint in exercising the convertibility privilege.

I floated this idea with the new U.S. Treasury team of Secretary Henry Fowler and Undersecretary Fred Deming, who seized on the suggestion. U.S. Treasury discussions with their British counterparts quickly produced an agreement in principle under which the British government would undertake to deal firmly with wage and price inflation, while the United States would take the lead in rounding up foreign central bank support for heavy purchases of sterling on a guaranteed basis.

As evidence of its determination to defend sterling, the British government announced on September 2 its intention to seek statutory authority to require advance notification and, if deemed necessary, temporary deferment of wage and price increases. On the guaranteed sterling arrangement, however, complications arose as the British Treasury took a hard bargaining line, calling for the foreign central banks participating to shift through market purchases a full 5 percent of their total reserves into guaranteed sterling. Moreover, the British Treasury now insisted that conversion of such guaranteed sterling would require 30 days' prior notice, plus consultations with the Bank of England.

The Bank of England cabled the British Treasury position to me on August 26, and I telephoned back my grave concern whether such a proposal would prove acceptable to the BIS group of central banks. I volunteered to make a quick trip to the Bank of Canada in Ottowa to test out Governor Rasminsky's reaction. As I expected, Rasminsky took a decidedly chilly view. But on returning to New York on August 28, I learned from Chairman Martin that the British Treasury had not only decided to stick to its proposal but had already transmitted it to the French, Italian, and German treasuries. The Bank of England had been instructed to open negotiations with the three central banks involved.

On arriving in Rome on August 30 to brief Hayes on developments during his absence on vacation in Corfu, I found that the British Treasury proposal had been categorically rejected by France, Italy, and Germany, who wanted no part of potentially long-term, if not frozen, credits to the British government. So I returned to New York on September 1, dismayed that the British Treasury had so grossly overestimated its bargaining power and had overplayed a potentially winning hand. But on September 2, I had a call from

Hayes in Rome indicating that Governor Carli had arranged for a special meeting of the BIS governors in Basel on September 5, to discuss the sterling emergency.

On arriving in Basel, Hayes and I found that the British Treasury proposals had thoroughly poisoned the air. Even though Cromer brought with him a new guarantee proposal, virtually coinciding with that originally recommended by the Federal Reserve, the other governors felt that the earlier British Treasury cable had only too clearly revealed the basic British intention to secure long-term credit through this device. With his unfailing negotiating skill, Hayes nevertheless managed to work out, with considerable help from Carli of the Bank of Italy and Blessing of the Bundesbank, a compromise arrangement under which the United States would honor its commitment to buy guaranteed sterling up to a projected total of $400 million equivalent, if the continental central banks, plus Canada, would provide an additional $600 million of support in whatever form the Bank of England was prepared to accept. The continental governors refused to make any immediate commitments but agreed to give further urgent consideration to the Federal proposal.

I then returned to New York and in a special telephone meeting of the Open Market Committee on September 8, secured FOMC authorization to buy in the market guaranteed sterling up to a maximum of $200 million. With a similar $200 million authorization previously supplied by the U.S. Treasury, the New York Federal now had $400 million of market ammunition in hand. On September 9 the Bank of England reported to us that it had managed to round up $600 million of new short-term credits from all the BIS central banks, with the notable exception of the Bank of France.

Sterling had responded favorably to the announcement on September 2 of the British government's move towards an incomes policy, and signs of market shortages of sterling began to appear. The stage was now fully set for a bear squeeze, and this official counterattack was launched on Friday, September 10. For several hours that Friday morning, we maintained an open telephone line between the New York Federal and the Bank of England, as Bridge and I consulted constantly with each other on market tactics.

At 9 a.m. New York time, 2 p.m. London time, the Bank of England announced "the negotiation with the central banks of Austria, Belgium, Canada, Germany, the Netherlands, Italy, Japan, Sweden, Switzerland, the United States, and the BIS of new arrangements which would enable appropriate action to be taken in the exchange markets with the full cooperation of the central banks concerned." Fifteen minutes later the Federal Reserve Bank of New York, operating for System account, simultaneously placed bids for sterling totaling the equivalent of nearly $30 million with all the major banks in the New York exchange market at the then prevailing rate of $2.7918.

This was very big money at the time. Moreover, the intervention technique itself, a sort of barrage of Federal Reserve bids for sterling, was a startling change for the market from the usual central bank tactic of supporting an exchange rate quietly, if not secretly, through the agency of a commercial bank trader. By thus choosing to operate openly, and so forcefully as to excite a market uproar, we had in effect made a major official commitment and placed our credibility on the line. Once having launched such an operation, there was no turning back. This position was fully understood and supported by both the Treasury and the Federal Open Market Committee.

As our traders telephoned in rapid-fire sequence their sterling bids to the market, the impact was electrifying. Those speculating in sterling suddenly felt air under their feet as a seemingly sure profit became transformed into the risk of a major loss. The sterling rate immediately reacted upward, and we pursued the rate with new and higher bids until a rate of $2.7934 was reached; at this point the market tested our intentions by selling us sterling, but only in moderate amount.

After allowing the sterling rate to stabilize on its own around these levels, we squeezed the bears still further by a second round of sterling bids. By the close of the day, the sterling rate had risen to $2.7945 at a cost of only $13 million equivalent in guaranteed sterling acquired by the Federal. Bridge, who had promptly dubbed our flamboyant intervention as the "Chinese Army tactic," was jubilant and predicted that over the following weekend market traders would conclude that a sterling devaluation was no longer an immediate risk. He was right. On the following Monday the bears ran for cover and bid the sterling rate up so strongly that the Bank of England intervened to slow the rise by buying dollars to replenish its reserves. As we conducted our market operations, Bridge and I found ourselves wishing more than once that we had an exchange rate band of 3 percent over which to maneuver, rather than the relatively narrow 1½ percent spread between the sterling floor of $2.78 and ceiling of $2.82. But despite this constraint, as the sterling spot rate approached the $2.80 par, Bridge drove the rate through the parity level and successfully induced a new wave of short covering.

The recovery of sterling after the bear squeeze of September 10 reflected not only such short covering but also a welcome improvement in the British balance of payments position during the fourth quarter of 1965. After the turn of the year, favorable seasonal forces also came into play, with the result that the sterling rate moved into new, high ground during January 1966. Meanwhile the Bank of England recovered more than a billion dollars of its earlier reserve losses.

As dollars flowed back to the Bank of England after September, the Bank scrupulously honored the maturity dates of its short-term borrowings. Of its total reserve gain of somewhat more than $1 billion from September 1965 to February 1966, the Bank of England devoted $890 million to repaying in their entirety credits received during the summer of 1965 from the Federal Reserve and U.S. Treasury. Simultaneously the Bank of England succeeded in liquidating a very substantial part of its forward exchange commitments and thereby strengthened its hand for dealing with new pressures in the forward market.

As a tactical maneuver, the sterling bear squeeze thus provided the Labor government with a six-month respite from exchange market pressures and ample opportunity for orderly planning of future policy. Central bank cooperation had done all that it could reasonably have been expected to do. But the ordeal of sterling was by no means over, and by midsummer 1966 the Labor government and its central bank creditors were confronted by still another speculative challenge.

8

The Devaluation of Sterling

At the BIS, the central bank governors acknowledged somewhat incredulously the spectacular success of the September 1965 bear squeeze in sterling. But they remained apprehensive that their support for sterling during the previous year might tempt the British government to delay or temper the harsh self-discipline needed to restore sterling to reasonable health. They were particularly fearful that new dollar credits to the Bank of England might be frozen by some new sterling disaster, thereby exposing them to charges of negligent management of the national reserves entrusted to their care.

As the six months' maturity of the September 1965 credit package approached, most of the European central banks accordingly indicated reluctance to renew these facilities, unless the Bank of England would agree to limit the use of such credits to financing reserve drains occasioned by liquidation of foreign-held sterling balances. In effect, the European central banks took the position that they would be prepared to provide short-term accommodation to the Bank of England to protect sterling against pressures arising out of its role as a reserve currency, but they would no longer provide assured financing of balance of payments deficits of the United Kingdom itself.

At the November 1965 BIS meeting, the governors accepted a Bank of England proposal that a technical committee analyze the sterling balance problem and various possible ways of dealing with it. Dr. Milton Gilbert, Economic Adviser of the BIS, was asked to serve as chairman of the group, which also included Maurice Parsons of the Bank of England, Rinaldo Ossola of the Bank of Italy, Bernard Clappier of the Bank of France, Otmar Emminger of the Bundesbank, and myself.

This study yielded several useful results. First of all, the Gilbert report swept away earlier illusions that the sterling balances could somehow be funneled into longer term obligations or otherwise disposed of. Instead, the sterling balances were the liquid assets of governments, central banks, and private individuals, constituting an integral part of the international financial system and had to be treated as such. Second, as the Gilbert report pointed out, "the essence of the matter was that a severe (British) balance-of-payments deficit, combined with a heavy flight from the currency, had left a position in which the reserves were about a minimum level, given that the ordinary sources of international assistance had been fully drawn upon. In these circumstances, any pressure on the reserves coming from the sterling balances would be a threat to the sterling parity."

After analyzing the major types of drain on the British reserves resulting from a running down of the sterling balances, the Gilbert memorandum concluded that "Potentially, drains on the British reserves generated by the sterling balances added up to somewhat in excess of $1 billion." This suggested "the order of magnitude of a cooperative arrangement that would be adequate to protect the U.K.'s reserves from losses arising out of fluctuations in the sterling balances themselves. If such assistance were known to be available, there is a good chance that not much of it would have to be used."

On the basis of the Gilbert report, a new joint credit arrangement was laboriously negotiated over subsequent months. Contributions to the new credit package made by the continental central banks, the Bank of Japan, and the Bank of Canada were subjected to a number of restrictive clauses, however, which limited Bank of England use of such credits to no more than 50 percent of reserve losses attributable to conversion or other attrition of the sterling balances. The creditor central banks also insisted, reflecting fears of their credits becoming frozen, that Bank of England drawings on the new credit package should at no time exceed by more than $250 million the amount of unused drawing rights of the United Kingdom on the International Monetary Fund. On the other hand, the agreement permitted the Bank of England to make drawings for a term of a full year, which market a liberalization of the six-month maturity limit of earlier credits. The agreed contributions of the central banks of Europe and Canada were as follows:

Bank	Millions of Dollars
Central banks of the European Economic Community	325
Bank of Canada	60
Swiss National Bank	50
Bank of Japan	40
Austrian National Bank	30
Swedish Riksbank	20
Total	525

The Federal Reserve representatives at the BIS negotiations took the position that neither the U.S. Treasury nor the Federal Reserve wished to participate formally and directly in a new credit package designed for so restrictive a purpose. On the other hand, we would not object if the Bank of England chose, as a result of negotiations with the European central banks, to earmark for financing reserve losses arising out of the sterling balances, a certain portion of the existing $1150 million total of Federal Reserve and U.S. Treasury lines of credit to the Bank of England. In the final agreement $310 million was so earmarked. Governor Brunet of the Bank of France indicated at the April BIS meeting that his bank could not participate in any scheme designed to preserve sterling as a reserve currency but probably would be prepared to extend to the Bank of England a direct, bilateral credit facility available for any mutually agreed use. In the end, $90 million was so provided by the Bank of France. With a further $75 million credit from the BIS, there was thus rounded out a billion dollar credit package designed to insulate sterling against fluctuations in the sterling balances.

In devising this sterling balance arrangement, the BIS governors had hoped that the market would respond favorably to such a demonstration of orderly contingency planning, in contrast to the last-minute scrambles to put together emergency credits for sterling in November 1964 and September 1965. And if they had wasted less time in quibbling over details, an early announcement of the sterling balance agreement might indeed have helped consolidate the strong recovery of sterling over the winter months of 1965–1966. But by mid-June 1966, when the agreement was finally announced, the sterling market had already relapsed into new speculative disorder, and the agreement appeared as just another emergency credit.

At the end of February 1966 the sterling rate had moved below par for the first time since September 1965, as the exchange markets became unsettled by the disappointing January trade results and the impending British general election scheduled for late March. The Labor party's decisive victory at the polls on March 31, 1966, produced little reaction in the exchange markets, which remained relatively quiet throughout April awaiting Chancellor Callaghan's new budget. The budget message was once more a disappointment to the market, and speculative selling of sterling broke out again. With support from both the Bank of England and the New York Federal, the market stabilized but remained vulnerable to any new setbacks.

In this atmosphere the British seamen's strike that began in mid-May 1966 was a devastating blow. Sterling fell off to about $2.7900 in heavy trading and, as the strike dragged on, the exchange markets became increasingly apprehensive. The announcement of a reserve loss in May heightened the general tension, and the first of a series of intensive and prolonged selling waves began on June 3. The announcement in mid-June of the Sterling Balance Agreement brought only temporary relief as increasing stringency in the Euro-dollar market left British interest rates not fully competitive, with consequent outflows from sterling in late June.

And as the maritime strike continued, market sentiment steadily deteriorated. Despite a 9 percent rise in exports in the five months before the outbreak of the strike, the United Kingdom's trade account had not improved significantly over the corresponding months of 1965 because imports had also risen strongly. Moreover, the Bank of England had revealed reserve losses of $372 million during the four months of March–June 1966, even after recourse to central bank assistance. Market fears were further heightened by heated disputes within the Labor party over the proposed tightening of incomes policy, an important element in the long-term resolution of Great Britain's payments difficulties. The resignation from the government of Frank Cousins, a veteran trade union leader, proved particularly disturbing to market confidence.

Selling pressures on sterling accordingly intensified, reaching very heavy proportions in mid-July. In the face of these sales, the Bank of England continued to provide firm support for the pound in both spot and forward markets. Moreover, on July 14 the Bank raised its discount rate from 6 to 7 percent and doubled the special deposits required of the London and Scottish banks. In the cynical mood prevailing, the market shrugged off the bank rate increase as merely a technical adjustment to rising interest rate levels abroad, and sterling continued to be sold off in both the spot and forward markets.

On July 1, 1966, Deputy Governor Leslie O'Brien replaced Lord Cromer as head of the Bank of England. Cromer's relationship with Prime Minister Wilson and other members of the Labor cabinet had become increasingly strained, thereby further complicating the advisory role of the Bank of England. O'Brien, who had made a brilliant record in a series of increasingly responsible career assignments at the Bank of England, brought to his new post broad experience in the financial markets, both domestic and foreign. He was particularly well trained in the art of jurisdictional infighting against political and other advisers to the British government. Chairman Martin of the Federal Reserve once characterized O'Brien as "a tough little scrapper."

Partly owing to O'Brien's strenuous efforts, the Labor government's anguished debates over economic policy were at last resolved. On July 20 the Government announced a sweeping austerity program imposing a wage freeze, restraint on prices and dividends, additional taxes, reduced travel allowances, and further curbs on public expenditures at home and overseas. The new program struck directly at the problem of excessive domestic demand and represented a remarkably courageous, if somewhat belated, effort by the Labor government to regain control of the situation. Washington warmly supported the new Labor program, and the Federal Reserve moved into the sterling market shortly after the July 20 announcement, to stem and if possible reverse the drain on the Bank of England's reserves. By July 22 the sterling rate had recovered from $2.7866 immediately before the announcement of the new program to somewhat above $2.7900.

At the July 26 meeting of the FOMC in Washington, I reported as follows on the new sterling crisis:

On the exchange markets, we have witnessed during the past month a speculative attack on sterling more sustained in intensity than that of November 1964, and in certain respects even more dangerous. Perhaps I can best summarize the magnitude of the crisis by noting that the drain so far this month on the British reserves has amounted to roughly $1.1 billion, and would have been $145 million more if we had not undertaken market operations to support sterling. In addition, the Bank of England entered into new forward contracts in the amount of approximately $750 million. All told, therefore, official intervention in the spot and forward markets for sterling from July 1 through 22 came to very nearly $2 billion, on top of similar intervention during June of $500 million or so.

The sheer magnitude of these figures suggest a remarkable wide swing of the leads and lags against sterling and the buildup of a huge short position. Before the new British program was announced there was some hope on both the British side and on our own that strong market action to push up the sterling rate might force some quick covering of short positions, as occurred last September. We undertook such operations on Wednesday, Thursday, and Friday of last week for a total of $145 million, and in the process pushed the rate up from $2.7875 to $2.7912. We encountered very strong resistance as sterling continued to be sold in heavy volume through the Paris Bourse and other European markets. Although our operations have not yet succeeded in inducing short covering, both we and the Bank of England feel that they have had a useful stabilizing effect during the period of acute uncertainty.

The skepticism of the market regarding the new British program does not seem to arise out of any widespread feeling that the program is not sufficiently drastic, which it certainly is. The continuing concern of the market, rather, springs from fears that the government may be confronted with a revolt of the trade unions and so be unable to carry through the most important element of the program, namely the wage freeze.

As some of you may know, we strongly urged the Bank of England at the end of June to minimize their use of the Federal Reserve swap line and to show a very sizable reserve loss so as to point up the cost of the seamen's strike, and thereby bring home to the British public the necessity of drastic corrective action. Right now, however, the markets are in such a speculative mood that I am very much afraid that a report of sizable additional reserve losses could trigger a panic which might quickly get out of control. We have, accordingly, been urging the Bank of England to round up central bank financing from all sides. The Treasury may be prepared to provide $200 million of this on an overnight basis, and I would be hopeful that we could provide them with the remaining $200 million, also on an overnight basis. In a situation as dangerous as this one I can see certain advantages in avoiding three-month commitments until we can be sure whether the tide has begun to turn.

In August 1966 selling pressure on sterling eased considerably as the new British economic program, further Federal Reserve intervention in the spot market, and Bank of England operations in the forward market relieved market fears of an imminent collapse of the pound. But new dangers were rapidly looming, and on August 18 I sent to both Secretary Fowler and the FOMC a contingency planning memorandum recommending several major policy actions:

The short position in sterling has now reached enormous proportions, but market apprehension of a breakdown in the British program or an exhaustion of central bank credit arrangements continues to frustrate any short covering. Unless the market is soon provided with some concrete indication of a turn for the better, there is a real risk that sterling may suffer a new relapse and, in the process, deplete most of the credit facilities remaining to the Bank of England.

The entire international financial system, and more particularly the dollar, simultaneously face the threat of a breakdown in the gold pool arrangements as a result of the heavy attrition suffered since the beginning of the year. Here again, the approach of the Fund and Bank meetings may well stimulate even heavier speculative buying of gold and further depletion of the Gold Pool's resources. We may be able to negotiate an increase in the Gold Pool from $270 million to $370 million at the BIS meeting in early September, but it looks as if the continental European central banks will be most reluctant to go any further along this route. This would confront the United States with the dilemma of either continuing to hold the London price, at possible heavy cost to the U.S. gold reserves, or of allowing the price to rise and thereby risk a panicky conversion of dollars into gold by central banks all over the world. These twin risks of a sterling crisis and a gold market crisis, both of which would have dangerous repercussions on the dollar, are further magnified by the heavy outpouring of dollars from our balance of payments deficit in the third quarter and consequent prospective pressure on our gold reserves and existing credit facilities.

We might thus be suddenly confronted, possibly within the next month, with a serious emergency in both the international gold and exchange markets. Assuming that such an emergency might be ignited by a new speculative attack on sterling, it is conceivable that we might be able to put together over the telephone still another credit package involving not only Federal Reserve and Treasury funds, but also new credits to the Bank of England from the continental European and other central banks which participated in the September 1965 package. Judging from the attitudes expressed by most of the foreign central banks during the past year, however, my own personal belief is that it would be virtually impossible to negotiate such a package. . . .

If a new sterling crisis should occur, therefore, the British government and the Bank of England will probably make a strong appeal to the U.S. government and the Federal Reserve for a sizable increase in the amount available under the Bank of England/Federal Reserve reciprocal currency arrangements, as their only hope of staving off disaster. If this should occur, the Committee would suddenly be confronted with the decision of whether to refuse further accommodation and let sterling collapse or to provide one final extension of new credit to stave off a probable breakdown in the international financial system. In such extreme circumstances I should be inclined to recommend Committee approval of a further increase in the amount but only on the following conditions:

1. Full adherence by the British government to the July 20 program.
2. British trade union acceptance, however unwillingly, of the wage freeze.
3. Specific assurances from the British government and the Bank of England of a full liquidation within the term appropriate to central bank credits of any credits provided by the Federal Reserve.

Even if all of these conditions were fulfilled, however, I would still be most reluctant to see a massive increase in the Federal Reserve/ Bank of England arrangements without roughly corresponding increases in the Federal Reserve arrangements with the Continental

European and other central banks. In developing the Federal Reserve network of reciprocal currency arrangements, we have tried to maintain a certain balance in the relationship of each arrangement to the others. As a result of a two-year ordeal of sterling, however, our arrangements with the continental European central banks provide in a number of instances for disproportionately small amounts compared to our $750 million line with the Bank of England. This distortion would be further aggravated by a unilateral move to increase the Bank of England's facility and could easily lead to the situation where we were lending out more dollars through the arrangement with the Bank of England than we were able to mop up by drafts upon our facilities with the Bundesbank and other foreign central banks. In general, just as the United States functions as a banker for the rest of the world under the gold exchange standard, so does the Federal Reserve function as a banker under the network of its arrangements. In this process, we must take care that our lending facilities in one direction do not overbalance our borrowing facilities in other directions.

. . .

In view of the magnitude of the danger to the international financial system involved in either a collapse of sterling or a breakdown of the gold pool, I think that we would be well advised to seek a major reinforcement of the reciprocal currency arrangements. . . . As a rough target, I should be inclined to recommend that we go for an approximate doubling of the present $2.8 billion total available under those arrangements, with more than proportionate increases in some cases and less than proportionate increases in others.

On the morning of August 19, 1966 Hayes and I called Governor O'Brien to talk informally of contingency planning in the event of new pressures on sterling. O'Brien indicated that he too had this problem very much on his mind, more particularly in view of the disappointing performance of sterling so far that month, and the risk that the approaching IMF annual meeting might from one moment to another set off a new wave of speculation. Hayes said that our thinking on contingency planning had narrowed down to two main alternatives. The first would be to make a major effort to put together another combined United States–continental package of direct credits to the Bank of England; we had serious misgivings, however, about whether it would be possible to induce the continental central banks to join in such an endeavor.

The Governor of the Bank of England fully concurred, pointing to the categorical refusal by the continental central banks during negotiation of the Sterling Balance Agreement to provide additional credit to the United Kingdom other than to finance liquidation of sterling balances. An approach to the European central banks for new money would probably result in their caucusing together and jointly refusing the appeal, and this rebuff might well leak out to the market. He further noted that the continental central banks plus those of Canada and Japan had already committed themselves under the Sterling Balance Agreement to provide $690 million, and some of them in addition had extended overnight credits of $175 million at the end of July. O'Brien felt that the most he could hope for would be to renew such overnight credits at the end of August.

O'Brien went on to express grave concern over the month-end problem, since it now appeared that they would be in deficit for August as a whole and at the end of the month would therefore be obliged either to show a sizable reserve loss or to have recourse to central bank credit in large amount. He was inclined at this stage to think it advisable to again show a relatively small reserve loss which would, of course, require the British government to acknowledge that there had been further recourse to central bank credit. The markets would probably deride the reserve figure published, but this course of action would probably be less upsetting to the market than publication of the true loss. In any event the September 2 reserve date might mark a turning point, probably for the worse, in market sentiment.

Hayes and I then turned to our alternative approach, under which we might increase the Federal Reserve–Bank of England swap line by a substantial amount and simultaneously seek to negotiate corresponding increases in the Federal Reserve swap lines with other central banks as a counterbalance. O'Brien replied that he thought this approach was promising and, moreover, constituted the only feasible way out. O'Brien reverted again, however, to the question of timing, stressing the importance of taking action soon enough to forestall any speculative reactions to the reserve figures to be published on September 2. He expressed regret that he seemed to be putting the whole burden on our shoulders, but he saw no alternative. I stressed the importance of maintaining airtight secrecy on any negotiating approach that might be undertaken by the Federal, pointing out that the sequence of our approaches to the various central banks would have to be very carefully timed and that a strictly bilateral basis would have to be maintained. O'Brien fully concurred.

The August 23, 1966 meeting on the Open Market Committee took up my recommendations for a near doubling of the swap lines in a mood of grave concern over the new and heavy responsibilities that were being thrust on the Committee. I was closely questioned about the emergency and alternative policy options. Various Committee members were particularly insistent that we have a categorical expression of full support from the Treasury before moving ahead. With that proviso, the Committee voted me full negotiating authority to proceed with the program I had outlined.

In discussions over the rest of the week with the Treasury and other interested Washington agencies, however, I encountered an unshakable insistence that the BIS group of central banks be asked not only to agree to major increases in their swap lines with the Federal Reserve but also provide at least another $400 million in direct credits to the Bank of England. I pleaded in vain that the latter requirement would probably torpedo the whole negotiation, and on August 29 I departed for the September BIS meeting with a negotiating brief leaving absolutely no room for compromise.

Arriving in Basel on Friday evening September 3, I found Governor O'Brien in the lobby of the Schweizerhof, and we gloomily agreed that we faced an extremely difficult negotiating session over the weekend. Our fears were fully realized. By Sunday night I had been forced to cut back the projected increases in the Federal Reserve swap lines by $700 million, while the additional Federal

Reserve request for $400 million of new European, Canadian, and Japanese credits to the Bank of England met with stubborn, even angry resistance. At one point at the Sunday evening governors' dinner I thought that our negotiations were on the point of collapse, but O'Brien, in a masterful display of personal diplomacy, kept the discussion going.

On Monday, September 5, I flew back to New York and over the rest of the week completed by telex exchanges increases in the Federal Reserve swap lines totaling $1.7 million, all of them still contingent on agreement by the BIS central banks to provide $400 million of new direct credits to the Bank of England. At the end of the week the BIS governors yielded to the take-it-or-leave-it bargaining stance of the U.S. Treasury, and on September 13, 1966, the Bank of England was able to announce the package of credits from the BIS central banks.

The same day, at the New York Reserve Bank, I gave my usual press conference on my semiannual report on Treasury and Federal Reserve operations through the end of August 1966. At the conference, I reported the general expansion of the Federal Reserve swap lines from $2.8 to $4.5 billion, a major increase in the Bank of England swap facility from $750 to $1350 million, of which more than $1 billion remained fully available. These unexpected assurances of new financial support for sterling apparently provided the capstone for the British economic program announced in July. The exchange market, which had become almost totally convinced of the imminence of a new British devaluation, now began to cover short positions in sterling. To reinforce the effect of these announcements, the New York Reserve Bank again moved into the sterling market, making moderate purchases for both Federal Reserve and Treasury account.

Within less than a week, as noted by the *London Times,* an "astonishing turnabout" in market sentiment occurred. "The new currency swap arrangements effectively lifted all fears of a forced devaluation of the pound." At the end of September 1966 at the annual IMF meeting in Washington, I ran into Gordon Richardson, then chairman of the London merchant bank, Schroder, Wagg, who told me that a major industrial bond issue, announced in London shortly before the swap line increases, had been oversubscribed 35 times. And Pierre-Paul Schweitzer, in his speech opening the IMF gathering, cited the expansion of the swap network as an example to governments of decisive action to deal with the problem of international liquidity. According to the London *Economist*, "Once more the central banks stepped in where governments were clearly not ready to tread."

By the end of September 1966 the sterling spot rate had moved up strongly from 2.7877 to 2.7911, and in succeeding weeks it continued to improve as further covering of short positions was encouraged by better trade figures. This pattern of gradual recovery was interrupted briefly at the end of November and early December because of the usual year-end window-dressing preparation of commercial banks in several continental centers. Such year-end window dressing drew funds from London to the countries repatriating funds or to an increasingly stringent Eurodollar market.

Concerted action by the Federal Reserve and the BIS helped to relieve the strain, however. The New York Reserve Bank supported the sterling spot market by buying $88 million against forward sales for delivery after the turn of the year. Even more effective, the BIS, with the agreement of the Federal Reserve, channeled $200 million of drafts on its swap line with the Federal Reserve into the Eurodollar market for the express purpose of countering year-end liquidity strains.

After the turn of the year the progressive relaxation of monetary restraint in the United States, Germany, and other countries pushed down Eurodollar rates and opened up a significant arbitrage incentive in favor of London. In addition, demand for sterling picked up as the British trade position improved. Reflecting the recovery of confidence, foreign money returned to London. As dollars flowed back to the Bank of England, the Bank rigorously devoted the bulk of the receipts to repayment of central bank debt, while adding only modest amounts to its reserves.

By the end of March 1967 the exchange inflow had enabled the Bank of England to liquidate completely $1.3 billion of credits borrowed during the summer of 1966 from the Federal Reserve and other foreign financial authorities, while remaining central bank credits linked specifically to changes in the sterling balances were paid off early in the second quarter of 1967. Over the two-year period, May 1965–April 1967 the United Kingdom thus had successfully resisted two major speculative attacks on sterling by borrowing from the BIS group of central banks some $2.5 billion, all of which had been repaid on time as the speculative waves receded.

But now a more powerful tide of events began to swing against sterling with gradually cumulative force. Shortly after the announcement on May 4, 1967, of the third cut in the Bank of England's discount rate since the beginning of the year, from 6 to 5½ percent, Eurodollar rates began to firm, and covered interest rate comparisons that had tended to favor London earlier in the year started to turn adverse. Even more disturbing were indications that Britain's foreign trade account was lapsing into new difficulties. The announcement on May 11 that the British trade deficit had jumped from $36 million in March to $115 million in April was followed a few days later by President de Gaulle's denunciation of Britain's application to join the Common Market. By mid-May these and other unfavorable developments had eroded the earlier recovery of confidence and brought the influx of exchange to a halt.

In this vulnerable situation new heavy burdens were thrust on sterling by the Middle East War in early June 1967. As the month progressed, market anxieties were aggravated by rumors of major withdrawals of sterling by Arab countries. In the latter part of June reports of shifts of Arab-held sterling balances to Paris triggered heavy selling of sterling, and the Bank of England suffered heavy losses in holding the rate at just under $2.7900. The market had also become concerned over the damaging effect on the British balance of payments of the closure of the Suez Canal, and the announcement at midmonth of disappointing trade figures for May created still more apprehension. Finally, the pull of foreign interest rates, particularly during a brief squeeze in the Eurodollar market at the end of June, exerted further pressure. To cushion the reserve impact of these developments, the Bank of England drew $225 million during June under its $1350 million swap arrangement with the Federal Reserve.

The mid-August announcement of a sharp swing in the United Kingdom trade balance in July—to a small surplus from a large deficit the month before—provided only a brief respite from the continuing pressures on the pound. To cover reserve drains, the Bank of England drew a further $425 million on the Federal Reserve during the third quarter of 1967, thereby raising its swap debt to $650 million.

The rearguard action being fought by Bank of England officials in the exchange markets became progressively more difficult and costly in October and November. In mid-October it was reported that Britain's September trade balance had deteriorated badly to a deficit of $146 million, the largest in 15 months. As expected, the Suez Canal closing had raised the cost of fuel oil imports, but one could also see a weakening trend in exports. The outbreak in late September of a strike on the Liverpool docks, which subsequently spread to London, raised justifiable fears that exports might show even sharper declines in October.

Even more important, the unremitting selling pressure on sterling since the Middle East war had fanned into lively debate long-smoldering doubts held by many responsible publications and private individuals, both in the United Kingdom and abroad, regarding the economic viability of the $2.80 parity. In this debate the basic government policy of seeking to shift domestic resources into exports by restraining domestic demand came increasingly under attack. In the eyes of the market, the lagging recovery of exports, the rise in unemployment, and the decision of the British government to ease installment credit controls in late August increasingly suggested that a policy impasse had been reached.

These market fears set off a new heavy wave of selling of sterling in the spot and forward markets during the first two weeks in October. Despite heavy intervention by the Bank of England, the sterling rate by October 12 had dropped to $2.7824. On October 19, the Bank of England raised its discount rate by half a percentage point to 6 percent on October 19.

But market reaction was one of disappointment that the British bank rate had not been raised a full percentage point, and heavy selling of sterling resumed, requiring very sizable intervention by the Bank of England in both the spot and forward markets that same day. In an effort to stabilize sterling quotations in New York, the U.S. Treasury initiated purchases of sterling at rates just under $2.7830. These operations, eventually involving total purchases of $47.1 million equivalent, continued through Monday, October 23, and seemed to calm the market somewhat during the final week of October.

The announcement on November 2 of a $75.6 million reserve gain for October, after credit for a loan of $103 million equivalent from Swiss commercial banks had been taken, was brushed aside by a market increasingly persuaded that a devaluation of sterling was imminent. Sales of sterling in preweekend trading were heavy, and on November 9 the Bank of England, for the second time in three weeks raised its discount rate by another half percentage point to 6½ percent.

To me, however, the most significant development was the sense I had from August onward that the Bank of England had begun to consider the policy alternative of devaluation. Similar hints of a shift in British government attitudes were also reaching the U.S. Treasury. And for skilled market analysts of the sterling situation, there soon began to appear fairly overt signs of a basic change of British official policy. In early September 1967 the Labor government's relaxation of consumer credits restraints struck an ebullient note strangely clashing with the dirge that was coming from the exchange markets. The long delay in raising the Bank of England's discount rate, and then only by ½ percent, similarly communicated its own message.

Not until the BIS meeting on Saturday, November 11, 1967, however, did I get any formal indication of the impending decision of the British government to devalue the pound. Governor O'Brien brought the message to a special meeting of the BIS governors in the office of President Jelle Zijlstra. The message took the form of a contingency planning exercise. Would the member governments there represented support a British effort to raise medium-term credits from the International Monetary Fund or other sources? Neither the Bank of England nor the British government was prepared to rely further on short-term central bank credits. If such medium-term credit were not forthcoming, the British government would have no alternative but to devalue the pound. In London's judgment, a devaluation of at least 14 percent would be required. If that proved unacceptable to Britain's trading partners, the British government would probably have recourse to a floating rate for sterling.

Governor O'Brien's negotiating brief was skillfully presented, but the bargaining devices of a promise to hold the $2.80 parity in exchange for sizable new credits from the IMF or, alternatively, the threat to let sterling float, were quickly stripped away. The governors perfunctorily pledged themselves to support a British application for new credits from the Fund. They also noted that the chances of Fund approval, in view of the heavy British debt already outstanding, were probably minimal. Nor did the threat of a floating rate for sterling elicit any particular concern; no one at that time considered it a viable option. Accordingly, O'Brien was quickly forced into pleading his case for 14 percent as the appropriate cut in the value of the pound, and he handled this unenviable assignment with dignity and finesse. By the end of the session he had the clear support of nearly all the governors present for a devaluation of that order. As for sterling, the die was now cast.

The following Tuesday, November 14, the British government reported that the trade deficit in October had jumped to $300 million equivalent, the largest ever recorded, as the dock strike choked off export shipments. Any remaining hopes in the market that the $2.80 parity could be held were now virtually extinguished. Even as sterling was about to go down, however, market rumors began to circulate that negotiations were in progress for sizable new international credits. Accordingly, traders began to hedge their exposed positions in sterling, and on Thursday, November 16, short covering pushed the sterling rate up.

That afternoon, however, Chancellor Callaghan refused in Parliament to confirm or deny that such negotiations were in progress. Financial markets throughout the world immediately concluded that the last hope of a turnaround in the sterling situation had disappeared. On the next day, Friday, the market was inundated by offers of sterling in the expectation that a decision to devalue that weekend had already been taken. To help meet the avalanche of offerings of sterling, the Bank of England, which had already made further use of the Federal Reserve swap line, drew the remainder available under this arrangement, bringing the total debt outstanding to $1350 million. The cost of keeping the sterling market open on that final day of the $2.80 parity was appalling.

On Saturday, November 18, Chancellor Callaghan announced the government's decision to devalue the pound by 14.3 percent from $2.80 to $2.40. To stiffen the defense of the new parity, the Bank of England raised its discount rate to 8 percent (the highest level in 53 years), while the government announced curbs on consumer installment credit, cuts in government spending, and an increase in the corporation tax. Reviewing the sterling devaluation and its aftermath in an address to the Overseas Bankers Club in early February 1968, Governor O'Brien of the Bank of England sternly noted:

> Those who so readily advocated devaluation before we had made any attempt to apply other correctives had scant regard for our obligations abroad, for the risks entailed for ourselves and others, and for the harsh medicine which must be taken to make devaluation work. All these things are now being made abundantly clear. Those who thought devaluation was a soft alternative to strict internal policies have been disabused.

Callaghan's behavior in accepting defeat and the personal consequences was exemplary, revealing qualities of character that continue to serve his country well. Meanwhile, the three year effort he had made to stabilize the domestic economy now provided a base for exploiting the competitive advantages gained by British exporters from the devaluation. But the initial impact of devaluation was severely adverse, in line with the familiar J-curve analysis under which a devaluing country initially suffers an immediate rise in its import costs until the subsequent correctives of declining import volume and rising export volume come into play.

During this interval of continuing postdevaluation pressure on sterling, central bank credit was again provided in heavy volume, both by the Federal Reserve which raised its swap line with the Bank of England from $1350 million to $2 billion, and by other central banks in the Basel group. In fact, new credits drawn by the Bank of England during the first full year of the $2.40 parity totaled more than $3.5 billion.

Over the years since the November 1967 devaluation of sterling, there have been a good many suggestions that the Labor government delayed too long in devaluing. Some of these suggestions emanate, of course, from apostles of the free-floating rate school, who would probably regard any fixed parity as an invitation to disaster. But there are also a number of disinterested economists who in hindsight have pinpointed certain earlier dates when in their view devaluation had become inevitable.

For the BIS central bankers, however, any advice from Basel that Britain should have devalued before November 1967 would have been a presumptuous intrusion into British political affairs. As Jelle Zijlstra, who headed both the Netherlands Bank and the BIS, said to me one day: "Any one of us can make a judgment that Britain is in some kind of a disequilibrium. What we cannot do is to prescribe the political solution, whether by adjustment of the exchange rate, domestic disinflation, or some combination of the two. This is a British political matter. And if the British government decides to try to resolve the problem by domestic measures alone, we cannot contest that sovereign political judgment." In effect, the Basel central bank group went the last mile with the British government. This, I think, is of more fundamental significance in an interdependent world than whether their financial support eventually proved unavailing.

9

The Breakdown of the Gold Pool

The chronic illness of sterling, and its implications for the world financial system, was watched with a vulture's eye by the London gold market. The Labor victory in the elections of October 1964 not only brought heavy selling pressure on the pound but simultaneously ignited a burst of speculative demand for gold. Buying pressure in the London gold market continued to mount in early 1965 as President deGaulle launched a strong attack on American financial policy and called for a return to the gold standard.

And in March 1965 the Gold Pool was beset by new troubles as the Chinese government for the first time suddenly appeared as heavy gold buyers in London. To ease the strain, Bridge of the Bank of England allowed the London gold price to move close to the now accepted ceiling of $35.20, and the Federal then requested a reactivation of the selling syndicate of the Pool. By August 1965, as sterling relapsed into a new speculative crisis, the Pool had spent more than $200 million in new intervention.

But once again fortune turned in our favor, owing partly to our own efforts and partly to sheer luck. In September 1965, as previously related, the Federal Reserve Bank of New York launched a successful bear squeeze on the sterling market, in conjunction with a new package of international credit assistance for the Bank of England. The subsequent strong recovery of sterling dampened speculation on the London gold market and relieved pressure on the Pool. Then late in 1965 new heavy offers of Russian gold for cereal imports required by still another poor harvest hit the London market. By the end of 1965 the Pool had succeeded in recouping the losses sustained earlier in the year and still showed a $1.3 billion surplus for its four-year span of operations.

Nevertheless, the more I studied the London gold market problem, the more concerned I became. In November 1965 I finally felt compelled to write personal letters to Secretary Fowler and Chairman Martin, warning that the remarkable success of the Gold Pool so far had been favored by a fortuitous series of events that was unlikely to continue. On the contrary, certain basic trends in the market seemed to be moving strongly against us and might precipitate a dangerous market situation within a matter of months. On the supply side, I pointed out, we had benefited during the previous three years by an extraordinarily sharp rise in the flow of gold reaching the London market.

The heavily increased flow of gold from South Africa and other Western producers reflected two main factors. First, production by the South African mines had been rising strongly since 1960, mainly because improved mining techniques had been introduced. Second, after withholding during the period 1961–1963 an appreciable share of mining production to build the gold reserves of the South African Reserve Bank, the South African Government had been forced in 1964, and again in 1965, to release to the London market sizable amounts of its gold reserves to help finance balance of payments deficits. The abundant flow of gold from South Africa had been heavily supplemented during the three previous years by unusually large Russian sales, reflecting wheat harvest failures in 1963 and 1965.

	Millions of Dollars		
Year	Russian Sales	South African and Other Supplies	Total
1962	207	743	950
1963	525	866	1391
1964	438	1137	1575
1965 (Jan.–Oct.)	336	1119	1455

There had thus been at work on the supply side of the gold market a combination of temporary factors that could hardly be expected to repeat themselves. New gold discoveries in South Africa and elsewhere remained a possibility, but the prospect was that South African output would begin to level off, depriving the gold market of the annual increases in supply that had helped to keep the market under control. Moreover, the South African government had recently taken action to correct its international payments deficit and was already beginning to set aside part of current gold production to replenish the gold stocks of the South African Reserve Bank.

It was quite conceivable, therefore, that the $200 million of sales from South African gold reserve stocks during the first half of 1965 might be replaced in 1966 by renewed accumulations of $100 million or more, which would mean a severe reduction in the annual supply of gold reaching the London market. Finally, we might expect to see the Russians sell possibly another $100 million to $200 million of gold to finance the rest of their grain import needs. They might then disappear for many months; following completion of their wheat purchase contracts with Canada in March 1964, the Russians did not return to the market until August 1965, a stretch of 16 months.

The danger of so abrupt a contraction in the market supply of gold was further highlighted by recent trends in the demand for gold. Demand on the London market had risen from $752 million in 1963 to $952 million in 1964, and in 1965 it soared to a record annual rate of $1.8 billion, fully absorbing the abnormally large supply of gold reaching the market that year. Demand for gold in 1965 had been swollen by such factors as the war in Vietnam, the sterling crisis, the Gaullist attack on the dollar and sterling, as well as Chinese buying. If all these sources of speculative pressure were suddenly to disappear, the demand for gold on the London market might recede sufficiently to match temporarily the prospective shrinkage of supply. But if, instead, the world continued to be troubled by political and economic crises of varying intensity, speculative demand for gold seemed likely to persist.

Even more troublesome, the underlying trend of private demand was moving strongly against us. Industrial consumption of gold was steadily rising each year, reflecting not only new technological uses such as the American space program but also the simple fact that gold was still selling at the official 1934 price after decades of inflation of alternative metal prices. And in the jewelry trade, fattened by the general rise in real income, gold was quite literally on the bargain counter. Similarly, the growth of real income throughout the world had enlarged the pool of investment funds that could be diverted to the gold market.

And meanwhile, managers of private investment portfolios all over the world had now recognized a new uncertainty, which might in the end prove even more disturbing to the gold market than the international and political tensions of recent years. This was the emergence of a full-dress international debate over reform of the international financial system. Right or wrong, the financial markets were expecting basic changes in the present system, whose cardinal weakness, as acknowledged by all the major governments involved, was a prospective shortage of gold for official settlements. Such an impending shortage of gold for official settlements seemed hardly likely to encourage confidence in the adequacy of gold supplies for private uses, rather it would breed market suspicion that central banks would become increasingly reluctant to squander such scarce resources on price stabilization operations in the London gold market.

Finally, the secrecy maintained on Gold Pool operations had largely disguised from the market the deterioration in the underlying situation. In fact, even in 1965 the market showed far greater confidence in the stability of the London price, and in the solidity of the Gold Pool arrangements, than was felt by any of the central bank officials involved in the creation and operation of the Pool. From time to time, however, leakages of information on Gold Pool operations had occurred, and a remarkably complete account of daily demand over the period February–September 1965 had appeared in the London *Economist*. Given a few more disclosures of this sort, skilled market analysts might readily put together an accurate picture of the market situation and set off a new wave of speculative buying.

In late 1965 I saw a major risk, therefore, that we might soon be confronted by an emergency situation in the London gold market that could seriously strain, even overwhelm, the Gold Pool arrangements. Accordingly I suggested to Secretary Fowler and Chairman Martin that we should move pretty quickly to get agreement within the government on some kind of damage control operation to deal with a new explosion in the London gold market.

Fowler and Martin took my warning seriously and immediately set the planning machinery going. In early 1966 several thoughtful commentaries on the London gold market outlook were prepared by staff members of the Federal Reserve Board and the Treasury. They counseled patience until we could get a better view of prospective trends of demand and supply. But by late 1966 the market picture had become chillingly clear.

For the first 10 months of 1966, South African deliveries plunged to $670 million from the figure of $1119 million during the corresponding period in 1965, while Russian sales declined to zero from the $336 million figure of the previous year. This decline of $785 million in gold supplies reaching the London market during January–October 1966 drove the Gold Pool into a deficit of roughly $285 million.

Moreover, the damage would have been much greater if we had not benefited from a concurrent and very sizable contraction in market demand. Thus net private purchases of gold on the London market during the first 10 months of 1966 fell off to approximately $1 billion from $1.4 billion level of the preceding year. But in the judgment of most of the BIS group of central banks running the Pool, the 1966 decline in private demand had been primarily attributable to acutely tight money in the world financial markets. Accordingly, demand for gold could be expected to resume its secular upward trend as soon as the credit markets eased.

More generally, it had now become clear to all the central bank officials directly involved in the Pool that we had probably crossed a watershed from surplus to deficit in the Pool's operations. Now we found ourselves facing the hard question of how much more official gold from the United States and other countries should be diverted to the London gold market before formally concluding that the game was up.

At the September 1966 BIS meeting I requested on behalf of the Federal Reserve a $50 million increase in the Pool's resources from $270 to $320 million, while also negotiating major new credit arrangements with our partners in the swap network. Over the winter months of 1966–1967, a strong recovery of sterling relieved gold market pressures somewhat. But then both sterling and the gold market were caught by the backwash of the Middle East war. In June 1967 the Federal had to request another $100 million addition to the Pool's resources to cover a deficit now totaling $365 million.

Demand for gold remained strong during the summer. Speculation arising out of the September 1967 meeting of the IMF in Rio de Janeiro, coupled with sagging confidence in sterling, pushed the

Pool deficit to $434 million by the end of October. Meanwhile, urgent and repeated Federal Reserve calls on Pool members to enlarge their participation as needed to finance such intervention were severely straining the solidarity of the central bank partnership.

In July 1967 the first break occurred, as the Bank of France regretfully indicated that it could no longer continue. The United States took over the French share. Reflecting the spirit of Basel, Bank of France representatives at the BIS monthly meetings were nevertheless kept fully informed of market developments and Pool operations. The other Pool participants clung to the runaway train but with mounting urgency pressed the Federal Reserve to suggest a disengagement plan.

Meanwhile, in Washington and New York a series of contingency planning discussions, with the Secretary of the Treasury and the Chairman of the Federal Reserve board personally participating, had thoroughly scouted the major policy options available. All were more or less distasteful, technically complex, and dangerous to negotiate.

The first approach, which the New York Reserve Bank developed, was to halt official sales of gold on the London market as soon as feasible but to try to temper the speculative consequences by prior negotiation of two damage-control measures. First, we argued for creation, by massive increases in the Federal Reserve swap lines, of a "defensive ring" of the major central banks. Combined with forward operations by the central banks concerned, this seemed to us to offer the best hope of absorbing the strain on exchange rates of the heavy flows of hot money that a breakout of the London gold price would probably set in motion.

Next the New York Bank urged an agreement to convert the London gold market, and all other European gold markets if possible, into purely commodity markets limited to officially licensed demand for industrial and artistic uses. The United States, the United Kingdom, Japan, and the Netherlands were already limiting gold imports to similar nonspeculative uses. Other European countries, the New York Federal argued, should now be asked to introduce similar gold import controls. To reinforce such gold import licensing, we suggested a general imposition of a new and sizable duty on gold imports, designed to minimize gold hoarding in the form of jewelry.

A certain amount of smuggling could of course be expected to continue, but here government policing would be simplified by the sheer physical difficulty of illegally transporting and selling big amounts of gold. A million dollar shipment of bar gold weighed a full ton, normally required not only insurance but also police protection, as well as the services of reputable metallurgical firms for processing into the small size bars, medallions, or coins suitable for the retail market.

In general, the gold traffic could not proceed without the professional services of European banks, airlines, shipping firms, insurance companies, refineries, and security police. If such services were now prohibited except under license, speculative buying of gold would be diverted to the Asian, Middle Eastern, and African bazaars. In those markets gold price quotations, however inflated, would have little relevance to the Treasury's official price.

In mid-1967 Secretary Fowler authorized me to explore this policy approach with several European central bank governors. My discreet soundings elicited strong support for the central bank defensive ring concept and some indication that gold import controls might be reluctantly accepted as an alternative to an uncontrolled breakout of the London gold price. One major question was whether the Swiss and also the French would refuse to join in such a scheme and instead take over from London the marketing in Zurich and Paris of South African and Russian gold. With a sufficiently strong expression of support by the United States and certain other members of the Pool, I think these problems could have been solved.

But there was a second and even more troublesome question, namely, whether South Africa would rebel against a licensing scheme, more particularly if accompanied by official surcharges on imports of gold for legitimate uses. I felt compelled to point out to Secretary Fowler, and to the other Washington officials involved in our contingency planning discussions, that any effort to limit gold demand to legitimate uses would probably necessitate eventually some bargain with South Africa. Such a bargain might involve a South African export tax, in combination with import taxes in the gold-importing countries, thus squeezing out from both sides the artificial stimulus to using gold for industrial purposes and jewelry at the $35 official price. As I feared, this forecast of technical necessities aroused indignant opposition from White House advisers and the State Department to anything resembling a deal with South Africa and quickly killed Washington support for the New York Bank approach.

The second major approach, which proved to be a splendid nonstarter, involved continuing Pool defense of the $35 gold price in London by compensating Pool members for their gold sales with gold value certificates, to be issued by some new and undefined legal entity. In effect, Pool members would be asked to give up real gold bars in exchange for a piece of paper that would allegedly preserve its value in terms of the official (as distinct from the free market) price of gold. This scheme, which used up countless hours of discussion time, captivated many Washington officials as a seemingly promising step toward creation of a new international reserve unit, then the subject of intensive negotiations by financial officials of the Group of 10. When finally presented to the European central bank governors in late November 1967, the gold certificate scheme was immediately and flatly rejected as nonnegotiable. I was not surprised.

A third policy approach recommended the separation of the gold market into a two-tier affair, with no flow of official gold either into or out of the private market. In effect, the central banks around the world would not only refrain from selling gold on the free market but would also refuse to buy newly mined or Russian gold. The main objective of this approach was to force South Africa to sell its entire gold exports on the private market, thereby avoiding the risk that South Africa might rig the London price at an artificially high level by diverting part of its current output to certain central banks at the official price.

Events now overtook our contingency planning. The sterling crisis, building steadily to a climax since the Middle East war of June 1967, culminated with the devaluation of the pound from $2.80 to $2.40 on Saturday, November 18. Confirming my repeated warnings to the Federal Reserve and Treasury over the previous two years, a tidal wave of speculation now swept through the London gold market, and over the following week beginning November 20 the Pool sustained the following crescendo of losses:

Period		Millions of Dollars
January–June, 1967		113
July		73
August		3
September		25
October		71
November 1–17		145
November 20 (Monday)	27	
November 21 (Tuesday)	45	
November 22 (Wednesday)	106	
November 23 (Thursday)	142	
November 24 (Friday)	256	
November 20–24		576
		1006

On Friday, November 24, our contingency planning group reconvened at the Treasury to assess the damage and review the old familiar policy controversies. Meanwhile, President Blessing of the Bundesbank had telephoned Chairman Martin to suggest an emergency meeting of the Pool members on Sunday, November 26, in Frankfurt. It was decided that Deming of Treasury, Daane, Hayes, and I of the Federal should constitute the American delegation.

At the governors' meeting that Sunday afternoon in Frankfurt, opinion was sharply divided. Both the Bank of England and the Swiss National Bank felt strongly that we should continue the Pool operation and meanwhile seek ways and means of repairing the weakness of the dollar, on which gold market speculation was now focusing. Dr. Erwin Stopper, President of the Swiss National Bank, reported that he had enlisted the cooperation of his commercial banks in severely curtailing credit and forward facilities for dealing in gold. With familiar eloquence, he insisted that these informal measures would check the drain on the Pool, and Parsons from the Bank of England strongly supported the Swiss view.

Governors Carli of the Bank of Italy, Zijlstra of the Netherlands Bank, and Ansiaux of the Belgian National Bank disagreed absolutely. In their judgment the game was up; continuation of Pool operations would subject them to progressive loss of gold and thereby increase their uncovered dollar positions. As Carli succinctly put it, we had abandoned a gold standard for the central banks and had substituted another for private speculators against the dollar.

Presumably following instructions from the White House, Undersecretary Deming threw our support to the Swiss-British proposal to hold the line, and Blessing of the Bundesbank reluctantly joined with him. As a compromise, the governors temporized by agreeing to continue all-out Pool intervention for another week before reaching a final decision. They also agreed to study proposals handed to them by Deming to compensate Pool members for sales of gold bars by fuzzily defined issues of gold certificates. Carli glanced over his copy and tossed it aside in disgust. The group then proceeded to the tricky job of concocting a communiqué that would leave the impression of complete solidarity in the Gold Pool without actually committing any Pool members to support operations of more than a week's duration. The problem was solved by addressing the communiqué primarily to the exchange market problem in the following words:

> The Governors of the Central Banks of Belgium, Germany, Italy, Netherlands, Switzerland, United Kingdom, and the United States convened in Frankfurt on November 26, 1967.
>
> They noted that the President of the United States has stated:
>
> I reaffirm unequivocally the commitment of the United States to buy and sell gold at the existing price of $35 per ounce.

They took decisions on specific measures to ensure by coordinated action orderly conditions in the exchange markets and to support the present pattern of exchange rates based on the fixed price of $35 per ounce of gold.

They concluded that the volume of gold and foreign exchange reserves at their disposal guarantees the success of these actions; at the same time they indicated that they would welcome the participation of other central banks.

Whatever the ultimate fate of the Gold Pool, there was now a major job to be done of checking hot money flows out of the dollar. With this in mind, I negotiated during and shortly after the Frankfurt meeting eleven increases in the Federal Reserve swap lines totaling slightly more than $2 billion. I also secured U.S. Treasury agreement to all-out operations in the forward exchange markets in defense of the dollar. To help guide these exchange market operations I remained in Frankfurt at the Bundesbank after the departure of the rest of the American team and from there conducted heavy operations in the forward markets for Swiss francs, Belgian francs, and Dutch guilders during the following week.

On the London gold market, the Frankfurt communiqué combined with our exchange market operations brought a brief respite, and Pool losses declined to no more than $100 million over the next few weeks. New problems were being generated, however, as politically inspired scare stories kept surfacing in the French press, and U.S. Treasury officials decided to take a direct and continuing hand in negotiations with the governors of the Pool. But here the Treasury encountered a very delicate problem of protocol. The European central bank governors had long regarded the BIS meetings at Basel as a nonpolitical sanctuary of technical cooperation. Not surprisingly, therefore, they were outraged by Undersecretary Deming's proposal to attend the December BIS meeting with the prime objective of pushing the American gold certificate scheme.

To make matters worse, all the European governors had meanwhile studied the gold certificate scheme distributed by Deming at the Frankfurt meeting and had found it impractical and unacceptable. Perhaps out of desperation, most of them had now turned toward the suggestions I had made earlier in the fall for conversion of the London gold bazaar into a licensed market restricted to authorized demand for industrial and artistic uses.

But the U.S. Treasury had veered sharply away from its earlier tentative support for controls on the London gold market for fear of involvement with South Africa. Thus, as Deming in his role of unwelcome guest at the December BIS meeting reiterated U.S. Treasury opposition to such control measures, this damage control route was also blocked. The United States and Europe had reached an impasse on contingency planning.

Moreover, the resentment of the European central bank governors over Deming's visit to Basel immediately leaked out and, with no negotiating progress to report, the Pool paid a heavy price on the London market the following week. On Tuesday, December 12, the Pool lost $75 million; on Wednesday, $121 million; and on Thursday, $175 million. As I stopped off at the Bank of England en route back to New York, I found a readiness even among those staunch defenders of the Pool to close the market and cut our losses.

The long ordeal of the Gold Pool was by no means over. On December 13, 1967, the White House sought to save the situation by belated decisions to raise income taxes to finance the Vietnam war, and to stiffen controls on outflows of capital. Meanwhile Martin and Fowler had become persuaded that Congressional removal of the gold cover requirement, freeing the entire gold stock for defense of the dollar, was the *sine qua non* of an orderly dissolution of the Pool. In late December 1967, a bill removing the gold cover was introduced in Congress. Under these circumstances, Martin secured by telephone the support of the European governors for continuing Pool operations and, on December 16, still another communiqué reaffirming such solidarity was issued.

From mid-December 1967 through February 1968 demand in the London gold market fell back from the crisis levels reached immediately following the sterling devaluation. President Johnson's announcement, on January 1, 1968, of a drastic new balance of payments program helped considerably to relieve buying pressure.

Pool losses in January and February 1968 were nevertheless sizable, amounting to $233 million for the two months combined. Moreover, market psychology remained highly inflammable.

As it happened, the spark that touched off a new explosion of demand was a speech on Wednesday, February 28, 1968, by Senator Jacob Javits, calling for a cessation of Gold Pool operations as well as other basic changes in our gold policy. Although the U.S. Treasury promptly disavowed the proposal, Pool losses on the following Thursday and Friday amounted to $118 million, subsiding somewhat on the following Monday as the weekend passed uneventfully. The worldwide publicity given to the Javits proposal nevertheless threatened further trouble, more particularly since the March meeting of the BIS was scheduled for the following weekend. In view of the risk of a snowballing of gold market speculation and possible further defections from the Gold Pool, the White House urged Chairman Martin to attend the March BIS meeting, and on Thursday night, March 7, I flew with him to Basel.

Saturday, March 9, in Basel, was largely devoted to private conversations, in one of which President Zijlstra came out vehemently for deciding that weekend to get out of the Gold Pool once and for all. As he put it, "We central bankers are behaving like a rabbit that has been hypnotized by a snake." The general tenor of opinion among the other central banks, particularly their foreign department men, was much the same.

On Sunday morning and afternoon, Chairman Martin met in private session with the governors of the European central banks and urged continuation of the Pool for a further short period, during which Congressional approval of lifting the gold cover requirement might free our entire gold stock for defense of the dollar. He was strongly supported by Governor O'Brien of the Bank of England, who was equally anxious to avoid a speculative upheaval that might frustrate a new British stabilization program shortly to be announced by Chancellor Jenkins in his first budget message.

Late Sunday afternoon, Martin and O'Brien returned together to the Schweizerhof, where the normally peaceful lobby was jammed with television cameramen, photographers, and reporters. A BIS communiqué just handed out stated that "The central banks contributing to the London Gold Pool reaffirm their determination to continue their support to the Pool, based on the fixed price of $35 per ounce of gold." Martin commented that he was "very satisfied indeed" with the day's discussions. O'Brien, asked whether he believed the agreement would stop the gold rush, replied with a straight face, "Yes, I think this will do the trick; I am sure it will." As O'Brien subsequently noted, a major duty of every central banker was to learn "how to exude confidence without positively lying."

The day's discussions had been wearying; and conversation at the Sunday evening governors' dinner was desultory. Before bringing the dinner to an unusually early end, however, President Zijlstra looked around the table and said "If we were commercial bankers, I wonder what advice we would give to our customers after reading the communiqué tomorrow. I suspect we would all urge them to go into the gold market and buy even more heavily than before." No one disagreed.

On Monday morning I accompanied Martin from Basel to Zurich Airport. Before boarding my flight to New York, I telephoned Max Iklé at the Swiss National Bank. Iklé said that the London gold fixing that morning had cost the Pool well over $100 million, and I passed this on to Martin, with the comment that Pool losses during the coming week could easily rise above $500 million a day.

On returning to New York I was invited to still another interagency meeting at the Treasury, on Wednesday, March 13, for further discussions on the gold market problem. As opinion around the table was canvassed, it quickly became apparent that even the staunchest supporters of continuing intervention were rapidly losing hope. The massive dimensions of the run on the Gold Pool had become all too clear. Losses on Monday, March 11, had amounted to $118 million; on Tuesday, $103 million; and on Wednesday $179 million. The only remnant of earlier contingency planning gaining any general acceptance was the idea of making a complete break between the official and private markets in gold by seeking foreign central bank agreement to boycott the private market in terms of not only sales but also purchases.

The Treasury meeting reconvened the next morning, Thursday, March 14, to find that the gold fixing in London that day had cost another $220 million and that Pool intervention after the fixing might well run the day's total to close to $400 million. Shortly thereafter, Bruce MacLaury, my deputy at the New York Bank, telephoned me to report that several Pool members had just placed with us gold orders clearly intended to replenish their recent losses through the Pool. Just before lunchtime the Treasury reached a decision to advise President Johnson to discontinue Pool operations. Around 3 o'clock the President agreed, and Chairman Martin telephoned Governor O'Brien of the Bank of England to request that the London gold market be closed on the next day, a Friday.

The time differential between New York and London led to more than the usual complications, including on this occasion the formal necessity of waking up Queen Elizabeth around midnight London time to get her permission to close the gold market, and the decision of British Prime Minister Wilson not to wake up his Foreign Minister, George Brown, with the curious result that the latter resigned in protest the following day.

Closure of the London gold market threatened to set off heavy speculative flows of hot money not only from New York but also from Canada and London into the Continental European markets. To deal with this problem, I had urged in the Treasury meetings an increase of between $2 and $3 billion dollars in the Federal Reserve swap lines, which would help to safeguard the dollar and to reinforce the British and Canadian defenses.

Considerable opposition to this approach was now voiced by members of both the White House staff and the Council of Economic Advisers, who argued that the continental central banks should instead be pressed to take in new dollar flows on an uncovered basis as their contribution to maintaining international financial stability. If they refused, it was asserted, the European central banks should be threatened with a "temporary" closure of the gold window to them.

These recommendations were forcefully rejected by both Secretary Fowler and Chairman Martin. That afternoon, a telephone conference of the Federal Open Market Committee approved my recommendation for across-the-board increases in our swap lines from $7 billion to $9.3 billion. Three of the seven members of the Board of Governors dissented from the decision.

Meanwhile Martin was calling the European governors of the Gold Pool to attend a special meeting in Washington at the Federal Reserve Board on Saturday, March 16, 1968. On Friday, as the European bankers were flying westward over the Atlantic for the meeting, we were confronted with an acute crisis of confidence in the exchange markets. The dollar plummeted to its floor against all the major continental currencies, while widespread reports appeared of European hotels, airlines, and exchange offices refusing to accept dollar currency. Although the London exchange market was closed for the day, sterling came under pressure in New York and other markets, but the New York Reserve Bank supported the pound in sufficient volume to keep the sterling market under control.

There was, however, one major piece of good news that came that day: Senate approval by a margin of only two votes of the bill to remove the gold cover entirely. Chairman Martin and Secretary Fowler had labored mightily to secure such legislative approval, and their judgment was now vindicated. Without this long-delayed action, the Washington meeting of the Gold Pool central bankers on the following day might have had a quite different outcome.

On Saturday morning, March 16, 1968, in the board room of Federal Reserve headquarters in Washington, the governors of the Gold Pool group convened for the last time. Everyone seemed solemnly conscious of a momentous crossroads of policy, and everyone had a strong view to express. Martin, serving both as host and chairman of the meeting, imperturbably followed his usual practice at Open Market Committee meetings of letting everyone talk himself out, interposing his own views only when needed to keep the discussion within the bounds of reason.

The British delegation was comprised of Governor O'Brien, Jeremy Morse, and George Preston of the Bank of England, together with Harold Lever and William Armstrong of the British Treasury. President Blessing and Tüngeler represented the Bundesbank; Governor Carli and Ossola, the Bank of Italy; President Zijlstra and Van den Bosch, the Netherlands Bank; President Stopper and Iklé, the Swiss National Bank; President Ansiaux, the National Bank of Belgium; Managing Director Pierre-Paul Schweitzer, the IMF; and Ferras and Gilbert of the BIS also appeared as unexpected guests, having been personally invited by Chairman Martin. The Bank of France, as previously noted, had dropped out of the Pool.

Martin opened the meeting by reaffirming the decision of the United States government to hold to the $35 parity and called on the Governor of the Bank of Italy. In his lucid way, Carli recalled his recommendations at the Pool meetings in Frankfurt in November and Basel in December that we should abandon the Gold Pool and let the free market price of gold find its own level. We should, he argued, seek a solution based squarely on the Articles of Agreement on the International Monetary Fund. He thought it essential to separate the gold market into official and private components. He pointed to the possibility under the IMF rules of settling official debts by repurchasing one's own currency with foreign exchange, with no necessity whatsoever for settling in gold or holding the London gold price at $35.

All that was needed, Carli continued, was for a group of central banks to agree to buy and sell gold among themselves at par, but not to deal in the market. This would not break the IMF rules. He believed it desirable for the central banks to buy free market gold if the price should decline below $35. The London gold market should not be reopened, since it had become a quasi-official barometer of confidence. He anticipated possibly huge flows of funds across the exchanges the following week but thought we had all the operational instruments needed to minimize their effects.

Sterling remained a major problem, but Carli believed that closure of the London gold market would not hurt sterling. On the contrary, closing the London gold market would deprive holders of sterling of one of their options for conversion of sterling and would correspondingly lessen the drain on the British reserves. In conclusion, he asserted that the European central banks could no longer justify to public opinion at home continuing intervention in the London gold market. There was the obvious risk that the financial markets would conclude that our hand had been forced. But we had to accept this risk and to try to live with it.

Carli's proposals were so balanced and reasonable that the group could easily have proceeded immediately to drafting a communiqué endorsing his conclusions. But the British delegation was there not only to settle the gold market question but also to press a major fund-raising campaign for sterling. Governor O'Brien made the dual proposal that the United States raise substantially the official price of gold and join with other members of the Pool and the IMF in putting up no less than $5 billion of medium-term money to backstop sterling; otherwise, he feared, the British government might be forced to let sterling float the following week. But the European governors were deeply divided on the gold price issue and were in no mood to join in a massive new underwriting of sterling. Wild counterproposals, such as having the British freeze the sterling balances, were thrown on the table. Chairman Martin finally closed the bazaar by firmly reiterating the United States position on the official gold price and deferring consideration of further credits for sterling until the gold market issue was settled.

By Sunday afternoon general agreement had been reached on termination of Pool operations, a temporary closure of the London gold market, and full resistance, through central bank cooperation on the exchange markets, to hot money flows across the exchanges. There remained the problem of a communiqué, which Martin was to read that evening before television cameras in an auditorium of the State Department across the street from the Federal Reserve.

Largely reflecting the fine hand of Carli and Ossola of the Bank of Italy, the communiqué was a masterpiece of stern adherence to the Bretton Woods agreement combined with delicate, nonetheless persuasive, hints of secret policy understandings to phase out gold in official settlements. The communiqué began in traditional style by noting the commitment of the United States government to continue to buy and sell gold at $35 per ounce in transactions with monetary authorities, further noting that legislation approved only a few days before by Congress made the whole of this gold stock available for defending the value of the dollar.

As a *quid pro quo* for such American commitments, the communiqué stated the intention of the European countries to encourage domestic expansion to avoid tight money markets and increases in interest rates, to cooperate even more closely than in the past to minimize destabilizing flows of funds across the exchange markets, and to offset, as necessary, any flows that might arise. (Such European commitments to counter hot money flows in the exchange markets were paralleled by a secret commitment, offered by Undersecretary Deming, to intervene forcefully in the spot and forward markets and to consolidate, in due course, any foreign currency debts arising from such United States government exchange operations by recourse to the International Monetary Fund.)

As for the London gold market, sales by the Pool would be terminated. Moreover, ". . . as the existing stock of monetary gold is sufficient, in view of the prospective establishment of the facility for special drawing rights, the governors no longer feel it necessary to buy gold from the market." Finally, the cooperation of other central banks in such policy was invited.

The main effect of the communiqué was to warn all other central banks in the world not to buy gold in the London market, nor to make special deals with South Africa or Russia; it also conveyed the impression that an understanding now existed among the Gold Pool central banks not to use the Treasury gold window but to wait for the special drawing rights to come along. Deming had in fact appealed to the Gold Pool central banks, as an example to others, to show forbearance in coming to the Treasury window. Although flatly rejected by the European governors, this appeal may have had some deterrent effect.

In any event, most of the central banks not represented at the Washington meeting seemed to get a warning message. Over the next few months our gold sales remained relatively small, in striking contrast to the billion dollar loss sustained during the fourth quarter of 1960 after the breakout of the London gold price. Thus, a major peril posed by withdrawal of official support of the London gold market had now been averted.

There remained the risk of simultaneous speculative pressures in the exchange markets on the United States dollar, sterling, and the Canadian dollar. As noted earlier, I had secured the agreement of the Open Market Committee the previous Thursday for increases totaling $2.3 billion in the Federal Reserve swap lines. My first opportunity to negotiate these increases came after adjournment of the Saturday meeting, when we all went over to the State Department for a reception, passing through a roped-off pathway from the street with reporters and television cameramen on both sides clamoring for attention.

At the reception I secured agreement from our foreign central bank partners to all the swap lines increases approved by the Open Market Committee. In this effort I had the volunteered assistance of Governor Robertson, despite his formal dissent from the Committee decision to increase the swap lines. This was typical of Committee procedures; once a majority decision had been made, the ranks immediately closed in a solid front. A telephone call to the Bank of Canada, which had not been represented at the Washington meeting, also produced agreement on a major increase in the swap line with the Bank of Canada.

There remained the hotly disputed question of how much more assistance, and in what form, to provide for sterling. After considerable bickering, the European central bank governors finally agreed to put up $425 million, on condition that the United States would extend another $700 million, for an overall package of $1.1 billion. I suggested to Chairman Martin and Undersecretary Deming that the Federal Reserve might take $500 million of the suggested American share through an increase in the British swap line, from $1.5 billion to $2 billion, with the Treasury providing the additional $200 million. This was immediately agreed to by Martin and Secretary Fowler and subsequently was approved by the Open Market Committee.

The European governors left for home on Sunday evening, with grave forebodings of an explosion of speculation when the exchange markets opened the next day. Nothing of the sort occurred. Curiously enough, with all the technical expertise assembled around the table in Washington, we had lost sight of the simple fact that the gold speculators were now saturated with inventory, and those vast additions to private gold hoards would result in a heavy overhang of supply in the gold market for many months to come. Most speculators had anticipated a new and higher official price, at which they might unload their gold and walk away immediately with the profit of their foresight. They now had the problem of finding new buyers to relieve them of their inventory.

As the London gold market reopened on April 1, the price settled around the $38 level in quiet and orderly trading, and for the rest of 1968 it did not rise above $43. In 1969, moreover, a renewed flow of gold from South Africa combined with the overhang of private hoards to break the price down to the official $35 parity. Mainly reflecting European pressures, an IMF agreement was then devised to effectively place a floor under the London gold price.

On the exchange markets, the Washington agreement was welcomed. By this time everyone was getting rather weary of the whole question of the gold, and a multilateral agreement to bury the question, at least temporarily, seemed to come as a relief. As in the past, the strengthening of the Federal Reserve swap network, together with the provision of additional credits to the British, was taken by the market as confirming official determination to keep the exchange markets under control. And so, on the exchange markets as well as on the gold market another crisis had been weathered.

10

Devaluation of
the French Franc

Although France had been traditionally a high gold ratio country, Bank of France officials in the late fifties were uncomfortably aware of the threat to the Bretton Woods system of a sudden general shift of central bank dollar holdings into gold. As speculative pressure on the dollar mounted in late 1960, the Bank of France had shown considerable discretion in converting dollar inflows into gold. Not surprisingly, therefore, French officials had been angered by the October 1960 breakout of the London gold price, which had seemed to challenge the official United States parity. But shortly thereafter French forbearance in buying gold had been vindicated as President Kennedy in early 1961 pledged himself to maintain the official gold price and to restore the strength of the dollar.

Throughout 1961 the Bank of France continued to refrain from buying gold from the U.S. Treasury. The Bank of France gave solid support to the creation of the Gold Pool in late 1961 and suggested, in March 1962, the first swap arrangement entered into by the Federal Reserve. Such French support of the dollar suffered considerable embarrassment in late 1961 and 1962, however, when the British Treasury, recovering dollar reserves after the speculative crisis earlier in the year, used them to buy gold from the United States rather than prepaying its debt to the Fund. Governor Brunet of the Bank of France bitterly asked a senior official of the Bank of England how long he thought French forbearance on buying gold could be sustained in the absence of cooperation elsewhere in the BIS group.

As France continued to run heavy payments surpluses in 1962, a shift of French policy to partial gold conversion of mounting dollar balances was partly a counsel of prudence, fully in line with traditional French financial policy. To temper the impact on the American gold stock, the Bank of France initially limited conversions to only slightly more than $30 million monthly. But as time went on, and President de Gaulle increasingly set himself not only against American action in Vietnam but even an American role in Europe, the gold policy of the Bank of France became integrated into the foreign policy of the French government.

Public opinion in the United States was already moving against the Vietnam commitment, and persistent but reasonably diplomatic pressure from de Gaulle at this stage might have been helpful to the American officials already alarmed over the eventual financial consequences of Vietnam. A courteous request to the United States to relieve the Bank of France of its surplus dollars by recourse to the IMF or other sources of international credit could have exerted a gradual and understandable disciplinary effect.

But de Gaulle's pronouncements served only to polarize the issue in a new and confusing dimension. And his advisers who urged him to put a gun to the American head by cashing in dollars for gold succeeded only in hastening the downfall of Bretton Woods and ensuring that gold would never again play the same role in international finance. Between 1962 and 1966 the French government bought nearly $3 billion of gold from the U.S. Treasury, shipped the bulk of its gold custody holdings at the New York Federal to Paris, and generally challenged the functioning of the Bretton Woods system.

Initially I could sense in foreign financial markets a certain admiration for de Gaulle's readiness "to stand up to the Americans" as one European financial official put it. But as French political maneuvering excited dangerous bursts of speculation in the gold and foreign exchange markets, financial opinion throughout the world rejected with mounting indignation the Gaullist campaign against the dollar.

Meanwhile, Bank of France officials, although subject to a tightening straitjacket of political constraints, maintained correct and helpful relationships with their foreign central bank counterparts. The machinery of central bank cooperation thus remained intact and available for use when the economic fortunes of France were suddenly reversed by "the events of May 1968."

As late as May 13, while passing through Amsterdam en route to the three-hundredth anniversary celebration of the Swedish Riksbank, Martin and I had been approached by Brunet and Clappier of the Bank of France as to the best way of handling a new French government request to buy $90 million of gold. But on May 17 at the Stockholm ceremonies we heard the startling news of the outbreak of rioting in Paris. By the time I had returned to my office at the New York Federal, a general strike in France had closed down even the operational departments of the Bank of France and had disrupted post, telex, and cable communications.

Telephone communications with the Bank of France were still possible, however, and we agreed on May 20 to accept from their senior officials telephoned instructions, without supporting telex confirmations, to pay out dollars for Bank of France account to defend the French franc at its floor rate in New York. Over the next eight days, such support operations in New York totaled more than $50 million, all based on telephone communications, without a scrap of paper to confirm their authenticity. Finally, on June 4, Brunet's daughter, who had flown to New York for other reasons, delivered to us the Bank of France's confirmations. Our Legal Department heaved a sigh of relief.

On May 29, I had a telephone call at my home from Bernard Clappier, who seemed to be in a somewhat pessimistic mood, as well he had a right to be. Earlier that day President de Gaulle had disappeared from Paris (to round up the support of the French army as it turned out). To Clappier, the fate of the French government, as well as the French franc, probably seemed to be hanging in the balance. He recalled our conversation in Amsterdam, noting that the situation had so completely reversed itself that the French were now prepared to sell rather than to buy gold. In view of probable further speculation against the franc, such gold sales might be fairly sizable. Most of the French gold holdings were now in the vaults of the Bank of France, however, as a result of earlier heavy repatriations from New York. Clappier said that he could sell gold *loco* Paris to a good many European central banks. But he felt that since French gold had originally been bought from the United States, we should also have the chance to buy it back if we should so desire. Specifically, he asked what we would be prepared to quote on French gold located in New York, London, or Paris. I replied that it seemed highly appropriate for the Bank of France to offer the U.S. Treasury an opportunity to repurchase gold previously sold to France. I would find out immediately what prices the Treasury was prepared to quote, depending on location.

I then called the Treasury, urging them to quote the price of $35 flat for gold located in any of the three cities. But I was deeply disappointed by their reply. The Treasury would quote a purchase price of $35 flat, *loco* either New York or London. For gold *loco* Paris, the price would be cut to $35 minus shipping costs to New York of probably 10 cents per ounce. I pointed out that the French would be able to find plenty of buyers for gold *loco* Paris at $35 flat if we refused to accept it there, and that the net result of the Treasury position would simply be to divert French sales to Germany, Italy, and other European countries. To no avail.

A solution turned up, however, in a telephone conversation shortly thereafter with Pierre-Paul Schweitzer, Managing Director of the International Monetary Fund. He expressed the hope that the United States would be able to secure a major share of French gold sales and was surprised to hear of the price quotation offered to the Bank of France. Schweitzer commented that the U.S. Treasury position seemed to serve no useful purpose, since there would be plenty of organizations, including the International Monetary Fund, that would be prepared to pay $35 flat for gold *loco* Paris. I asked him if the Fund would be prepared to exchange on a flat basis gold *loco* New York for gold *loco* Paris. He replied that he saw no difficulty whatsoever, since the Fund had relatively little gold in Paris compared with New York. Accordingly, the Treasury agreed to buy French gold *loco* Paris at the $35 parity price on condition that it be exchanged ounce for ounce with Fund gold deposited at the New York Federal. Through this device, French gold sales to the United States in 1968–1969 eventually totaled $925 million.

On May 30, Memorial Day, I again spoke over the telephone with Clappier. Though he seemed somewhat less depressed than the previous day, he seemed still worried over the problem of ensuring that the Bank of France would have on hand the dollars needed to cover further heavy reserve drains. He said that the French government was approaching the International Monetary Fund to draw both its gold and supergold tranches. But he also seemed concerned over possible delays in setting the Fund machinery in motion. I noted in passing that if he should become severely pressed for funds, the $100 million swap line of the Bank of France with the Federal would be readily available; we could credit the Bank of France account immediately on their telephone request.

Late in the afternoon on May 30, I had a telephone call from Roy Bridge of the Bank of England, reporting the warm reception given de Gaulle's television announcement that he intended to hold firm, and the appearance for the first time since the crisis began of large-scale public demonstrations in the president's favor. He felt that on the previous day the French financial position had skidded close to the edge of disaster, with ominous implications for sterling as well.

Shortly after the opening of business in New York on Friday, May 31, Clappier called to inquire how things were going. I reported that selling pressure on the franc after the New York opening had been immediate and intense, and I gave him the latest figures of our intervention. Clappier replied that the French government was fully prepared to deal with whatever losses might be incurred in defense of the franc. But he then asked, in view of the prospectively heavy drain and possible last minute delays in the French drawing on the Fund, whether we would permit a French drawing of the full $100 million available under our swap line. I replied that we would credit their account immediately.

During the BIS weekend in early June, I again talked with Clappier, who said that the only saving grace of the present situation, from his point of view, was that it would destroy the "myth," as he put it, of gold transactions becoming a one-way street, with the Bank of France acting as the only major buyer and the United States as the only major seller. Heavy gold sales by the Bank of France, which now seemed likely, would serve to restore the role of gold in international finance to a more natural and normal perspective.

I replied that we would be gratified by a replenishment of our gold stock. On the other hand, it seemed to me that big flows of gold in either direction tended to be an unsettling element in international finance, more particularly when they acquired political overtones. I noted that when sterling, the Italian lira, and the Canadian dollar had come under speculative attack, the provision of central bank facilities had effectively served to prevent a snowballing of speculation that otherwise might have occurred if the central banks concerned had been forced to publish massive reserve losses. Clappier listened noncommittally, without giving me the usual French official rebuttal regarding the pitfalls and hazards in the use of official credit.

That same day I had a brief chat with Carli, who confirmed that the Bank of France had sounded out the Bank of Italy as a possible buyer of gold. Carli indicated that the Bank of Italy would be a ready buyer but at the same time professed concern over what seemed to him to be an undesirable revival of the role of gold internationally. He noted that not only France but the entire international financial system would now be in a much stronger position if the French had joined in as a major partner in the swap network. I concurred and said that we would have welcomed French participation in the successive enlargements of the swap network in recent years.

I telephoned Clappier on July 1, the day after the final French election had brought de Gaulle a sweeping majority. I started by asking whether the election returns were not likely to have a stabilizing effect on the exchange market. Clappier replied with some asperity that the elections had "settled absolutely nothing" and that the Bank of France was fearful of further heavy drains on the French reserves. In particular, he was concerned over the prospective market impact of the publication on Wednesday, July 3, of reserve losses for June totaling nearly $1.2 billion. He and his colleagues had been giving a great deal of thought to ways and means of countering speculative pressure on the franc.

Specifically, Clappier wished to know whether the Federal Reserve would be prepared to participate in a network of swap facilities with the Bank of France totaling $1.3 billion. He envisaged that this total might be divided in roughly equal proportions between the United States and the Common Market countries, with the Federal Reserve swap line moving up from $100 million to $700 million, while the Bundesbank would provide $300 million, Italy $200 million, and Belgium and the Netherlands $50 million each. The BIS would also be asked to put up $100 million. He felt it would be desirable to combine such French access to short-term credit with further sales of French gold in the amount of $300 million, of which $150 million would be sold to the United States, $75 million to Germany, $50 million to Italy, and $12.5 million to both the Netherlands and Belgium.

At the previous meeting of the FOMC I had in fact already raised the question of a possible increase in the French swap line and had received a fairly sympathetic response. With the support of Chairman Martin, I now secured by telegram FOMC approval of a $600 million increase in the French swap line, which became available to the Bank of France the following day. France's Common Market partners and the BIS thereafter supplied a further $700 of similar credit facilities. Announcement on July 11 of this $1.3 billion credit package relieved considerably earlier selling pressure on the franc.

Meanwhile, however, the French government had conceded in June wage increases of more than 10 percent to settle the strike while also shifting to a much more stimulative fiscal and monetary policy designed to revive industrial production. These decisions eventually proved fatal to the parity of the franc, as subsequent price inflation gradually eroded the competitive strength of French foreign trade. During the late summer of 1968 recurrent rumors of a German revaluation exacerbated selling pressure on the franc. By September the Bank of France had drawn $490 million under the $700 swap line with the Federal, while also using up other credit facilities and selling gold.

In early November 1968 events moved swiftly toward a climax as a new wave of speculation on either a mark revaluation or a franc devaluation flooded through the exchange markets. By November 20 the reserves of the Bundesbank showed a gain over the previous three months of more than $4 billion, while the French and British had lost more than $2 billion. With Bank of France drawings on the $700 million Federal Reserve swap line now exceeding $600 million, I came to the BIS meeting on November 16 with a strong feeling that the Bundesbank should take a major responsibility for rechanneling, or recycling, back to the Bank of France and the Bank of England the speculative inflows from Paris and London.

I quickly got the impression, however, that Bank of France officials, presumably with the agreement of the French Treasury, had concluded that further defense of the franc parity was hopeless. French policy now sought simultaneous devaluation of the franc and revaluation of the mark. In further conversations that weekend, the governors unanimously supported such a combined move and vigorously urged President Blessing of the Bundesbank to seek his government's approval.

In the normal course of events, quiet negotiations between the French and German governments might have yielded this eminently desirable solution. But as luck would have it, Treasury Secretary Fowler and Undersecretary Deming were making a farewell swing around the major European capitals, and on Monday, November 18, they arrived in Bonn. On their arrival, a message from the White House instructed Secretary Fowler to request an immediate meeting of the G-10 finance ministers to negotiate a combined revaluation of the mark and devaluation of the French franc. Fowler and Deming then secured what they thought were assurances from the German government that the question of a mark revaluation would be treated as an open issue. Thus it was agreed that Minister Schiller, as Chairman of the G-10 ministerial group, would urgently convene a meeting. This, as it turned out, was a prescription for disaster.

Meanwhile, I had driven from Basel to Frankfurt in company with Johannes Tüngeler, whose chauffeur was still trying to break the record for the trip. In Tüngeler's office the next day, we heard that the three German parties had formally voted against a revaluation of the mark, thereby throwing the full burden of adjustment on the French franc. At that point the best solution would probably have been to downgrade the Bonn G-10 meeting to a brief, perfunctory affair, while pursuing further negotiations on rate realignments through other and quieter channels.

Instead the Bonn Conference turned into a spectacular political sideshow as the United States delegation continued to press for a revaluation of the mark while the German politicians, including G-10 Chairman Schiller, took full advantage of television and press coverage to pose as stalwart defenders of the mark against a foreign conspiracy. As the conference dragged on from November 18 through 20, the proceedings increasingly took on a Kafkaesque quality. The meeting place itself, the Ministry of Economics at Bonn, had a huge glass entrance that was besieged from morning to night by hundreds of press correspondents, television men, and pickets carrying signs saying "Save the Mark!" In full view along the main corridor inside, dozens of G-10 officials wandered aimlessly about, as waiters proffered glasses of champagne and unidentifiable canapés in aspic, which seemed to be the only provender in the Ministry's kitchen.

Prominent among the corridor standees were the central bank governors, periodically banished from secret meetings of the Finance Ministers that sometimes went on until 3 a.m. On arriving, Pierre-Paul Schweitzer of the IMF incredulously surveyed the scene and commented, "I would never have dreamed of attending a financial meeting from which Bill Martin would be barred." Meanwhile, Chairman Martin and Governor Daane of the Federal and Otmar Emminger of the Bundesbank played ping-pong to pass the time. Others, including myself, grew famished as mealtimes came and went and even the supply of canapés began to fail. On one occasion, the Governor of the Bank of France and I both hungrily eyed a sole frankfurter remaining on a waiter's tray, agreed to divide it, and toasted each other in the ever-flowing champagne.

The finance ministers from time to time allowed the central bankers to attend their sessions, and it became clear to us that little progress was being made. At the opening session Chancellor Jenkins indiscreetly cited his impression that the recent central bank meeting at Basel had favored a revaluation of the mark. Schiller turned in fury on President Karl Blessing of the Bundesbank, inquiring what authority he had to discuss such matters with foreign officials and demanded from BIS President Jelle Zijlstra of the Netherlands Bank a full report on the Basel discussions. Zijlstra, a former prime minister of the Netherlands, politely told Schiller to go to hell. A total impasse on the question of German revaluation had clearly been reached, and the attention of the conference accordingly turned to the French franc, where the risk now emerged that the French government might devalue the franc so sharply that pressure would be put on other major currencies. As Finance Minister Ortoli of France sat quietly chain-smoking and reserving his position, the other ministers urged him not to go beyond an 11 percent devaluation and promised new financial support for the franc if this limit were observed.

Regarding financial assistance to France, the finance ministers naturally looked to the central banks for the funds needed. To my amazement, I watched my suggestion at the previous Basel meeting of a recycling of hot money flows suddenly blossom into what came to be the only major recommendation in the final communiqué of the Bonn Conference. The central bankers agreed to study the recycling problem energetically, but at the instance of Zijlstra met for lunch on Friday, November 22, to decide what immediate reinforcement could be provided for a French franc presumably to be devalued over the weekend. I say "presumably" because at least one participant in the conference still thought the French position on devaluation was somewhat unclear. As we went to lunch, Bill Martin said to me, "I still don't see just what the French have committed themselves to do."

His vision was totally clear, but everyone else in their anxiety to get out of the Bonn Ministry of Economics by the next plane readily accepted the general assumption that the French would have no alternative but to devalue to the full 11 percent maximum agreed by the finance ministers. And so at the central bank lunch on Friday, November 22, Zijlstra conducted a fund-raising campaign for the postweekend, devalued French franc that yielded within a half-hour $2 billion of reasonably firm credit commitments. For the United States share, I suggested an increase in the Federal Reserve swap line with the Bank of France from $700 million to $1 billion and a special Treasury credit of $200 million. Both Fowler and Martin agreed, the latter with a distinct lack of his usual cheerful assurance in such matters.

Thus the ill-fated Bonn Conference ended. The French and British governments, and somewhat reluctantly, the German government as well, had wisely decided to close down their exchange markets until the political polemics at Bonn on exchange rate realignments had subsided. But over the month as a whole, the speculative drain on the more vulnerable currencies was severe. During November the Bank of England was forced to draw another $750 million on the Federal Reserve swap line, and the drain on the reserves of the Bank of France had been even heavier. But much more damage had been done to the process of orderly negotiation of exchange rate policy problems by the major trading nations.

Late Friday afternoon our delegation left for Washington in one of those converted Air Force tankers with no windows. IMF Managing Director Pierre-Paul Schweitzer was our guest. He was expecting to preside at a special Fund meeting the following Saturday morning to give formal approval to the new devalued parity of the French franc.

Late the next morning I awoke at my home in Green Village, New Jersey and early in the afternoon picked up a radio broadcast of the Harvard–Yale game. The game went badly for Harvard, eventually trailing 29 to 13 with less than a minute to play. At that moment the phone rang. Federal Reserve Board Governor Daane was calling from Washington, but as I greeted him wild bursts of cheering from the radio distracted my attention. I asked him to hold on and found that Harvard had suddenly scored 8 points. With less than 20 seconds of the game remaining, I thought that Daane could wait that long and so I listened to that fantastic scoring by Harvard of still another 8 points to tie the game at 29–29.

Somewhat bemused, I returned to the telephone. What Daane had to tell me was hardly less astounding than the last minute élan of the Harvard football team. President de Gaulle had decided that the French franc would not be devalued, and the United States government had already publicly supported his decision. To say the least, I was dismayed. Two billion dollars of central bank credit pledged to support a devalued franc, which now would not be devalued. There was nothing to be done, of course, and shortly afterward I so counseled several very angry central bankers who called me from Europe and elsewhere.

President de Gaulle meant what he said, and the very next day began to tighten up all the screws through which the French bureaucracy can temporarily exert its will. In addition to new fiscal and monetary restraints, exchange controls were stringently enforced. French importers, for example, were actually forced to abrogate a substantial portion of their forward contracts to buy foreign exchange, and French banks were required to sell to the Bank of France the foreign currencies held as cover against those contracts. Through these and other harsh measures, the capital outflow from France was temporarily checked. By early March 1969 the Bank of France had regained sufficient reserves to pay off $300 million on its swap debt to the Federal as well as to liquidate a substantial amount of debt to other central bank creditors.

The capital inflows induced by the tightening of exchange controls soon tapered off, however, and the deep deficit in the French payments accounts once more began to drain away French official reserves. Moreover, de Gaulle decided to stake his political future on a constitutional referendum on April 27. The referendum defeat and de Gaulle's resignation further intensified selling pressures on the franc. Then in early May 1969 a new wave of speculation on a revaluation of the mark swept through the exchange markets. The forward discount on the French franc rose to 32 percent before the forward market dried up completely. The Bank of France financed these reserve drains by heavy new drawings on the credit lines made available at the Bonn Conference in November 1968. Despite its strained circumstances, the Bank of France remained fully mindful of the short-term nature of these facilities. As its $460 million debt under the Federal Reserve swap line approached the one-year traditional limit, the Bank sold $275 million of gold to the U.S. Treasury to help finance a complete repayment of its debt to the Federal Reserve.

On August 8, 1969, the long ordeal of the French franc came to an end as the French government, in a cleanly executed maneuver managed by Finance Minister Giscard d'Estaing, suddenly devalued the franc by 11.1 percent, roughly in line with the maximum cut agreed at the Bonn Conference. The defense of the franc over the preceding 15 months had cost France reserve losses of roughly $5 billion.

11

Defense of the Dollar, 1965–1968

The main thrust of American policy during the 1961–1964 Dillon-Roosa administration of the Treasury was to substitute mutual credit facilities for international gold settlements. By the end of 1964 the Federal Reserve swap network and other central bank credit arrangements, the Roosa bonds, and the greatly expanded lending capacity of the International Monetary Fund formed a spectrum of short- through medium-term credit facilities available to all the major trading countries for financing temporary deficits in their foreign payments. Speaking before the annual IMF meeting in Tokyo in September 1964, Dillon urged an enlargement and elaboration of such credit facilities rather than further increases in the overall supply of reserves.

This policy stance of the Treasury gradually crumbled, however, in the face of incessant and broadening demands in the latter half of the sixties for creation of some kind of new international money to supplement gold and the reserve currencies. The crusade for a new international reserve unit, which came to be colloquially labeled "paper gold," enlisted in its ranks a broad range of normally clashing policy interests, each one visualizing some variant of a new world money that would serve his special needs.

The less developed countries seized on the proposal of Maxwell Stamp for generous allocations of new reserve money as a fresh source of development aid. In the United Kingdom, both Conservatives and Labor were hot on the trail of a monetary device that would both replenish the shrunken reserves of the British government and permit a hiving off onto the International Monetary Fund of the overhang of sterling liabilities. On the other hand, French and other Continental European officials could envisage a bargain in which creation of new international reserve money would be traded against a severe curtailment of the reserve currency roles of both the dollar and sterling.

Most university economists focused on the simple truth that the secular growth of world trade would require an expansion of international liquidity. They generally felt both distaste and distrust of informally negotiated credit facilities. Such credit arrangements probably seemed to leave too much to the human factor. Academic views accordingly leaned strongly toward a comprehensive and formalized scheme of liquidity creation in the form of a new reserve asset. As allocations of such new reserve assets expanded in tempo with liquidity needs, central banks would be relieved of policy pressures to run balance of payments surpluses to meet their reserve growth needs.

In early 1965 the new team of Fowler and Deming took over the reins at the Treasury. They inherited the impending escalation of Vietnam and the budget, balance of payments, and inflationary consequences of the new burdens of military spending abroad. They were worthy successors of the Dillon-Roosa Treasury. Fred Deming, formerly President of the Reserve Bank of Minneapolis, had participated in all of the FOMC policy discussions of Federal Reserve operations in the foreign exchange markets and was thus already well briefed on his new responsibilities. Deming had the same decisive qualities as Roosa and moved fast in any emergency. Secretary Fowler brought to his post the careful, orderly thought of a skilled lawyer as well as a forceful dedication to international financial cooperation. One of the most respected figures in world financial circles, "Joe" Fowler conducted Treasury policy during 1965–1968 with wisdom and integrity.

Fowler and Deming anticipated pressure on the dollar, the American gold stock, and the London gold pool. To complicate matters still more, earlier Treasury reliance on mutual credit facilities to finance balance of payments strains was now challenged by Gaullist insistence on payment in gold and nothing else.

Not surprisingly, therefore, the new Treasury team not only took an active interest in the liquidity debate but soon evolved its own set of proposals tailored to American needs. But nearly five years of arduous negotiations among the G-10 countries were to elapse before the creation in 1969 of the special drawing rights (SDR) in the International Monetary Fund.

The New York Federal did not play any role in the SDR negotiation, although we had ample opportunity to do so. For my own part, I could not help feeling that the SDR edifice, however carefully constructed, would nevertheless be balanced on a razor's edge. If, on the one hand, the fiat money attribute of the SDR were to be emphasized, I found it hard to believe that money issued by the International Monetary Fund or any supranational agency would prove to be a generally acceptable alternative to the dollar, much less gold. And if, as was eventually agreed, the SDR was endowed with a categorical gold guarantee to enhance its acceptability, the SDR would inevitably be dragged along in the wake of whatever happened to gold itself.

Thus during the SDR debate almost no attention was given to the question of what would happen to the SDR with its gold guarantee if the American gold window should be closed, with the United States continuing to maintain the fiction of an official price far below free market gold price levels. As I pointed out to Treasury and Federal Reserve officials before closure of the gold window, the effect would be to immobilize all official gold holdings. No central bank would sell gold until the official gold price was raised, either *de facto* or *de jure,* close to the prevailing free market level. Similarly, official holdings of any reserve asset guaranteed as the SDR in terms of gold would suffer the same paralysis. Finally, official action to substantially raise the price of gold as a means of reactivating official gold stocks would create a vast new amount of international liquidity, undercutting the very rationale of the SDR, which was designed to overcome a prospective shortage of such liquidity.

Accordingly I devoted myself to a continuing effort to strengthen the swap network and other machinery of central bank cooperation. Nor did Secretary Fowler's espousal of the "paper gold" concept diminish Treasury support for Federal Reserve efforts to protect through credit facilities both the dollar and the currencies of our major trading partners from speculative attack. In fact, as the Vietnam conflict took its toll of the dollar's strength in the late sixties, and both sterling and the French franc succumbed to domestic inflation, central bank cooperation met with a series of unprecedented challenges.

By the end of June 1964, as noted earlier, the Federal Reserve had completely liquidated swap debts of $1.3 billion incurred over the previous two years. During the second half of 1964, however, heavy outflows of bank credit and longer term investments from New York brought new selling pressure on the dollar. Morever, as the 1964 sterling crisis moved toward its climax, the dollar was caught in the backwash of the flood of hot money rushing from London into the continental financial centers.

As surplus dollars piled up on the books of the continental central banks in late 1964, the Federal forestalled huge gold losses for the United States by borrowing under the swap lines $750 million of Swiss francs, German marks, Belgian francs, Dutch guilders, and Italian lire. We also joined with the Treasury in forward market sales of guilders, Swiss francs, and lire of somewhat more than $800 million equivalent. These defensive operations, totaling $1550 million by the Federal and the Treasury in the spot and forward exchange markets, enabled the dollar to ride through the speculative storm that finally subsided in the late spring of 1965.

While Federal Reserve operations in the exchange markets thus protected our gold stock from the main impact of the speculative onslaught, gold settlements nevertheless continued on a diminished scale. United States gold sales between October 1964 and June 1965 totaled $1.5 billion, largely reflecting the shift of French gold policy to a more aggressive stance. But there were also included a number of gold transactions designed to settle payments outflows or swap debt that seemed irreversible to both the Federal Reserve and its foreign central bank partners. Similarly, the U.S. Treasury in July 1965 made a $300 million drawing of five European currencies from the IMF, primarily to enable the Federal to pay off swap debt approaching maturity. And, as the British government made a $1.4 billion drawing on the IMF in May 1965, in the form of not only dollars but European currencies as well, the Federal Reserve was enabled to acquire sizable amounts of lire, guilders, and Belgian francs in which we had debt positions outstanding.

By and large, however, the great bulk of Federal Reserve swap debt and Treasury and Federal forward commitments was liquidated by a major reversal of hot money flows as speculation against the dollar receded. By July 1965 all but $48 million of the Federal's swap debt had been repaid, while its forward commitments had also been reduced to minor proportions.

In general, therefore, Federal Reserve exchange market operations during the crisis-ridden winter months of 1964–1965 closely conformed to the policy objectives and limitations we had set for ourselves. In our lending operations we had provided the Bank of England with emergency credits totaling $1250 million while more or less simultaneously borrowing $750 million from other partners in the swap network. The short-term maturities of all these swap credits had been meticulously honored. Insofar as reversals in the flow of funds did not suffice to finance swap debt repayments on time, the two governments had enabled their respective central banks to discharge their swap obligations through governmental sale of gold or recourse to medium-term borrowing from the IMF. To many of us in the BIS group of central banks, there now seemed to be a fair chance of converting the capriciously harsh discipline of the Bretton Woods system into more sophisticated machinery capable of controlling speculation.

Yet as I pointed out in my semiannual report on exchange operations in early March 1965, successful management of this new machinery depended on one basic assumption: "that both the British and the United States governments would quickly put in motion forceful corrective programs to eliminate their payments deficits."

In the case of the dollar, much of the trouble arose from capital transfers abroad. Though the dollar had benefited by a strong growth of our trade surplus from 1961 through 1964, a rising tide of capital outflows had largely offset the gain on trade account. The unrivalled capacity of the American financial markets to supply capital funds over a broad maturity range had become a magnet for foreign borrowers.

Moreover, New York rates were consistently cheaper, reflecting not only the country's greater reliance on low interest rates as an economic stimulus but also the cartel and other restrictive practices prevalent in a number of European financial markets. American portfolio investment in foreign stocks and bonds and bank lending abroad were further swelled by a rapid growth of direct investment of American corporations in manufacturing facilities in foreign markets, as well as in traditional raw material development projects.

In mid-1963, as the continuing balance of payments deficit generated further heavy flows of dollars into the European central banks, the Kennedy administration had introduced the interest equalization tax (IET), which was designed to squeeze out the rate differentials favoring American investment in foreign bonds. Quite aside from the tax deterrent it imposed, the IET exerted a high degree of moral suasion on institutional investors and generally proved to be an effective constraint.

American bank lending and corporate investment abroad continued to surge ahead, however, and by the fall of 1964 were subjecting the dollar to considerable strain in the exchange markets. In November of that year the sterling crisis vividly illustrated the vulnerability of the dollar and the urgent need for new defensive action. Accordingly, with the full support of the Federal Reserve, the Johnson administration announced in Feburary 1965 new capital-control measures to limit the balance of payments impact of both direct investment and bank lending abroad.

Restraint on bank lending was secured in the form of a voluntary program sponsored by the Federal Reserve under which banks undertook to limit their foreign lending within certain designated ceilings. The cooperative response of the banks was excellent and immediately relieved pressure on the dollar coming from that source. On the other hand, the Commerce Department program of restraint of corporate direct investment abroad was a loosely designed affair that was administered even more loosely.

On balance, however, the capital-control measures taken in February 1965 provided much needed protection for the dollar as sterling relapsed into new speculative difficulties in the summer of 1965. As a result, Federal Reserve and Treasury credits of $890 million to the Bank of England during the summer of 1965 were accompanied by Federal Reserve drawings of no more than $180 million on our swap lines with the Italian, Dutch, and Belgian central banks. By the end of February 1966, moreover, the sterling bear squeeze of the previous September had routed the speculators. Return flows of hot money to London and New York enabled both the Bank of England and the Federal Reserve to clear away completely the $1.1 billion of swap debt thus incurred during 1965 by the two central banks.

During the spring and summer months of 1966, the dollar was supported by a further substantial rise of interest rates in the New York market as the business expansion fueled by Vietnam gathered momentum. But again in July 1966, the British experienced another and even more violent speculative attack on sterling. The swap network was once more called on to absorb the shock. The Federal Reserve again came to the aid of the Bank of England with new swap credits and supporting bids for sterling in the market, as related in Chapter 8. Meanwhile, the swap network readily accommodated new drawings by the Federal during the summer and autumn months of 1966 of slightly more than $700 million equivalent in Swiss francs, Dutch guilders, Belgian francs, Italian lire, and German marks. The proceeds of such drawings were immediately employed to absorb surplus dollars convertible into gold on the books of the continental central banks concerned. But the risk to the dollar as sterling teetered on the brink of collapse also urgently called for an across-the-board strengthening of the swap facilities of the Federal with the continental central banks. And so in early September 1966, I hurriedly negotiated over a Basel weekend an increase of the swap network from $2.8 to $4.5 billion. Moreover, the September 1966 announcement of the swap network expansion, coupled with further direct credits to the Bank of England, effectively broke the speculative onslaught on sterling. As the speculators retreated and earlier hot money flows reversed themselves, both the Bank of England and the Federal succeeded by early 1967 in again paying off the swap debt incurred in the defense of their currencies. In the case of the Federal's lire debt, however, the strong balance of payments position of Italy seemed likely to frustrate any return flow of funds, and the U.S. Treasury agreed to liquidate the debt by drawing $250 million of lire from the IMF.

By the early spring of 1967, the fifth anniversary of the swap network, all the lines were clear, and the Federal and its partners in the network could look back on a total of $7.7 billion of central bank credits extended and repaid in their entirety. Slightly more than 90 percent of such credits had been repaid within six months and no drawing had remained outstanding for as long as a year. In those five years the Federal Reserve swap network had transformed the financial machinery of Bretton Woods by creating a major new source of international liquidity for the major trading nations and encouraging a progressive substitution of mutual credit facilities for gold settlements.

During those years, moreover, the cooperation of the BIS group of central banks with the Federal Reserve was by no means confined to credits extended through the swap network. The Eurodollar market had also become a potential trouble spot. Many European commercial banks used the Eurodollar market as a major outlet for their secondary reserves, and at the customary window-dressing dates, such as June 30 and year end, made large scale repatriations of such Eurodollar placements. Such window dressing in turn brought about severe seasonal squeezes and sharp rate increases in the Eurodollar market. Such seasonal stringencies then pulled money out of New York and the London sterling market, thereby aggravating whatever other ailments currently afflicted the two reserve centers.

The Eurodollar market, functioning as it did as a truly international money market, could not, like a national money market, rely on the support of any single central bank to relieve temporary stringencies or knots in the market. There was a great deal, however, that the BIS group of central banks could do in an informal, *ad hoc* way to alleviate temporary strains on the market. Such a seasonal stringency in the Eurodollar market appeared on November 29, 1966, for example, when year-end window-dressing activities suddenly pushed up the one-month rate by nearly a full percentage point with sympathetic reactions on other maturities. On the very same day, concerted actions to deal with the situation was taken by several central banks and the BIS.

First, the Swiss National Bank announced that it would be prepared to enter into dollar–Swiss franc swaps over the year end with its commercial banks. Under such swap contracts, the Swiss National Bank bought dollars spot against a forward resale contract. The dollars so acquired by the Swiss central bank were immediately channeled back into the Eurodollar market, offsetting the window-dressing withdrawals of the Swiss commercial banks. This technique, originally pioneered by Max Iklé of the Swiss National Bank, has subsequently become standard practice. Second, the BIS, with the encouragement of the Federal Reserve, began drawing on its $200 million swap line with the System for the express purpose of channeling these funds into the Eurodollar market to counter year-end strains. During December 1966 the BIS employed in such operations the full $200 million facility, while also shifting $75 million of its own investment funds into the Eurodollar market.

Finally, the New York Federal immediately moved into the sterling market, where the constellation of interest and exchange rates had opened incentives to move money from New York into sterling and also from sterling to the Eurodollar market. By executing $88 million of one-month swap contracts—purchases of sterling spot against resale contracts one month hence—the Federal helped insulate sterling against the year-end strain.

Another illustration of central bank cooperation in relieving potential strains on the Eurodollar market was provided by the Bank of Italy in 1965, after the introduction of capital controls by the United States posed the risk that American banks and corporations would increase their borrowing demands on the Eurodollar market while simultaneously pulling back deposits to conform with the regulations. Italy had meanwhile staged a strong recovery from its crisis of 1964. In the words of Deputy-Governor Paolo Baffi of the Bank of Italy:

> Now that we are in the upswing and approaching a total gold and foreign exchange reserve of $5 billion, we have not chosen to add to that distinction by making ourselves a nuisance. . . . Just to give an instance, we have extensively used the recent surplus in our balance of payments to reduce drastically our borrowing in the Eurodollar market. This reflow of dollars from Italy to the Eurodollar market

was partly due to market considerations, but was also the result of the readiness on the part of the monetary authorities to provide to our banks alternative facilities.

These facilities took the form of Bank of Italy swaps of dollars with its commercial banks (i.e., sales of dollars against a repurchase contract, which effectively channeled a high percentage of Italian reserve gains into the Eurodollar market). To assist the Italian authorities in this endeavor, the U.S. Treasury and the Federal Reserve shared a sizable portion of the forward liabilities thus assumed by the Bank of Italy.

By far the most extensive use of this technique of rechanneling official reserve gains into the Eurodollar and other private markets, however, was made by the Bundesbank. On occasion, such "swapping out" of inflows of dollar reserves served also to mop up unwanted increases in domestic liquidity. But at other times, when inflows of dollars into Germany were largely speculative in origin, such rechanneling of Bundesbank reserve gains into the Eurodollar market sometimes tended to produce a "carousel" effect by providing fresh Eurodollar financing for further speculative buying of marks.

However successful the BIS group of central banks in thus strengthening and refining the machinery of international finance, the fate of the whole system still depended on the quality of national management of the individual major currencies, and more particularly, the dollar. In this area of managing the national currency, central banks have far less authority or even influence than is commonly supposed. At the Basel meetings, little if anything in the way of coordination of national monetary policy was ever accomplished. Each governor reported his problems but rarely forecast policy recommendations. In most countries, monetary policy is a major political as well as technical issue, and the decisions eventually taken frequently reflect the most intricate political negotiations. Moreover, fiscal policy, incomes policy, and national security policy often prove far more decisive in shaping the fate of national currencies than monetary policy, which is then dragged along in the train of other decisions made at the highest political level.

Thus as a result of such political decisions—and sometimes lack of decisions—the machinery of international financial cooperation constructed by the BIS group of central banks became subject after 1967 to mounting strains. Only two months after the Bank of England had completely repaid all central bank debts incurred in the speculative crisis of 1966, the Middle East war in June 1967 cut short the convalescence of sterling. The new speculative drive on sterling, the fourth such attack in less than four years, developed comparatively gradually over the summer months, perhaps reflecting a caution instilled by market losses incurred in selling sterling short in earlier crises. But meanwhile British government thinking was quickly shifting toward acceptance of the devaluation policy alternative. As this message filtered through to American officials, we began to concentrate on shielding the dollar from the consequences.

Vietnam had been taking an increasing toll of the dollar's strength. Quite aside from the direct balance of payments cost of American involvement in Vietnam, the delay in raising taxes and consequent deficit financing of heavy new military outlays marked the beginning of a decade of inflation. The federal budget deficit had soared from $1.6 billion in the fiscal year 1965 to $3.8 in 1966, $8.7 in 1967, and $25.2 in 1968. Consumer prices, which had risen by only 1 percent in 1964, gradually moved up to an annual rate of increase of 5 percent by 1969. As inflation gathered momentum, the balance of payments consequences of Vietnam were further magnified by a loss of American competitive strength in world trade and weakening market confidence in the future of the dollar itself.

And now, as sterling slid toward the brink of devaluation, we faced the further possibility of an imminent breakdown in the Gold Pool. In reports to the FOMC over the previous year, I had several times compared the twin risks of a sterling devaluation or a breakdown of the Pool to two time bombs imbedded in the Bretton Woods structure. An explosion of either one would probably set off the other, rocking the very foundations of confidence in the gold parity of the dollar.

These fears were not misplaced. The devaluation of sterling on November 18, 1967, after the Bank of England had run through its entire $1350 million swap line with the Federal, set off an avalanche of demand for gold on the London market. Treasury insistence on keeping the Pool going until March 1968 cost $1.9 billion of our gold reserves, thereby further eroding confidence in the dollar. Meanwhile, as hot money took flight from London and New York, the continental financial centers were swamped by unprecedented inflows of dollars, most of which had to be absorbed by the central banks of the countries concerned.

As long as the U.S. Treasury gold window remained open, I was responsible for minimizing gold conversions of these surplus dollar holdings of the European central banks. Accordingly, at an emergency meeting of the governors of the Gold Pool in Frankfurt on November 26, 1967, I negotiated major increases in our swap lines totaling $2 billion, expanding the overall swap network to slightly more than $7 billion. With these strengthened credit facilities in hand, we proceeded to absorb through swap drawings the bulk of the hot money flow that had swollen the dollar reserves of our partners in the network.

By late December 1967 such Federal Reserve swap debts had risen to a record level of $1.8 billion: $650 million in Swiss francs, $500 million in Italian lire, $350 million in German marks, $170 million in Dutch guilders, and $121 million in Belgian francs. These swap operations were strongly reinforced by central bank intervention in the forward markets, specifically designed to induce reflows of hot money into the Eurodollar market. At the Frankfurt meeting I had urged a coordinated launching of such central bank operations in the forward market and had secured from Secretary Fowler unlimited authority to so intervene on behalf of the Treasury. During November and December, forward operations by the Bundesbank rose to a total of $850 million. Similar forward operations by the central banks of Switzerland, the Netherlands, and Belgium, with forward cover supplied by the Federal and the Treasury, not only helped to arrest further speculative inflow but also induced outflows to the Eurodollar market of somewhat more than $100 million.

Even as the rush of speculative capital flows began to subside in early December 1967, however, the approach of the year-end window-dressing period again produced heavy repatriations of European commercial bank placements in the Eurodollar market. As in previous years, a joint effort was made by the Swiss National Bank and other European central banks to maintain orderly conditions in the Eurodollar market by rechanneling such funds back to the market. Reinforcing these European central bank operations, the BIS, at the suggestion of the Federal Reserve, drew dollars on its swap line with the System for placement in the market. By the end of 1967, such BIS placements had risen to $342 million. In response to such smoothing operations, the Eurodollar market continued to function efficiently, with no more than a seasonal rise of rates. In the aggregate, central bank operations protecting the Eurodollar market after the devaluation of sterling totaled $1.4 billion.

The shock effect on the dollar of the sterling devaluation was thus met and contained by Federal Reserve and other central bank operations totaling $3.2 billion. To help stabilize sterling at its new devalued parity of $2.40, a further $1.5 billion of new credit facilities was made available to the Bank of England. These stabilizing operations served their purpose as a holding action. After the turn of the year into 1968, the markets settled down as the British and United States governments announced drastic new measures to bring their respective external accounts under control. As the speculative tides receded, the Federal Reserve took full advantage of every market opportunity to buy up the foreign currencies in which it was indebted and by early March 1968 had succeeded in repaying nearly $900 million of swap and forward commitments. Where return flows were slow to develop, the Federal pressed the Treasury to issue Roosa bonds and draw needed currencies from the Fund. In this manner another $366 million of Federal Reserve debt was paid off, thus reducing the total outstanding to $577 million.

The Washington meeting in mid-March 1968, dissolving the Gold Pool and allowing the London gold price to find its own level, threatened new serious disturbances in the exchange markets. At that final meeting of the Gold Pool, I negotiated further increases in the Federal Reserve swap lines of $2275 million, thereby expanding the swap network to an overall total exceeding $9 billion. This strengthening of official credit resources had a salutary effect on market confidence. But we were again obliged to mop up through new drawings on the swap lines further flows of speculative money to the continental financial centers; it was also necessary to resume intervention in the forward markets. Our swap debt and forward commitments thus ballooned out once more to $1.1 billion as of late April, 1968. But again we managed to completely clear away this debt as confidence in the dollar recovered, and we made arrangements to buy sizable amounts of European currencies made available by first French and then British government drawings on the IMF. As of early July 1968, the Federal Reserve had borrowed and fully repaid during the preceding six years $5.8 billion of foreign currencies in defense of the dollar.

Over a stretch of eight years beginning in early 1961, the governments and central banks of the major trading countries had thus accomplished a major reform of the Bretton Woods system. Though gold at the official United States price of $35 remained the *numeraire* and lynch-pin of the fixed parity system, the previously disruptive role of gold as an official settlements medium had been subdued. Over the eight-year span, official credit facilities ranging from the swap network to a greatly strengthened IMF had taken over the major role of settling payments imbalances.

Finally, the bright new hope of the SDRs promised to create a further source of international liquidity and reduce still more the role of gold in international settlements. The very fact of intergovernmental agreement to take the SDR route had immensely facilitated the termination of Gold Pool sales on the London gold market, and the subsequent breakout of the London gold price had left the dollar relatively unscathed. French governmental efforts in the mid-sixties to reassert the primacy of gold had foundered during the riots of May 1968. The Bank of France would thereafter buy only minimal amounts of gold for reserve purposes, instead participating actively in the network of central bank credit facilities.

Thus reformed and strengthened, the Bretton Woods system had absorbed the shock of the sterling devaluation in late 1967 and would subsequently shrug off the impact of a similar devaluation of the French franc in August 1969. Shortly thereafter, the German mark would be revalued with none of the speculative consequences following the 1961 revaluation.

More generally, the eight-year reform effort had created a network of instant communications among the major governments and central banks and had encouraged a flourishing of official cooperation in the exchange markets. At that point in mid-1968 the major trading countries had in their hands all the authority, the financial resources, and the communication facilities needed to protect the world financial system against the risk of a national currency crisis escalating into a worldwide financial explosion.

Yet within little more than three years, the Bretton Woods system broke down, not so much from inherent weaknesses left uncorrected as from the crushing burdens thrust on it by emerging policy conflicts among its major member governments. First and foremost, the Nixon policy of "benign neglect" of our balance of payments rejected the cooperative procedures of Bretton Woods and invited massive speculation against the dollar. Second, the 1970–1971 clash of easy money in this country and tight money in Germany was left unreconciled. And finally, the emerging necessity of a realignment of the dollar, mark, and yen exchange rates was frustrated by an apparent breakdown of communications among the governments concerned.

12

Collapse of
the Dollar

*You do not know, my son, with what
little wisdom the world is governed.*

OXENSTIERNA

As the Nixon administration took office in January 1969, the Federal
Reserve Bank of New York was abruptly cut off from Washington
discussions of foreign financial policy. President Hayes of the New
York Bank was never again invited to Treasury meetings, and his
role as the chief representative of the Federal Reserve System at
the Bank for International Settlements was progressively curtailed.
The policy influence of Chairman Martin also waned as the end of
his term in early 1970 drew nearer. His successor, Dr. Arthur Burns,

brought with him little prior experience in international finance, and several years were to elapse before his redoubtable intellect found time to focus on the foreign financial scene. Meanwhile, as the foreign role of the Federal Reserve was temporarily eclipsed, Washington policy planning became increasingly dominated by political considerations, much like French policy under de Gaulle, with growing disregard for the structure of intergovernmental cooperation built up during the previous decade.

Initially the Nixon administration had at hand no available substitute for the operational role of the New York Bank in the foreign exchange markets. And so we continued, much as before, to conduct exchange operations on behalf of both the Treasury and the Federal Reserve, and to maintain liaison with the foreign central banks in Basel and in bilateral meetings. But the cordial and candid working relationships with Treasury officials I had enjoyed under Secretaries Dillon and Fowler soon withered away. Despite frequent visits to the Treasury during those early years of the Nixon administration, I was cut off like Hayes from Washington policy meetings. Nor could I even discern who was in charge of foreign financial policy. The new Treasury team seemed indecisive and lacking in initiative, and frequently gave the impression of simply executing policy instructions originating elsewhere—presumably in the complex of White House advisers. But the veil separating the White House men from my Treasury contacts was impenetrable, and remained so.

During its first year in office the Nixon administration not only failed to develop any coherent foreign financial policy but also displayed a seeming lack of concern over the underlying deterioration in the United States balance of payments. Initially this relapse of policy into an aggrieved acceptance of whatever the future held in store did not do much visible damage. During 1969 the erosion in the strength of the dollar was temporarily disguised by a severe tightening of Federal Reserve credit policy that artificially buoyed the dollar in the exchange markets by pulling money into New York from all the European financial centers.

This determined attack by the Federal on inflationary psychology relied heavily on squeezing bank liquidity through the device of Regulation Q, which imposed ceiling interest rates on bank time deposits. As market interest rates rose well above the Regulation Q ceilings, the major American commercial banks suffered sizable and sustained losses of time certificates of deposit, while loan demand continued to grow. Virtually all Federal Reserve officials at the time conceived of Regulation Q as providing "the sharp cutting edge" of credit restraint. As a lone dissenter concerned over the whipsaw effects internationally, I could find no one who took my worries seriously.

But the major American banks had alternatives to passively accepting the Regulation Q squeeze, and one of these was to borrow heavily in the Eurodollar market through their overseas branches. From a peak level of $7.5 billion in 1968, Eurodollar borrowing of American banks rose to the $15 billion level by late 1969. As a result of such aggressive New York bidding for international money, which drove the three months' Eurodollar rate from 8 to 12 percent during 1969, the dollar strengthened more or less across the board. Our payments balance shifted into a surplus for 1969, the Federal Reserve reduced its swap debt to no more than $215 million during the year, while the Treasury paid off $840 million of Roosa bonds.

In January 1970 Arthur Burns succeeded William McChesney Martin as Chairman of the Federal Reserve Board. From both parties, political pressure on the Federal to ease credit had become intense. At the swearing-in ceremonies at the White House, President Nixon concluded his introduction by pleading with a big smile: "Dr. Burns, please give us some money!"

With the support of most of his associates on the Federal Open Market Committee, Chairman Burns proceeded to do just that. As Federal Reserve credit policy was progressively eased throughout 1970 and early 1971, the three-month certificate of deposit rate of the New York banks fell from 7½ percent in September 1970 to only slightly more than 3½ percent in the spring of 1971. Meanwhile Eurodollar rates on comparable maturities were generally quoted more than 1 percent higher.

In response to these strong incentives to interest arbitrage, short-term money flowed in heavy volume from New York to the Euro-dollar market and from there to the national money markets and central bank reserves of Europe. The great bulk of this flood of short-term money represented repayment by American banks of earlier borrowings of foreign-owned funds from the Eurodollar market. Thus the Eurodollar debt of American banks to their over-seas branches plummeted from a peak of $15 billion outstanding in October 1969 to less than $8 billion at the close of 1970 and below $2 billion by early August 1971.

The Federal Reserve took various technical measures in late 1970 and early 1971 designed to slow the repayment by the banks of their Eurodollar borrowings. And during the first few months of 1971 the Export-Import Bank and then the U.S. Treasury in re-sponse to suggestions by the New York Federal made successive issues totaling $3 billion of short-term securities to the foreign branches of American banks, thereby absorbing Eurodollars no longer wanted by their head offices. But these belated measures were overwhelmed by a continuing flood of hot money outflows abroad that were motivated not only by interest arbitrage but eventually by speculation against the dollar.

The highly expansionary fiscal policy of the Nixon administra-tion further undermined the international value of the dollar. The budget deficit ballooned out to $23 billion in fiscal 1971 from the surplus of $3 billion registered in 1969. Meanwhile the price-wage spiral gained further momentum as the administration rejected any form of incomes policy. Thus the competitive strength of the United States in world markets continued to erode.

Such bland disregard by the Nixon administration of the weak-ening dollar soon bred charges not only in foreign financial circles but also in the American press that the administration was pursuing a policy of so-called "benign neglect" of its international financial responsibilities. Such charges were generally indignantly denied by spokesmen of the Nixon administration. But curiously enough, one member of the President's Council of Economic Advisers subse-quently volunteered a candid acknowledgment that benign neglect had been imbedded in the policy thinking of the Nixon administration from the very beginning.

The CEA member was Prof. Houthakker of Harvard University. In a note published by the *Wall Street Journal* on March 1, 1973, Houthakker confirmed the Nixon policy of "benign neglect" in the following passage:

> This policy, first formulated by a Republican preelection task force in 1968 under the chairmanship of Professor Gottfried Haberler of Harvard, was aimed at forcing a depreciation of our overvalued dollar. At that time there was no possibility of devaluing the dollar unilaterally, since several other countries had made it clear they would devalue by an equal amount, thus nullifying our move. These countries therefore had to be persuaded by a continuing accumulation of inconvertible dollar balances.

I think it doubtful that Haberler, Friedman, and other economic advisers to Nixon ever exerted so direct and controlling an influence on administration policy as Houthakker has implied. In all fairness to Treasury officials at the time, some of them seemed to be fully aware of the shattering consequences of a collapse of the dollar and continued to explore ways of averting the evil day. Secretary David M. Kennedy's statements at the annual meetings of the Fund and World Bank in 1969 and 1970 gave no hint of any basic change in national policy. And in 1969 Treasury officials successfully pushed through the activation of the SDR arrangements previously negotiated by Secretary Fowler. Moreover, until closure of the gold window in August 1971, the Treasury regularly honored without delay or haggling all foreign central bank requests for conversion of surplus dollars into gold, SDRs, claims on the IMF, or foreign currency claims on the Treasury or the Federal Reserve. Meanwhile there were innumerable interagency meetings at the Treasury to discuss a possible widening of the exchange rate bands, crawling pegs, and other proposals designed to reform rather than to destroy the Bretton Woods system. But such exercises generally represented no more than a spinning of the policy wheels while distracting attention from the more fundamental issues of domestic inflation and the dollar-yen exchange rate.

The benign neglect doctrine found fertile ground, however, in the honest conviction of many Nixon officials that the country was suffering from widespread and deliberate discrimination and other unfair practices by our major trading partners. Domestic political pressures for tariff or quota protection of our textile, steel, and other industries had become intense, while the agricultural policy of the Common Market became a prime target of complaints from the farm bloc. There were, of course, many such abuses. But our foreign trading partners, notably the Common Market, had compiled a similar lengthy list of tariff and other trading practices on our part that they found equally objectionable. Analytical studies by various Washington agencies seeking to prove that the Common Market pot was blacker than the American kettle have not, to the best of my understanding, been particularly persuasive.

But whatever might have been the rights and wrongs of this controversy, the Nixon administration took the hard line, as subsequently related by one of its senior officials, that "the U.S. was being done in by its major trading partners. They were the villains of the piece and it was up to them to straighten it out." The doctrine of benign neglect thus provided an intellectual rationale for all the accumulated frustrations of the Nixon administration in the trade policy area. In this general sense, benign neglect had a corrosive and generally demoralizing influence on the will of the Nixon administration to take any decisive action to protect the dollar in the exchange markets. In effect, benign neglect seemed to emerge as United States policy in 1970 more or less by default.

As a policy, benign neglect was based on two major assumptions, both factually incorrect. At the time the doctrine was developed by the Haberler Committee in 1968, the dollar was clearly overvalued, as were many other currencies, vis-à-vis the German mark. Every central bank represented at the G-10 conference in Bonn in November 1968 was fully agreed on that point and within two years would associate the yen with the mark as pressure points on the Bretton

Woods system. But there was no factual case for regarding the dollar as generally overvalued in 1968. In Europe neither sterling, the French franc, nor the Italian lira could legitimately be regarded as inherently stronger than the dollar, nor were the broad range of Scandinavian, Latin American, Middle East, and Far East currencies generally undervalued in relation to their dollar parities. The progressive weakening of the United States foreign trade position during the early years of the Nixon administration was instead a reflection of trouble developing in our relationship with three of our major trading partners: Canada, Japan, and Germany. Between 1965 and 1971, 85 percent of the deterioration in the United States foreign trading position was accounted for by trade with these three countries.

The second erroneous assumption underlying the Haberler-Houthakker doctrine was that foreign governments were implacably opposed to any correction of exchange rate disequilibria and would be persuaded only if they were deliberately swamped with inconvertible dollars. A general devaluation of the dollar, whether by a surprise, unilateral decision or with prior consultation, indeed presented major technical obstacles, more particularly if the gold window were to remain open. But there was also available to the United States the alternative policy route of quietly pressing for a selective realignment of exchange rates against the dollar through individual revaluations or upward floats of a relatively small number of major foreign currencies such as the mark, the yen, and the Canadian dollar.

The Bonn Conference of November 1968 had shown the danger and the futility of open confrontation on exchange rate issues. But in 1969 and 1970 the German and Canadian governments in fact took such action to appreciate their currencies on their own initiative. With a sufficiently strong expression of concern by the United States, the Japanese government might have been induced to follow suit. Yet no Federal Reserve representative attending the BIS meetings in 1970–1971 was ever asked to urge on senior Bank of Japan officials the importance of revaluing the yen. Nor, as far as I could ascertain, were Nixon officials using other channels for negotiation of a yen revaluation. Senior Japanese financial officials have since confirmed to me that there were no American approaches to them at the time for a revaluation of the yen.

Such misconceptions underlying the doctrine of benign neglect in turn produced a tactical approach to the exchange rate problem that was a prescription for disaster. In the first place, the doctrine of benign neglect, and the resultant paralysis of any action by our government to restore and maintain the international competitive strength of the American economy, naturally tended to become a self-fulfilling prophecy. If the dollar was not overvalued when the doctrine was conceived, a policy of neglect guaranteed that it eventually would become so. To foreign governments, American policy thus seemed to thrust on them the entire political burden of exchange rate adjustment, with no assurance that the exercise would not have to be repeated as neglect continued to take its toll of the country's competitive strength. In effect, the Nixon doctrine of benign neglect thoroughly discouraged foreign officials from considering exchange rate concessions they otherwise might have been prepared to yield.

Second, the assumption that the dollar had to be devalued generally rather than selectively led directly to the conclusion that the United States government had to use the shock tactics of renouncing its Bretton Woods commitments, suspending convertibility of the dollar, and confronting our trading partners with a choice between world monetary disorder or yielding under duress to our demands for a general revaluation of foreign currencies. The United States paid a heavy price, not least in official credibility, for this flagrant breach in the code of international behavior it had spent a quarter-century in promoting. A more precise focusing of American policy objectives on the revaluation of only two or three strong currencies, more particularly the yen, might have yielded effective results with minimal damage to the code of Bretton Woods and the reputation of the United States.

Finally, the doctrine of benign neglect was an open invitation to exchange traders to speculate against the dollar and here again eventually became a self-fulfilling prophecy. In due course, the dollar exchange markets came to resemble a sort of disorderly casino with the odds rigged in favor of the gamblers instead of the house. But the invitation was at first received warily, if not incredulously by the market as running contrary to all the dictates of common sense. Moreover, financing by the United States of the huge payments deficit of $10 billion in 1970 was facilitated because a substantial part of dollar reserve gains abroad favored the countries that were in process of rebuilding exchange reserves depleted in 1969 or anticipating scheduled debt repayments to American agencies or the IMF. As of the end of 1970, Federal Reserve swap debt amounted to no more than $810 million. Market confidence in the dollar was remarkably well sustained.

Early in 1971, however, world financial markets began to sense an imminent crisis of the dollar. As interest rate differentials between the United States and Europe widened still further, outflows of short-term funds from New York to the European markets accelerated and forced most European currencies hard against their ceilings. Then as the weekly figures on foreign central bank reserve gains repeatedly confirmed the weakness of the dollar, overt speculation further swelled the torrent of dollars flowing to foreign markets.

Although the developing weakness of the dollar now became generalized across the European currency exchanges, the German mark was particularly exposed to speculative buying pressure in view of the continuing strength of Germany's trade surplus, a severely restrictive credit policy that kept German interest rates well above international levels, and the lack of restrictions on German borrowing abroad. During the period February–April 1971, German corporate borrowings abroad amounted to roughly $2.5 billion, nearly equivalent to total business lending by the entire German banking system over the same period.

In February 1971 the Bundesbank tried to squeeze out the interest-arbitrage incentive to short-term capital inflows by driving the forward mark to a sizable discount through forward sales conducted through the agency of the Federal Reserve Bank of New York. In the absence of firm official commitments to maintain the mark-dollar parity, this experiment proved excessively costly and was quickly abandoned. The German government still faced the dilemma of making its restrictive credit policy effective while simultaneously allowing its business corporations unfettered access to the Eurodollar market.

Early in May 1971 a report by the major German economic research institutes, recommending either a floating of the mark rate or revaluation as the best solution to this and other policy dilemmas, was greeted sympathetically by Schiller and other German political officials. The market seized on this apparent shift of policy and speculative funds flooded into Germany. The Bundesbank was forced to buy dollars in mounting volume, more than $1 billion on May 3–4 and a further $1 billion in the first 40 minutes of trading on May 5. At that point the Bundesbank withdrew from the market and allowed the mark to float.

To protect themselves against the backwash of the German float, the central banks of the Netherlands, Switzerland, Belgium, and Austria similarly terminated official support of the dollar that same morning. Over the weekend the Swiss franc and the Austrian schilling were revalued by 7.07 and 5.05 percent, respectively; the German mark and Dutch guilder continued to float.

The Japanese yen had also come under very heavy buying pressure. For several years before 1971, Japan's balance of payments had strengthened dramatically, mainly reflecting a growing trade surplus. Japanese exports had become increasingly competitive in world markets, with particular success in the United States. In 1970 Japanese shipments to the American market rose by 20 percent. Japan's overall balance of payments surplus jumped to $1.4 billion in 1970 and would have been even larger in the absence of measures taken by the Japanese authorities to curtail capital inflows.

A slowdown in the Japanese economy in early 1971 served to aggravate still further the surplus in the Japanese payments accounts.

Imports slackened, while exports expanded even more rapidly than before. Accordingly the Japanese authorities turned to more stimulative policies, and the Bank of Japan made a further cut in its lending rates in 1971. Even so, the decline in Japanese interest rates did not match that in the United States and in the Eurodollar market. To avoid capital inflows, the Japanese authorities doubled the yen facilities available to their banks for financing import credits. They also eased some of the controls on outflows of funds and imposed additional barriers against inflows. Market demands for yen remained strong, however, and Japanese reserves rose by nearly $1 billion in the first quarter of 1971.

With market expectations of a yen revaluation now mounting, Japan was particularly vulnerable to the wave of speculation that hit the European exchange markets in late April and early May 1971. Japanese customers abroad rushed to cover their yen commitments; there were particularly heavy yen prepayments for ships under construction in Japanese yards. Japanese official reserves rose by nearly $2 billion in the second quarter and by a further $325 million in July.

At this point, as traders all over the world sensed a total breakdown of policy coordination between the United States and its major trading partners, the exchange market situation slipped completely out of control. The continuing flotation of the mark and the guilder suggested that the German and Dutch governments had abandoned the dollar as the unmoving center of the world currency system. Furthermore, as the mark and the guilder floated upward, they tended to become barometers of weakening confidence in the dollar. Monthly figures on the performance of the United States economy were deteriorating, and the foreign trade balance slipped into a deepening deficit in April and subsequent months. The trade deficit for the second quarter was $1.0 billion, while the overall United States payments deficit for the first half of 1971 soared to $11.6 billion on an official settlements basis. In July and early August 1971, events moved inexorably toward their climax as speculative anticipations reached throughout the full range of trade and investment decisions in the market.

On Friday, August 6, a Congressional subcommittee report asserted that the dollar had become overvalued and called for corrective action through a general exchange rate realignment. On the same day, the U.S. Treasury reported a loss of gold and other reserve assets totaling more than $1 billion, mainly reflecting British and French repayment of debt to the IMF. Over the following week, the flight from the dollar accelerated still further as $3.7 billion moved across the exchanges and into foreign central bank hands.

As the speculative onslaught gathered force during the spring of 1971, the New York Federal repeatedly warned Washington of the impending collapse of the dollar. We consistently encountered a blank wall. It became increasingly clear that the Nixon administration had either lost or abandoned any semblance of control of the situation.

With dollars flooding into the foreign central banks, we faced the risk of a major run on our gold stock or, alternatively, a massive buildup of Federal Reserve debt in foreign currencies if our partners in the swap network called on us to make swap drawings as an alternative to gold conversions. But despite mounting hysteria in the markets, the foreign central banks displayed a remarkable degree of coolness and forbearance. Each knew that a major gold purchase might trigger a run on the U.S. Treasury gold window and force its closure. But even if closure of the gold window eventually proved unavoidable, this would not necessarily bring the dollar down. There would still be available to the United States for sustaining dollar convertibility the immense credit resources of the IMF, the Roosa bonds, the Federal Reserve swap network, and the newly activated SDR facility. Not to mention $10 billion of United States gold whose value might be raised to levels closer to its commercial value. Moreover, to most of the foreign central banks the disequilibrium in the exchange markets still seemed primarily attributable to an undervaluation of the German mark and the Japanese yen rather than a generalized overvaluation of the dollar. Finally, there remained abroad an abiding faith in American leadership and the ability of the government to regain control of its affairs whenever it chose.

Reflecting such forbearance by our foreign central bank creditors, United States gold losses from January until closure of the gold window in mid-August 1971 came to no more than $845 million. Of this, only $413 million represented foreign central bank switches from dollars to gold; the rest were IMF debt transactions. Nor was the Federal Reserve forced into massive drawings on the swap lines until the very last week before the gold window was closed.

It is true that in the spring and early summer of 1971 the Federal had to make recurrent drawings of moderate size in Belgian francs, Swiss francs, and Dutch guilders on our swap lines with the central banks concerned. But on these and earlier drawings, where reversals in the flow of funds now seemed increasingly unlikely, I had pressed the Treasury to settle the debt on maturity through sales of gold and SDRs, or by American drawings on the IMF. Through these and other devices, swap repayments totaling $1.3 billion were made between January and July of 1971. As of late July 1971, Federal Reserve swap debt outstanding had in fact been reduced to no more than $605 million from the $810 million outstanding as the year began. The suggestion occasionally heard that the Federal Reserve swap network somehow disguised the weakening of the dollar and so delayed corrective action is a misreading of the factual record.

By midsummer, however, the risk to the Federal of being pushed into massive borrowings under the swap lines was mounting rapidly. As certain of the swap lines approached exhaustion, the Open Market Committee approved increases in the lines only after requesting from the Treasury official assurances that it was in the national interest to do so. On Friday August 6 I went to Washington to give both Treasury and Federal Reserve officials my judgment that the market situation could turn into a panic within a matter of days, and to plead once more for drastic policy action. On my rounds, I found that others were also becoming alarmed, not least of all because Secretary Connally was apparently still scheduled to leave on vacation that weekend. One distinguished Federal Reserve figure, who should have been privy to all the contingency planning of the government, said to me as I entered his office that Friday, "I don't know about you, but I'm getting scared!"

During the following week, nearly $4 billion of hot money fled the country. To protect the gold stock, the Federal Reserve, again after formally requesting Treasury approval, was forced to draw another $2.2 billion on the swap lines, increasing the total outstanding to $3 billion by Friday, August 13. On Sunday night, August 15, President Nixon announced in a television address the closure of the gold window. Alfred Hayes, President of the Federal Reserve Bank of New York was not consulted, nor even informed of the decision.

The decision to close the gold window, together with a hastily devised price-wage freeze, a border tax, and cuts in government spending, was reached at a secret meeting of President Nixon and a small group of top advisers at Camp David. William Safire's book, *Before the Fall*, reveals that Chairman Burns vigorously protested the Treasury recommendation to close the gold window. According to Safire,* the following dialogue ensued:

Burns: "At the right moment I want to question the judgment of closing the gold window."

The President: "Arthur, your view, as I understand it, is why is it not possible to do all the things that get at the heart of the problem and then go to close the gold window if needed. The Treasury objection to that is that reserve assets will be depleted quickly."

Burns: "I think they are wrong. If they are right, you can close it a week later. You will be doing something dramatic—a wage and price

* William Safire, *Before the Fall*. New York: Doubleday & Co., Inc., 1975. Pp. 513–514. Used by permission.

policy, a border tax. You will order a cutback in government spending. These major actions will electrify the world. The gold outflow will cease. If I'm wrong, you can close the gold window later. . . . If we close the gold window . . . we are releasing forces that we need not release."

Connally: "What's our immediate problem? We are meeting here because we are in trouble overseas. The British came in today to ask us to cover $3 billion, all their dollar reserves. Anyone can topple us—anytime they want—we have left ourselves completely exposed."

As someone in close touch with the exchange markets and the major foreign central banks, I think that Burns was entirely correct in his appraisal. The effect on the international market of an announcement by Nixon of drastic action to stabilize wages and prices, impose a border tax, and cut government spending would have sufficed to turn the speculative tide. Then, in a calmer atmosphere, a revaluation of the already floating German mark and a forceful recommendation that the Japanese government follow suit could have accomplished most of the exchange rate realignment required. Connally's citation of the eleventh-hour British request for $3 billion of exchange cover as an example of imminent foreign attacks on the dollar is a travesty on the facts. The Bank of England request for cover, quickly agreed in the amount of $750 million rather than $3 billion, was a direct consequence of justifiable British suspicion that the Treasury was on the verge of closing the gold window. In company with the other foreign central banks, the Bank of England would have refrained gladly from putting any pressure on the dollar if the United States government had given any signal of readiness to defend it. But as Safire also noted, Budget Director George Shultz and others in the Camp David meeting favored a floating dollar, while "Connally's advice was usually to take the chance, to press the luck, to go for broke."* Thus Burns, outnumbered, lost the argument and the dollar was cast adrift.

---

* Safire, *op. cit.*, p. 506.

Nixon's speech was a skillful effort to thrust the main burden of responsibility for the dollar crisis on the "unfair exchange rates" being maintained by our trading partners. He concluded with the absurd promise that an inconvertible dollar would never again be a prey of international speculation. But now the main task of defending and executing administration foreign financial policy fell to Treasury Secretary John Connally who held in late August a press conference that was a political *tour de force.* None of his questioners laid a glove on him as he sidestepped such complaints as the prospectively higher cost of foreign goods and services, with the bland reply that under a floating dollar such foreign exchange costs might just as easily go down as up.

Connally had long ago made clear his conviction that the United States had for decades shown a woolly minded disregard of our foreign trading interests and that the time had come to pound the table and set the accounts straight. He took a particularly harsh view of the Common Market and seemed to have written off Bretton Woods and the International Monetary Fund as a total loss. An executive director of the Fund told me that on Connally's first visit to that institution he had treated it "as a museum in which anything that wasn't already stuffed ought to be." And at a meeting sponsored by the American Bankers Association in Munich in June 1971, Connally had displayed a belligerently aggressive style that raised hackles even among those personally sympathetic to American policy demands. Now, as the United States dramatically denounced its convertibility obligations under the Bretton Woods agreements, Connally moved to the front of the world financial stage and became immediately embroiled in a series of adversary relationships with the finance ministers and central bank governors of all our major trading partners.

Somewhat accidentally, perhaps, Connally had become the prime spokesman for the doctrine of benign neglect that now reached its fullest flower in the policy slogan: "The dollar is our currency but your problem." No American effort would be made to support the dollar through a return to convertibility or even through Federal Reserve operations in the exchange markets. And when, after several weeks, our official spokesmen finally revealed what they were after, they bypassed the simple, obvious need for correcting the German and Japanese trade surpluses and produced a laundry list of specific revaluations embracing the entire G-10 group of currencies. This shotgun approach naturally evoked the indignant reply abroad that generalized revaluations by our trading partners might more naturally be accomplished by a devaluation of the dollar through an increase of the $35 gold parity. Pierre-Paul Schweitzer, Managing Director of the IMF, in fact publicly suggested at this point that the United States might share in the exchange rate realignment process by a minor increase in the gold price; he was immediately moved into the most-wanted category on the Nixon administration's enemy list. Meanwhile, however, as Connally pursued his strong-arm tactics during the late summer and autumn of 1971, the entire international financial system was rapidly sliding toward disaster.

For a full week after Nixon's closure of the gold window, the major European governments kept their exchange markets closed as they sought to develop some joint policy response to the United States *démarche*. These negotiating efforts failed, and on Monday, August 23, the European governments had no alternative but to reopen their exchange markets on an uncoordinated basis. While each government continued to adhere to its pre-August 15 parity, all but the French government suspended their commitments to defend the previous upper limits of their exchange rates.

In Tokyo it was Monday morning with market trading already under way when President Nixon's Sunday night closing of the gold window was announced. Seemingly paralyzed by the "Nixon Shokku", the Japanese authorities kept their market open the rest of that day and for two more weeks as well. This was not only an exercise in total futility but also a revealing commentary on the state of communications between the two nations. Before August 1971 was over, the Bank of Japan had been forced to absorb nearly $4.5 billion dollars. Despite a reinforcement of exchange control policies, Japanese banks liquidated their long position in dollars by converting into yen dollars borrowed from every possible source in the United States as well as from the Eurodollar market. Finally, on August 28, 1971, the Japanese authorities gave up the struggle. The yen joined the now generalized float of all the major currencies.

Over the next few months the spot exchange rates of Europe and Japan moved to widening premia over their old parities; by mid-December 1971 the mark had risen by 12.5 percent, the yen by 12.3, and even sterling and the lira by 5.4 and 4.1 percent, respectively. Market speculation remained rampant, focused on the question whether the United States would participate in a rate realignment in the form of an increase in the United States official gold price. As market expectations clustered initially around a 5 percent gold price increase and, after the November G-10 meetings in Rome, at a figure closer to 10 percent, foreign currency rates tended to move up to levels consistent with such projected gold parity adjustments.

More generally, the exchange market atmosphere progressively deteriorated from mid-August until the G-10 meeting in Rome revived hope of an early alignment of new parities. Serious operating problems were posed for market participants during the floating rate period, more particularly for those dependent on efficiently functioning forward markets. Moreover, mounting uncertainties and anxieties arising from the proliferation of exchange controls, as well as fears of potential trade restrictions and retaliation, had severe and far-reaching repercussions on business confidence in the major trading countries, particularly where exports contribute heavily to gross national product. As noted by Chairman Burns:

. . . the dangers were growing of a recession in world economic activity, of increasing recourse to restrictions on international transactions, of a division of the world economy into restrictive blocs, and of serious political frictions among friendly nations. Prompt resolution of the crisis was clearly necessary, and intensive international discussions therefore got underway in the autumn of 1971.

These international discussions culminated on December 18, 1971, in the Smithsonian Agreement of the Group of Ten countries. The agreement specified an exchange rate realignment based on an increase in the $35 United States official gold price by 8.57 percent to $38 per ounce. This devaluation of the dollar was accompanied by much smaller devaluations of the Swiss franc, the Italian lira, and the Swedish krona against gold, thus slightly reducing their effective appreciation against the United States dollar. The German mark, the Japanese yen, the Dutch guilder, and the Belgian franc were revalued upward by differing amounts, further increasing the appreciation of these currencies against the dollar. The pound sterling and the French franc remained at their previous gold parities, producing an appreciation of these currencies of 8.57 percent against the dollar. The Canadian dollar continued to float. Finally, it was agreed that the trading bands surrounding these new central rates would be widened to 4.5 percent.

Currency	Percentage Appreciation of Parity Against United States Dollar
Belgian franc	11.57
British pound	8.57
French franc	8.57
German mark	13.58
Italian lira	7.48
Japanese yen	16.88
Netherlands guilder	11.57
Swedish krona	7.49
Swiss franc	6.36

Announcement of the Smithsonian Agreement was greeted with relief by the exchange markets, rates for a number of major currencies settled at or close to their new floor levels, and sizable reflows of funds to the United States developed through the year end. Following the turn of the year, however, market optimism gave way to an anxious and even skeptical mood as traders began to ponder the long negotiating path to a restructured international financial system. A devalued dollar might be devalued again; the unthinkable had now become possible, and even plausible. Moreover, the dollar remained inconvertible, with no undertaking by the United States to defend its new, reduced value by exchange market or other support operations. Market concern accordingly focused on the risk that certain foreign central banks might suddenly withdraw from their Smithsonian commitments to defend their currencies at the new upper limits by buying inconvertible dollars in unlimited amounts. Successive waves of speculation in January and February 1972 drove the mark, the guilder, the Belgian franc, and the yen close to or hard against their official ceilings. The central banks concerned intervened decisively and without hesitation, however, and this demonstration had a reassuring effect.

In early March 1972 expeditious Congressional action to increase the gold price removed another source of uncertainty that had been breeding unsettling market rumors. Simultaneously, the German government took action through the "bardepot" arrangement to control borrowing abroad by German industrial firms (which had been a major source of buying pressure on the mark over the previous three years), while the Japanese government reinstated controls on speculative buying of the yen. Finally, the interest rate gap between Europe and the United States began to be squeezed out from both sides, as the U.S. Treasury bill rate rose significantly and discount rate cuts were announced in Germany, Belgium, and the Netherlands. The dollar showed some strength and resiliency throughout most of the spring months of 1972, as a return flow of short-term funds largely offset continuing deficits in other components of the United States balance of payments.

This encouraging trend was abruptly reversed midway in June 1972, however, as sterling was suddenly swept off its Smithsonian parity by a speculative wave that had been gathering force for many months. In allowing sterling to float on June 23, the British authorities indicated that the defense of sterling during the previous six days had cost the equivalent of $2.6 billion.

Such official intervention to defend sterling was almost entirely conducted in Common Market currencies, in accordance with a

British undertaking on May 1 to join with its prospective Common Market partners in maintaining a spread of no more than $2\frac{1}{4}$ percent between sterling and any other Common Market currency. This European Community (EC) agreement had thus created a dual system of exchange rate limits in which the $2\frac{1}{4}$ percent Common Market band became colloquially described as the "snake" in the "tunnel" represented by the $4\frac{1}{2}$ percent Smithsonian band. A critical feature of the Common Market $2\frac{1}{4}$ percent band was that intervention in dollars was to be confined to circumstances in which a weakening Common Market currency should decline the full distance to its Smithsonian floor or a strong currency should rise to its Smithsonian ceiling. Otherwise, maintenance of the $2\frac{1}{4}$ percent Common Market band was to be carried out by each country intervening in the other's currencies. There was a major technical deficiency in this arrangement, which soon revealed itself.

As sterling came under selling pressure in June, 1972 the Bank of England was called on to offer marks and whatever other Common Market currencies were being quoted at rates $2\frac{1}{4}$ percent above sterling, while its European partners bought sterling with their currencies. The general effect of such intervention to maintain the $2\frac{1}{4}$ percent Common Market band was to brake the decline of sterling toward its Smithsonian floor of \$2.5471, while simultaneously pulling the stronger EEC currencies well below their Smithsonian ceilings. In this strained pattern of rates, the markets saw a two-way speculative opportunity to go short of sterling and long of continental currencies in the hope of profiting on both. The "snake in the tunnel" arrangement became a shooting gallery for the speculators.

Following the British decision to float the pound on June 23, 1972, the other Common Market currencies immediately rebounded to their Smithsonian ceilings, reflecting market fears of a severe tightening of capital import controls, a joint float of the Common Market currencies, or some combination of both. The European currency markets were then closed down, and an emergency meeting of the EC finance ministers was set for the following Monday in Luxembourg. At that meeting Denmark formally withdrew from the EC monetary agreement, while Italy secured a temporary authorization to keep the lira within the $2\frac{1}{4}$ percent band by intervening in dollars rather than European currencies. The finance ministers reaffirmed their determination to defend both the Smithsonian parities and the Common Market band.

Despite this reaffirmation, and subsequent drastic controls imposed by Switzerland and Germany to ward off unwanted capital inflows, rumors of a European joint float continued to incite heavy speculative selling of dollars against the stronger European currencies and the yen. By Friday, July 14, 1972, the sterling crisis had generated not only the previously noted flight of $2.6 billion of funds from sterling into other Common Market currencies but also additional flows totaling over $6 billion from dollars into various European currencies and the yen.

The sterling crisis of 1972 forcefully illustrated the fatal weakness of the Smithsonian Agreement, that is, the total absence of any commitment by the United States to help defend the new structure of parities. The entire burden of protecting the dollar-mark parity fell on the Bundesbank, the dollar-franc rate on the Bank of France, and so on throughout the parity network. In effect, the rest of the world had formally accepted a dollar standard and in so doing had abandoned effective control of the money-creation process in their own countries. The money supply in Switzerland, for example, now depended more directly on the Federal Reserve Open Market Committee than on the Swiss National Bank.

The Nixon administration had hailed the Smithsonian Agreement as a negotiating triumph, but such one-sided agreements reached under duress generally turn out to be bad bargains for all concerned. In the months following the Smithsonian, I had repeatedly warned Treasury and Federal Reserve officials of the urgency of demonstrating our support of the Smithsonian parity for the dollar by forceful intervention in the exchange markets. The Treasury had flatly rejected these proposals. Then, as the United States government stood idly by while the Dutch, German, and other central banks sought to beat back successive speculative waves, the exchange markets began to suspect that the Nixon administration either had no confidence in the new dollar parity or might in fact welcome a further depreciation of the dollar.

Virtually alone among Washington officialdom, Chairman Burns had recognized the danger inherent in the Treasury policy stance. In a widely-acclaimed speech delivered in Montreal in May 1972, he had called for immediate efforts to reinforce the fragile Smithsonian structure, only to have his recommendations repudiated by a Treasury official speaking from the same platform. But as the sterling crisis brought the Smithsonian Agreement to the verge of collapse, Treasury officials finally recognized the gravity of the situation. In a brief meeting with Treasury officials on July 18, Burns and I secured their agreement in principle to a limited resumption of Federal Reserve exchange market operations in defense of the dollar by reactivating the Federal Reserve swap network.

I remained in Washington the following day. Market reports from the New York trading desk of a more buoyant dollar quickly persuaded me that immediate support operations by the Federal Reserve might help to consolidate a revival of confidence. After seemingly interminable arguments with fearful Treasury officials, I was finally conceded a small supply of Treasury balances in German marks to conduct a pilot intervention in that currency. In a brief telephone discussion, Tüngeler of the Bundesbank welcomed our projected initiative. And so from Washington I asked David Bodner, my deputy at the New York Federal, to launch the operation. After listening over the telephone to the encouraging early reaction to our mark offerings, I authorized Bodner to operate more forcefully at his discretion and caught the next shuttle flight to New York.

On arriving in New York I found that Bodner, although operating on only the shoestring of the Treasury authorization, had conducted a brilliant technical maneuver, driving the bears to cover while inducing a significant rise in the dollar rate. In so doing, he had spent only $2.5 million of the Treasury's mark balances. Press inquiries were meanwhile referred to Chairman Burns, who firmly acknowledged the operation as a move by United States authorities to play their part in restoring order in the foreign exchange markets and upholding the Smithsonian Agreement, just as other countries were doing. Burns also promised that the operation would continue on whatever scale and whenever transactions seemed advisable.

This initiative by the Federal Reserve was hailed by the press the following morning, so much so apparently as to cause considerable embarrassment to the Nixon administration. At the opening of the New York market, the New York Trading Desk put in an offer of a small amount of marks to check any serious slippage from the closing levels of the previous day. To our amazement and disgust, a peremptory telephone message from the Treasury suddenly ordered us without explanation to pull back the offer and suspend all further market operations. Since we were using Treasury money, we were in no position even to argue the case, and we most reluctantly complied. In a confused market, the dollar rate fell back sharply but stabilized as market traders guarded against a sudden reappearance of the Federal.

Over subsequent months the timing of our July 1972 intervention was fully vindicated when the dollar showed an increasingly buoyant trend as our trade figures improved, United States interest rates rose, and earlier speculative outflows reversed themselves. By the autumn of 1972, the German mark had fallen below par. The Federal had meanwhile proceeded to accumulate nearly $170 million of mark balances to guard against renewed speculative pressures against the dollar, while also completing arrangements for reactivation of its swap credit line with the Bundesbank if necessary.

Shortly after the turn of the year, however, a series of troublesome events suddenly snowballed into a new crisis of confidence that left the Smithsonian Agreement in ruins. On January 20, 1973, the Italian authorities sought to relieve heavy selling pressure on the lira by introducing a two-tier exchange market system that channeled current account and capital transactions into separate markets, the former officially supported and the latter allowed free rein. The

Swiss franc immediately came under speculative buying pressure. To stave off inflationary dollar inflows, the Swiss authorities decided to allow the franc to float temporarily.

Speculation then spread to other currency markets including the mark and, as luck would have it, was exacerbated by publication on January 24, 1973, of an erroneous figure showing a sharp deterioration of the United States trade position in December. (The figure was later revised to show an improvement, which continued over subsequent months.) With Treasury agreement, the Federal Reserve intervened in the market to slow the rise of the mark. By Friday, February 2, we had spent all our own holdings of marks and begun to draw on the Treasury's modest balances. Nevertheless, the market problem was primarily psychological and on Friday afternoon buying of marks abated. At that point, the situation was still controllable, and a strong statement of German-American solidarity in holding the line might have settled things down.

As it happened, just the opposite occurred. As I read the *New York Sunday Times* that weekend, I saw prominently displayed the following report from Bonn of a press conference given by the Finance Minister of Germany.

> Finance Minister Helmut Schmidt today ruled out another upward revaluation of the West German mark. . . . According to Mr. Schmidt, the new monetary crisis was basically due to the dollar's "worldwide frailness." . . . the Finance Minister, who telephoned the United States Treasury Secretary, George P. Shultz and the French Finance Minister, Valéry Giscard d'Estaing, before last night's Cabinet meeting, said that Mr. Shultz had recommended the floating of the mark to ward off the new onslaught on the German currency. "Had we followed his advice," Mr. Schmidt said, "this would have driven France up the highest tree."

As I read, I thought to myself "The ball game is over." Although denied several days later by both Schmidt and Shultz, the *Times* report had the ring of authenticity and could be expected to inflame the exchange markets on their Monday opening. The consequences were even worse than I feared. The Bundesbank was swamped the following week by hot money inflows approaching $6 billion, far and away the heaviest speculative attack recorded up to that point. Meanwhile, no defensive policy action by the Nixon administration was forthcoming. And so I confined further Federal Reserve intervention during that week to drawings of only slightly more than $100 million on our swap line with the Bundesbank.

It was just as well I did, for unknown to the New York Federal, the Treasury had reached a decision on Tuesday of the same week to dispatch its Undersecretary for Monetary Affairs to Toyko, Bonn, and Paris with instructions to negotiate a further 10 percent devaluation of the dollar. The monthly BIS meeting fell on the following weekend. Not until our Sunday afternoon meeting in Basel on February 11 did I hear the specifics of the American devaluation proposal. Deputy-Governor Clappier of the Bank of France shook his head sympathetically as he brought me up to date.

At that Sunday afternoon meeting of the badly shaken central bank governors, I felt as never before the tragic and unnecessary degradation of the dollar. The following week nearly all the major countries retaining par values for their currencies accepted the full devaluation of the dollar, while the Japanese yen was allowed to float upward to a still higher level. Even the Brazilian cruzeiro appreciated against the dollar. Hope was expressed in some official quarters that the second dollar devaluation within 14 months would somehow clear the air. What it instead accomplished was the near-total destruction of American official credibility. But there were still further depths to be plumbed.

Within a week the dollar had fallen to its new floor against the mark, the French franc, the guilder, and the Belgian franc. On Thursday, March 1, 1973, a new flight from the dollar forced the continental central banks to take in more than $3.6 billion in maintaining the ceiling rates on their currencies. That night they announced that their exchange markets would remain closed until further notice.

Emergency meetings of the European Economic Community and the G-10 finance ministers were convened and quickly yielded two major policy decisions. On March 11, 1973, five members of the EEC—Germany, France, Belgium, the Netherlands, and Denmark—agreed to maintain fixed rate relationships among themselves within a $2\frac{1}{4}$ percent band. Their central banks would refuse, however, to buy dollars, which meant that their exchange rates would be allowed to float as a bloc against the dollar. Norway and Sweden subsequently joined this European currency bloc. The Japanese yen, the Swiss franc, the pound sterling, and the Italian lira each continued to float independently. The disintegration of the Bretton Woods system was now nearly complete.

The decision by the European Community to engage in a joint float against the dollar raised a major question of whether such a float would be "clean" or subject to intervention by the EEC central banks and the Federal Reserve at their discretion. This policy issue was taken up by the Paris meeting of the G-10 finance ministers, including Secretary Shultz, who issued on March 16, 1973, a communiqué reiterating their determination to ensure jointly an orderly exchange rate system. The ministers agreed in principle that official intervention in the exchange markets might be useful at appropriate times to help maintain orderly conditions. To ensure adequate resources for such official exchange operations, enlargement of some of the existing swap facilities was envisaged.

With these new but ill-defined rules of the game, the markets were officially reopened on March 19, 1973, and some reversal of earlier speculative flows sustained the floating dollar over the next two months without Federal Reserve intervention to which the Treasury remained adamantly opposed. But by mid-May a new speculative attack on the dollar had erupted in which soaring gold prices, rampant inflationary pressure, sliding Wall Street stock prices, and a weakening dollar all fed on one another.

In the exchange markets the Federal Reserve trading desk watched in helpless fury a cascading of dollar rates as exchange traders sought to protect themselves against further depreciation of the dollar. All too often in preceding months, traders had suffered losses whenever they held a long dollar position overnight and, conversely, had realized profits from shorting the dollar. In the frenzy that now gripped the market, a moderate-sized offer that in normal conditions could have been handled without any discernible rate movement was now passed like a hot potato from one dealer to the next. Traders, hoping to make their rates unattractive to dollar sellers, widened the spread against marks, for example, by as much as 200 points, as compared with a normal spread of 10–20. But even these wide quotes failed to check the dumping of dollars. By early July 1973 the dollar was plunging each day by 2 percent or more against the European currencies.

As these speculative pressures reached a climax on July 6, the German mark had been bid up by some 30 percent above the central rate established in February, the French franc and other EC currencies by 18 to 21 percent, while the London gold price had shot up to $127. Meanwhile, trading conditions in the exchange markets had become increasingly disorderly. By Friday, July 6, 1973, a number of New York banks were refusing to quote rates on the major European currencies. Exchange trading was grinding to a standstill. The brief experiment in a free-floating dollar thus ended in a fiasco.

Nor was the damage confined to the exchange markets. Worldwide inflation had gathered momentum as the successive devaluations and depreciation of the dollar set off speculative buying in the world commodity markets and particularly intensified inflationary pressures in the United States and in other countries whose currencies had moved downward with the dollar. Countries whose currencies had correspondingly appreciated gained some protection from imported inflation, but they simultaneously saw in such appreciation a potential threat to their competitive position in world markets. Meanwhile, the European countries that had been, in Prof. Houthakker's words, "persuaded by a continuing accumulation of inconvertible dollar balances" to accept two devaluations and the downward float of the dollar, had suffered a grossly excessive expansion of their money supply with inevitable inflationary consequences. And raw material producers, ranging from Australia to Venezuela, who had generally invoiced their iron ore, oil, and other major exports in dollars had incurred enormous losses. This was an explosive situation from almost every point of view, and was so recognized in press commentary around the world.

At a meeting of the BIS group of central banks in Basel on the following weekend, I completed earlier negotiations providing for major increases in the Federal Reserve swap lines while my deputy Scott Pardee made new arrangements to share exchange risks on swap drawings involving floating currencies. On Sunday night, July 8, 1973, the governors issued a statement noting that all the necessary technical arrangements had been made for official intervention to maintain orderly markets. I then flew back to New York, going from the airport to a telephone meeting of the FOMC which approved my recommendation of a resumption of exchange operations.

The stage was now set for a dollar bear squeeze that might have restored some degree of market faith in the ability of the central banks to maintain orderly markets. The market in fact seemed to be anticipating such a squeeze. By the following Tuesday afternoon, when the Federal Reserve announced an increase in the swap network from $11.7 billion to nearly $18 billion, a strong recovery of the dollar was already under way. At Treasury insistence, however, the Federal Reserve trading desk was confined to a series of defensive operations, which cost far more than a forceful approach by conveying to the market an impression of timidity and continuing lack of official confidence in the future of the dollar. Nevertheless, Federal Reserve intervention totaling slightly more than $270 million in July helped to settle things down, and the swap debt thereby incurred was quickly paid off in August. Over subsequent weeks developments in the Watergate scandal and other troubles required new swap drawings totaling nearly $240 million. But here again the debt was fully paid off by the end of October.

Then in late 1973 the oil crisis exploded in the form of the Yom Kippur war, cutbacks in oil supplies, and successive, steep price increases by the oil-producing countries. The long-smoldering resentment of the Middle East oil-producing countries over earlier heavy losses sustained in selling off a precious natural resource in exchange for depreciating paper money, first sterling and then the dollar, now found an excuse for retaliation in the form of price demands that went far beyond the bounds of reason. But here again was another by-product of the breakdown of the world financial order, originating five years earlier in the policy of benign neglect.

The first impact of the oil crisis favored the dollar. The market initially took the view that the United States could more readily cope with oil supply restrictions and absorb the payments burden of costlier oil. Moreover, it was widely anticipated that a major share of the oil producers' higher revenues would be attracted to dollar investments. Suddenly the dollar was in strong demand, as short-term funds moved out of the major European currencies and the Japanese yen into dollars. Sharply rising dollar exchange rates were accelerated by a large-scale unwinding of long-standing speculative positions in foreign currencies. By mid-January 1974 the German mark and the Swiss franc had fallen by roughly 23 percent from their peak levels of July 1973.

Just as suddenly, the complete elimination of United States capital controls on January 29, 1974, thoroughly reversed the flow of funds through the exchange markets. As foreign governments rushed to launch dollar borrowing programs to meet anticipated balance of payments deficits, they were met with open arms by American bank lending officers now free of Federal Reserve controls. Between February and May 1974, claims on foreigners reported by American banks ballooned by a record increase of well over $9 billion. In effect, the United States had taken on the burden of financing not only its own oil cost increases but those of many other countries as well.

As a result, dollar rates against most European currencies fell steadily during February 1974 to levels more than 10 percent below the January high. The Federal Reserve then resumed intervention in German marks but, in accordance with administration policy, remained limited to no more than day-to-day smoothing operations. By mid-May 1974 the dollar had fallen 21 percent below its January high against the mark.

En route to the May 1974 BIS meeting, I stopped in Zurich for discussions with my old friend, Fritz Leutwiler, the newly appointed President of the Swiss National Bank. In Basel the next day we joined Tüngeler of the Bundesbank for our regular monthly lunch together and reached tentative agreement on a program of concerted exchange market operations to counter excessive speculation against the dollar. Reports of this agreement appeared on the news tickers on May 14 and immediately brought about a scramble to cover short dollar positions. Over the summer months of 1974, improving trends in our balance of payments position reinforced the change in market psychology. Meanwhile, the exchange markets were buffeted about by the successive troubles of the Franklin National and Herstatt banks and the dénouement of the Watergate affair. But by August 1974 the dollar had risen against the mark to a level 10 percent above the lows reached in early May.

The roller-coaster progress of the dollar then crested and plunged into a new slide over the winter months of 1974–1975 as American interest rates fell faster in response to enveloping recessionary trends than rates in the European markets. By November 1974 market sentiment toward the dollar had again turned bearish, and speculative buying pressure on the mark and Swiss franc reappeared. The rise of the mark and of the Swiss franc tended to be mutually reinforcing, and to set off a general upsweep of currency rates against the dollar. From mid-December to late January the exchange markets were subject to an almost unremitting diet of gloomy forecasts for the American economy, and dollar rates slipped lower almost every trading day.

Meanwhile throughout 1974 the Trading Desk of the New York Federal remained confined by the straitjacket of administration policy limiting intervention to no more than braking an excessively sharp decline of the dollar on any single day. Total intervention by the Federal during all of 1974 came to no more than $1 billion.

As the depreciation of the dollar continued during the closing months of 1974, European exporters became increasingly concerned over an emerging undervaluation of the dollar that would leave them at a competitive disadvantage in world markets. In earlier months, most European governments had tolerated if not welcomed the appreciation of their currencies against the dollar as a reinforcement of their anti-inflationary programs. But now as the chill winds of recession began to blow, they could no longer disregard the mounting complaints of their export trades and in various official statements noted that the dollar had fallen to unrealistically low levels in the exchange markets.

For my own part, I had become increasingly concerned over the absurd and damaging gyrations of the dollar against the Continental European currencies during the previous two years. Over that 24-month span the dollar rate against the mark first plummeted by 31 percent, rebounded by 30 percent, slumped again by 17 percent, rose once more by 12 percent, and fell off again by 10 percent. U.S. Treasury spokesmen had continued to voice publicly their opposition to anything more than daily smoothing operations in the exchange markets, however, for fear of seeming to buck fundamental trends. But the roller-coaster pattern of exchange rates between the dollar and the continental European currencies over 1973–1974 could hardly be regarded as an accurate market reflection of fundamental forces that were changing equally abruptly. In fact, the fundamentals often seemed to be pointing in the opposite direction, as evidenced by the surging rise of American exports during the latter half of 1974 while the dollar continued to fall.

The wild swings of dollar rates against the European monetary bloc had instead reflected the volatile reactions of the exchange markets to a series of short-run disturbances, ranging from Watergate to Herstatt, to temporary interest arbitrage, to rumors that certain OPEC countries were planning to buy another chunk of German industry or salt away a few more Swiss francs. Skilled foreign exchange traders earn their salaries and bonuses by correctly anticipating short-term rate movements. In the jargon of the trade, betting on the long-run fundamentals is an excellent way of losing one's shirt.

Meanwhile, since the breakdown in early 1973 of the Smithsonian

Agreement, we had seen not only the hardy survival of the European fixed-rate bloc of currencies, the so-called snake, but also the emergence of a "dollar bloc" of currencies. The major trading partners of the United States—notably Canada and Japan—had for months at a time virtually pegged their currency rates to the United States dollar by intervening as heavily as necessary on both sides of the market. When chided by a journalist for such backsliding from "clean" to "dirty" floating, Finance Minister John Turner of Canada had succinctly replied: "Two dirties make a clean!"

There had thus emerged by early 1975 a polarization of most currencies into two major blocs, one based on the dollar and the other gravitating around the mark, with trade and investment inside each bloc facilitated by either fixed or tightly managed exchange rates within each group.

The only major area of currency instability remaining was the volatile rate relationship between the European bloc and the dollar bloc, where policy constraints on intervention had allowed the dollar-mark rate to roll back and forth like loose cargo on a ship. The potential dangers of such wild swings of currency relationships between the vast trading area of the dollar bloc on the one hand and the huge economy of Europe on the other, still seemed to be lost on most Washington officialdom with the potent exception of Chairman Arthur Burns of the Federal Reserve. Although Burns and the New York Federal disagreed on many things, we shared an acute distaste and distrust of free-floating exchange rates, and market experience over the past two years had thoroughly vindicated our judgment. In late January 1975 I made a particularly strenuous appeal to Burns for more forceful exchange market operations in support of the dollar, and he secured the necessary policy clearances within Washington.

And so, on February 1, 1975, Burns and I met with President Leutwiler of the Swiss National Bank and President Klasen and First Vice-President Emminger of the German Bundesbank in a small conference room on the third floor of a hotel at London's Heathrow Airport. Mutual convenience had suggested the locale: Burns was attending a weekend conference of the Ditchley Foundation near Oxford; Leutwiler was scheduled to make a speech the next day in the London Guildhall; the Germans flew in from Frankfurt and I from New York. Our conference room overlooked the head of one of the runways at Heathrow. As an unending succession of jetliners roared away to overseas destinations, it seemed to me somehow appropriate that we should be meeting at that crossroads of world traffic to discuss the problem of stabilizing currency exchange rates.

Burns and I opened the meeting by proposing a major stepping up of joint Swiss, German, and American intervention in the exchange markets. Leutwiler, who had acquired a thorough understanding of the foreign exchange marketplace during his previous assignment as head of his bank's foreign operations, strongly and skillfully supported our proposal, and Klasen warmly concurred. Within little more than an hour, agreement on operational techniques had been reached, we shook hands, and departed for our respective destinations.

Over the next six months Federal Reserve intervention was stepped up to $1 billion, the Swiss National Bank and the Bundesbank also intervened heavily, and selling pressure on the dollar was finally arrested. By late spring the fundamental fact of the undervaluation of the dollar was finally recognized by the exchange markets. Dollar rates moved up strongly over the summer months by roughly 13 percent against the mark and other currencies of the European monetary bloc.

At the end of February 1975 I elected to take early retirement from the Federal Reserve Bank of New York with a sense of encouragement that we were on the road back toward some new, restructured system of international finance. Through informal cooperation, the major central banks had quietly reactivated much of the machinery developed during the sixties to control speculation and otherwise assist an orderly functioning of the exchange markets. Since the United States government abandoned in July 1973 its disastrous experiment with a free-floating dollar, the major central banks had intervened on the exchange markets to the extent of more than $100 billion. The sheer magnitude of such central bank intervention during the past three years suggests the violence of the speculative storms that would otherwise have swept across the exchanges. In the absence of exchange stabilization operations on such a scale, it is hard to visualize how the exchange markets could have continued to function. Meanwhile, the central banks have generally avoided the trap of defending for too long exchange rates that have become untenable. Sterling, for example, has been periodically allowed to depreciate further so as to reflect the relatively high British rate of inflation and other changes in the fundamentals.

In effect, managed rather than free floating of the key exchange rates has now become the order of the day. As inflation in the major trading countries subsides, such managed floating will probably gradually evolve into a reasonably stable system of *de facto* adjustable parities linking up the dollar with the other key currencies. Meanwhile, intergovernmental agreements from time to time will hopefully consolidate the progress achieved through operational experience. The Rambouillet Agreement in the fall of 1975, calling upon the G-10 central banks to "counter erratic fluctuations of exchange rates," was a step in the right direction. And early in 1976, the Jamaica Agreement gave a formal IMF stamp of approval to coordinated official intervention in the exchange markets. Such evolutionary reform will be far more productive than political bargaining over the blueprint of a new Bretton Woods.

Meanwhile, new compulsions have been driving governments toward better coordination of exchange rate policy in the interests of a more orderly international financial system. During the inflationary outburst of 1972–1975, the risk of floating exchange rates generating competitive depreciations was minimized. Germany and other strong economies frequently welcomed appreciations of their currencies as a defense against imported inflation while Britain, Italy, and others in a deficit payments position desperately struggled to raise sufficient funds to support exchange rates that were clearly overvalued. Allowing the market to set its own rates on the pound or the lira in such circumstances would have invited still further inflationary disasters.

By 1976, however, subsiding inflation, lagging recovery from re-cession, and idle export capacity had considerably transformed the economic policy options. In certain major countries, exchange depre-ciation could now be visualized as the key to an export-generated recovery of business activity, if their foreign trading rivals did not follow suit, and so the spectre of competitive depreciation in search of an export-trading advantage began to recall memories of the thirties. During the early months of 1976, the domino sequence of the sudden depreciations of the lira, sterling, and the French franc vividly illustrated the risks of allowing market speculation to deter-mine exchange rates. Governments can escape neither the necessity of deciding for themselves what exchange rate is appropriate to the underlying trade realities, nor the equally compelling necessity for reaching temporary agreements with their major trading partners on target exchange rates acceptable to both. Money does not manage itself, no more so internationally than in the domestic markets.

Index

Anderson, Robert B., 12, 51, 53—54
Angotta, Anthony, 105
Ansiaux, Baron, 27, 79, 162, 169
Armstrong, William, 169
Asbrink, Per, 27

Baffi, Paolo, 197
Beattie, Robert, 117
Blessing, Karl, 27—28, 127, 161—162,
    169, 182, 184
Blough, Roy, 18
Bodner, David, 226
Braun, William, 40
Bridge, Roy, 28, 37, 58—59, 63, 65,
    79, 82, 103, 114—115, 124—125,
    129, 153, 179
Brimmer, Andrew, 73
Brooks, John, 21—22, 122
Brown, George, 167
Brunet, Jacques, 134, 175—177
Burns, Arthur, 71, 204—206, 217—218,
    221, 226—227, 236—237
Callaghan, James, 112—115, 123, 135,
    149—150

Carli, Guido, 27, 30, 35, 39, 51, 84,
    127, 162, 169—170, 180
Clappier, Bernard, 132, 176—180, 229
Cobbold, Lord, 27, 37, 52—53, 78,
    107—109, 111
Connally, John, 1, 93, 217—220
Cousins, Frank, 135
Cromer, Lord, 78, 86, 111, 113, 119,
    121—123, 127, 136

Daane, Dewey, 73, 161, 185—186
deGaulle, Charles, 1, 96, 110, 120, 145,
    152, 175—177, 179—180, 186
Deming, Fred, 125, 161—164, 171—172,
    182—183, 189—190
Dillon, C. Douglas, 15—18, 34, 37—38,
    60—61, 71, 88—89, 106, 117, 119,
    188—189

Emminger, Otmar, 28, 31, 132, 183,
    236

Ferras, Gabriel, 28, 169
Friedman, Milton, 71, 208

241

Fowler, Henry, 16, 125, 138, 153,
156, 159, 164, 168, 173, 182,
189—191, 200, 208

Gilbert, Milton, 28, 132, 169
Giscard d'Estaing, Valéry, 187, 228
Guindey, Guillaume, 28, 60
Guth, Wilfrid, 31

Haberler, Gottfried, 208—210
Havenga, Nicholas, 45
Hayes, Alfred, 23, 30, 51, 54, 60,
62—63, 73, 97, 100—101, 111—112,
114, 117, 119, 122, 127, 140, 161,
204, 217
Heffelfinger, William, 38
Holtrop, Marius, 10, 27, 38, 62, 79
Houthakker, Hendrik, 208, 210

Iklé, Max, 28, 35—38, 80, 82, 90, 166,
169, 197
Jacobsson, Per, 23, 89
Javits, Jacob, 165
Jenkins, Roy, 165, 184
Johnson, Lyndon, 97, 106, 164, 167

Kennedy, David M., 208
Kennedy, John, 15, 18—20, 49—50,
60, 66, 79, 82—83, 89, 91, 93,
96—98, 102—105, 175
Keynes, Lord, 3, 9
Klasen, Karl, 236—237
Koszul, Julien-Pierre, 28, 74—75, 77

Larre, René, 28
Leontief, Wassily, 4
Leutwiler, Fritz, 234, 236—237
Lever, Harold, 169

MacLaury, Bruce, 167
Martin, William McChesney, 23, 37,
51, 53—54, 61, 69—71, 73, 82—83,

86, 89, 100, 102, 117, 126, 136,
153, 156, 161, 164—170, 172—173,
181, 183—185, 204
Maudling, Reginald, 110, 112
Mayekawa, Haruo, 120
McCracken, Paul, 18
Mitchell, George, 73
Morse, Jeremy, 169

Nixon, Richard M., 15, 49, 206, 217,
219—220
Norman, Montagu, 3

O'Brien, Lord, 25, 136, 140—143,
148—149, 165—167, 169—170
Ossola, Rinaldo, 28, 132, 169—170

Pardee, Scott, 232
Parsons, Maurice, 51, 55, 108, 119,
132, 162
Preston, George, 55—56, 169

Ranalli, Emilio, 28, 39, 90
Rasminsky, Louis, 81, 117, 126
Raw, Rupert, 25
Richardson, Gordon, 143—144
Robertson, Louis, 73, 172
Roche, Thomas, 54
Roosa, Robert, 16—20, 23, 31, 34,
37—38, 40—41, 60—61, 71—72, 83,
85, 88—89, 100, 102, 117, 120, 188

Safire, William, 217—218
Schiller, Karl, 2, 182—184, 213
Schmidt, Helmut, 228
Schwegler, Walter, 27, 35, 80, 120
Schweitzer, Pierre-Paul, 144, 169, 178,
183, 185, 220
Shultz, George, 218, 228, 230
Sproul, Allan, 4, 18, 21, 23, 45, 122
Stamp, Maxwell, 189
Stopper, Erwin, 162, 169

Strauss, Franz Josef, 2
Strong, Benjamin, 3, 22, 75

Tungeler, Johannes, 28, 32–35, 65, 82, 90, 103, 169, 182, 226, 234
Turner, John, 236

Vandenbosch, Count, 28, 40, 169

Waage, Thomas, 121–122
Williams, John H., 4
Wilson, Harold, 112–113, 115, 136, 167

Young, Ralph, 71–72, 102

Zijlstra, Jelle, 148, 150, 162, 165–166, 169, 184–185